A Speaking Part

A Speaking Part

Lewis Casson and the Theatre of his time

Diana Devlin

HODDER AND STOUGHTON
LONDON SYDNEY AUCKLAND TORONTO

British Library Cataloguing in Publication Data
Devlin, Diana
    A Speaking Part
    1. Casson, Sir Lewis   2. Actors—Great
    Britain—Biography
    I. Title
    792'.028'0924   PN2598.C/

ISBN 0 340 28090 5

Hodder and Stoughton Editorial Office: 47 Bedford Square, London WC1B 3DP

For the other grandchildren: Anthony, Penny and Jane;
Glynis and Bronwen; Dirk, Teresa, Tom and Ben.

Acknowledgments

I first researched my grandfather's career for a doctoral dissertation at the University of Minnesota. My thanks go to my advisors there, Dr. Arthur Ballet, who made it possible for me to be there, and Dr. Charles Nolte, who transmitted his support and encouragement unstintingly across the Atlantic.

I am grateful to the staff of the Arts Council of Great Britain, the B.B.C., the British Theatre Centre, the College of St. Mark's and St. John's, Glasgow Central Library, the John Rylands Library, Manchester Central Library, and the Theatre Department at the Victoria and Albert Museum, for access to valuable materials, and to Raymond Mander and Joe Mitchenson for their help with illustrations. The late Elizabeth Sprigge allowed me to use an unedited transcript of an interview with Lewis and an unpublished biography of Lewis by the late Kenelm Foss sometimes set me on the right path of enquiry. I am grateful, too, for letters from Max Berner and T. Byron Place about Lewis's activities in the First World War.

My warm thanks go to the friends who helped, through information and discussion, to build up a picture of Lewis and his work, in particular: Freda Gaye; Mary Glasgow, who, especially, clarified the background to C.E.M.A. and Lewis's relationship with Keynes; the late Tom Honeyman, especially for information and papers about the Scottish Playgoers Ltd; the late Margaret Webster. And it would be difficult to measure the help I have received from members of the family who delved into their memories and their archives to enlarge or modify my understanding of Lewis: my cousin Peggy Reed, who gave me much information about the Casson family; my uncles and aunts John and Patricia Casson, Ann Casson and Douglas Campbell; my father, William Devlin; my mother and stepfather, Mary and Ian Haines; my late grandmother, Sybil Thorndike, with whom I had many enthralling and moving conversations about Lewis.

Finally, special thanks to my agent, Dinah Wiener of Curtis Brown Ltd, my editor, Ion Trewin, and his father, John Trewin, for their kindness and support to a new writer.

I knew Lewis only in the last quarter of his life. Others may find gaps and distortions in this biography. I hope they will accept it as one selective interpretation of an immensely rich life.

Contents

Illustrations

Between pages 118 and 119

Lewis aged about four
The Casson family
Lewis and Sybil[1]
The family at Dymchurch
Lewis as Dante in *Beatrice*
Lewis in *Latitude 15°S*
The tent scene from *Saint Joan*[2]
Lewis as Shylock[2]
Lewis as Socrates
Lewis as Professor Linden[3]
The French court in Lewis's production of *Henry V*[2]
Lewis as Macbeth, Sybil as Lady Macbeth
Lewis as Father-General, Sybil as Teresa in *Teresa of Avila*[4]
Lewis about 1955

ACKNOWLEDGMENTS

1. The Gaiety Theatre Manchester Annual, 1909
2. Raymond Mander and Joe Mitchenson Theatre Collection
3. Houston Rogers, Victoria and Albert Museum
4. Anthony Buckley

Prologue

Inside the grandfather clock which always stood in Lewis Casson's home, and now stands in his son's, is a note in his handwriting, explaining its origins:

> This clock was the property of "Wonderful Walker", Vicar of Seathwaite in the Duddon Valley, North Lancashire, for sixty-seven years, until his death in 1802 at the age of 92. He was my great-great-great-grandfather. In 1745 he hid this clock in a slate quarry when the Young Pretender was marching south from Scotland . . .

On the other side is a simplified diagram of the family tree. In retracing his ancestry Lewis always liked to begin with this character, whose longevity, industry and enterprise he himself was to rival, though in very different spheres. I too shall begin with "Wonderful Walker", because Lewis did, and also because he was, as we shall see, a remarkable man, with many of the same qualities as Lewis.

Robert Walker was born at Seathwaite in 1709, the youngest of twelve children, and his family decided to "breed him as a scholar" since he was too delicate for bodily labour. So he was taught to read and write in Seathwaite Chapel, where he would later teach and preach himself. He became a schoolmaster at Loweswater and then acquired enough classical knowledge to take holy orders. In this, his career was paralleled by his descendant, though Lewis changed course before becoming a priest. Upon his ordination Walker was offered two curacies and chose Seathwaite because, as well as the five pounds per annum it carried, a cottage went with the cure and this enabled him to marry the girl he had set his heart on. He married and took up his position in about 1735. Both he and his wife lived to their ninety-third years and died after sixty-seven years of marriage: Lewis and his wife lived to their ninety-fourth years and celebrated sixty years of marriage. Robert Walker remained healthy and alert to the end, with all his senses except his sight: Lewis too, eyesight apart, largely kept the use of all his faculties.

A vivid description of Robert Walker at home survives:

I found him sitting at the head of a long square table . . . dressed in
a coarse blue frock, trimmed with black horn buttons; a checked
shirt, a leathern strap about his neck for a stock, a coarse apron,
and a pair of great wooden-soled shoes plated with iron . . . with a
child upon his knee, eating his breakfast; his wife and the re-
mainder of his children, were some of them employed in waiting
upon each other, the rest in teazing and spinning wool, at which
trade he is a great proficient; and moreover when it is ready for
sale, will lay it, by sixteen or thirty-two pounds' weight, upon his
back, and on foot, seven or eight miles, will carry it to market,
even in the depth of winter.

In keeping sheep as well as his parish he was a pastor in two senses,
and cared equally for both his flocks, as well as for his flock of eight
children. Thus, spiritual, social and domestic tasks were all combined, just as they were for Lewis. One may perhaps find some
resemblances too in this description of Robert Walker's character:

A man who, with his candour and meekness . . . his soundness in
principle and practice, is an ornament to his profession and an
honour to the country he is in; and hear me if I say that the
plainness of his dress . . . the simplicity of his doctrine, and the
vehemence of his expression have a sort of resemblance to the
pure practice of primitive Christianity.

"Wonderful Walker" has been remembered in three ways: in a stone
memorial in Seathwaite churchyard, in several Wordsworth poems,
and in his name pronounced by more than a century of his descendants, since I, his great-great-great-great-great-granddaughter, heard
it from my grandfather Lewis. And now Lewis himself is com-
memorated in stone in St. Paul's Church, Covent Garden, and in
the words spoken and written by those who knew him.

The slab of stone commemorating "Wonderful Walker" and his
wife is of blue slate from the Vale of Ffestiniog in North Wales, sent
as a mark of respect from one of their descendants. And the stone
commemorating Lewis in St. Paul's Church, Covent Garden, is
from the same place, for it was from this Welsh branch of the family
that he came. One of "Wonderful Walker's" granddaughters, Esther
Wilson, married Thomas Casson, who quarried slate and ran a farm
in Seathwaite. In about 1800, Thomas Casson heard with interest
from a Welsh friend that there were great quantities of slate in

Merionethshire which had not been touched, just waiting to enrich the men who would quarry them. Determined to take the opportunity, he set off on horseback, with his wife riding pillion, on the long journey from Seathwaite to Blaenau Ffestiniog. And that ride was how the Cassons came to Wales—presumably the clock came later.

Thomas Casson helped to found the slate-quarrying industry in North Wales, though soon after he arrived he himself went off to the Napoleonic Wars, leaving his wife to run the quarries herself, as she did with great competence, organising soup-kitchens and doing many other things that were, as Lewis said, "supposedly modern". The slate was carried by mules to the little harbour of Portmadoc in Caernarvonshire and exported from there. The industry thrived and soon the Cassons could invest in a windjammer schooner to carry the slate. Buying land in San Francisco, they built a sort of early housing estate, but this venture was not a success; the land was devastated in an earthquake. They settled in Portmadoc, but did not forget their roots in the Lake District, and every Christmas Thomas Casson would raise his glass and drink "To all old friends round Walla Barrow Crag!" This toast was handed down the family and is still drunk by Cassons who have never seen Walla Barrow Crag, let alone had friends there.

Thomas and Esther had two sons, the elder of whom, William, inheriting his father's impulsiveness, eloped to Gretna Green to marry a rich heiress, while the second, John, inheriting the business sense, founded the Casson Bank, with branches in Portmadoc, Ffestiniog and Pwllheli. William Casson had three sons: the second was Lewis's father, and so the line from Lewis to his "great-great-great-grandfather" is drawn. Lewis's father, Thomas II, was born in 1843 and brought up in Portmadoc with his two brothers, William, who, like him, joined his uncle's bank, and Randal, who became a prosperous and respected solicitor. In 1870 he married Laura Ann Thomas, the daughter of a retired sea-captain from the nearby village of Talsarnau. The story of Laura Ann's mother is a short but poignant chapter in the family history. She was a distant cousin of her husband, Captain Lewis Holland-Thomas, living in a quiet little Cheshire village, which, until her marriage, she had never left. Immediately after the wedding Captain Thomas took her on board his schooner anchored at Liverpool and set sail for the Pacific. For four years they sailed up and down the Pacific coast. Laura Ann was born at Valparaiso, and later another daughter. At last they returned to Liverpool where Mrs. Thomas fell ill and died. So, her whole life was spent in her native village and at sea. Captain

3

Thomas later married again and settled in Wales to bring up his family. He wrote an account of that four-year voyage for his daughters to read when they were old enough and this log has been handed down to the family like the tales of "Wonderful Walker", yet another commemoration of Lewis's ancestry.

1

Early Scenes
1875–1900

Lewis Thomas Casson, born to Thomas and Laura Ann Casson on October 26th, 1875, was the third of seven children. Frances (Fanny) and William (Will) were born in Portmadoc. Then the Casson Bank was taken over by the North and South Wales Bank, and Thomas and his older brother went up to work in the head office in Liverpool. Lewis was born in Birkenhead while his father was training for bank management. When they returned, Thomas was appointed to the branch in Denbigh, and there the family was completed, with the births of Esther, Randal, Elizabeth (Elsie) and Annie. At first they lived in the Bank House but later moved a little further out to "Cae Derw" meaning "oak field".

Lewis's childhood was spent in the quiet steep-streeted little town of Denbigh, looking out over the gentle River Clwyd, where he swam, and the low Welsh hills around it, where he first learnt to love walking and thinking and talking. The family was closely united in affection but Lewis's intimate companion was his brother Will. Fanny was the eldest, and although the Cassons were progressive enough to give their daughters as much education as they could afford, family life centred on the boys, of whom great things were hoped. Their closeness in age inevitably made them rivals but it was always a friendly rivalry. Towards the younger children Lewis felt both affection and responsibility and was always happy to keep them entertained.

Besides the usual pursuits of a rural childhood there was church; the Cassons, devout Anglicans, attended St. Dolgau's in nearby Llanrhaiadr; and there were frequent trips by rail to Portmadoc where their Casson uncles lived, and Talsarnau where numerous Holland-Thomas aunts and cousins resided. Randal Casson, by now quite prosperous, had delayed marriage for ten years until he could afford the kind of house he wanted for his family. At last he brought his bride, Lucy Nesbit, to Bron-y-garth ("Garden ridge"), a fine and spacious mansion above the harbour at Portmadoc, with a splendid view across the bay, the Traeth, towards Harlech, and there they lived in considerable comfort and dignity. They had only one child, Randal Alexander Casson (Alec). Portmadoc and surrounding mountainous countryside, with Snowdon in the distance, were as familiar to Lewis as Denbigh. In later life when he contemplated the glories of a mountain landscape, one saw the same rapt expression on his face as when he listened to well-loved music. These were his Welsh roots.

Most integral to his life was the dramatic activity at home. Thomas Casson had been a keen amateur actor in Liverpool; he and Laura Ann had both been in several Gilbert and Sullivan productions, and he introduced his children to Shakespeare at an early age by reading *Macbeth* to them. When Lewis was six, Fanny, Will and he gathered a company together for a nursery version of *As You Like It* in which he played Orlando. It was marred only by Rosalind getting cramp in her toe. The following year they performed *Box and Cox*, with the love interest removed. But with their appetite for theatre whetted, Will and Lewis constructed a most elaborate toy theatre, with a complete auditorium, a row of real gas jets along the front and real gas for the battens and floats. They were unperturbed by the fire hazard; when during one of their splendid pantomimes, the inevitable happened and the theatre caught fire, they solemnly lowered the cardboard "safety curtain"—a recent innovation in the theatre—before proceeding to put out the blaze. They bought the traditional "penny plain" books by mail from a shop in Great Queen Street in London, coloured them and invented their own scripts. Later their amateur activities extended beyond the house and they performed their plays in the local infirmary and asylum.

The almost complete self-sufficiency of Denbigh in musical and dramatic entertainment influenced Lewis in two ways. Theatre, always his enthusiasm for he developed no musical skill though he loved to hear music, was associated from the first with a mixture of huge fun and service to the community, whether this meant the rest of the family who were to be entertained, or the more needy people in the neighbourhood. Lewis would never be stage-struck, any more than a member of a Welsh male voice choir would be in awe of an international opera singer. Comradely respect would be in order, and a shared love of the art itself. For from the age of six, he recollected, he was always concerned in some way or another with the preparation or performance of a play.

Of his parents, his mother was the more intellectual—under her influence all the children read copiously for enjoyment and for education—and his father more practical and something of an inventor, interested in all sorts of scientific developments which he

6

would take up with great amateur enthusiasm. But his overriding interest was in the organ. Already a music-lover, he met in Liverpool a well-known organist, W. T. Best, and they fell into long discussions about the merits and demerits of various kinds of organ and the methods of powering them. When Thomas settled in Denbigh he pursued this interest avidly and spent much of his spare time conducting experiments in designs and methods of organ-building. He took out several patents and his first big success was the organ he built at the church in Llanrhaidr, powered from a stream running alongside the churchyard. At first adult members of the family looked with indulgence on these activities as a pleasant but eccentric and often expensive hobby. Later, they were more impressed when he published a short book, *The Modern Organ*, in 1883, and then built an entire large church organ to his own design which was accepted for the Inventions Exhibition in South Kensington in 1885. It was said that he would have got a gold medal for this, but the other organ-builders objected because the organ, built entirely in his own workshop in Denbigh, was not finished in time—the first and ominous sign that his brilliance was not matched by his efficiency.

The short-term result of Thomas Casson's success was exciting for Will and Lewis, for they were taken down to London to see the exhibition. For the first time they encountered the noise and bustle of the capital. Impressed, but fearless in the company of his father and brother, Lewis was more intent, as most ten-year-old boys would be, on the scientific inventions he had come to see. They saw at South Kensington an early typewriter, the machine that would revolutionise careers for women, and there were demonstrations of electric light and illuminated fountains. Lewis saw his own hand in X-ray, and he and Will were so fascinated by the electric telegraph machine that their father promised them a toy set as soon as they had learnt Morse, and with it they sent each other messages from room to room. Just as exciting was the proud sight of their father standing in front of his organ, expounding its virtues so enthusiastically and guilelessly that half the people listening left the exhibition fully able to steal his designs, and some probably did.

Luckily for Will and Lewis their immediate ambitions could be fulfilled, for their school was quite unusual in already possessing a well-equipped laboratory. A year earlier they had entered Ruthin School, eight miles from Denbigh. There were free places for boys from the little town of Ruthin itself, and fees for other day-boys and boarders, most of whom were, like the Cassons, from professional and tradesmen's families. The boys had to be English-speaking, although the school was designed to educate Welsh boys. They studied a broadly-based curriculum, including Classics, Divinity, French, History, English and Mathematics, examined through the Oxford and Cambridge Certificate; and, to the delight of the Casson boys, the school had recently converted an old coach-house into a chemistry laboratory, equipped with a sink, bunsen burners, and what Lewis later referred to as "a miscellaneous collection of glass-ware". In due course Lewis elected for this chemistry course and as a result of examinations "solemnly invigilated by the local draper", achieved a pair of noble certificates in Elementary and Advanced Chemistry from the City and Guilds Central Technical Institute (later to become the Imperial College). This achievement increased Lewis's ambition to become a scientist, especially as Will had already started training at the City and Guilds. Though Lewis later tended to dismiss his efforts as a schoolboy, he and Will had both done well at Ruthin, gaining high examination results and several prizes, and Lewis had joined in plenty of other activities such as sports, plays and concerts.

So, in 1891, at the age of nearly sixteen, he left school all set to become a scientist. But instead he began a period of more than ten years of vacillation, changes of fortune, changes of ambition, domestic turmoil and spiritual upheaval, which would end only when he finally committed himself to the totally different profession of theatre.

At the time that Lewis intended to begin his scientific career, his father was coming to the end of a long struggle in which he had tried to reconcile himself to the secure position of bank manager, when his true vocation was becoming ever clearer—organ-building. He saw himself as an organ-reformer. His talks with organists, particularly with W. T. Best; his study of the organ itself and of its repertoire, had convinced him that most organ-builders, unaware of the instrument's potential and its difficulties for players and composers, were constructing machines often huge and costly and yet not technically adapted to the skills and artistry of the musicians. Determined to change all this, he geared his inventions to solving both musical and technical problems. At the Inventions Exhibition six years before, where his large organ had created such a stir, he had met two men eager to start their own firm of organ-building in London, and equally keen to enlist Casson in their enterprise. He had remained in touch with them ever since; now at last he decided to accept their overtures. He invested his "modest estate" and became a partner and supervisor of the Michell and Thynne Organ-Building Company in Shepherd's Bush. For the time being he kept on his position at the bank, travelling to London as often as possible to oversee the work.

Organ-building was traditionally a family enterprise and so it was more or less taken for granted that Will and Lewis would join the business. Certainly Lewis never questioned it. (Indeed he was inclined to operate in the same way with his own children, tacitly assuming that they would join in his ventures.) It was arranged that Will would first finish his course at the City and Guilds, but that Lewis would join the firm almost at once. So, instead of starting an independent career, he was apprenticed to a local foundry and spent three months training in the lathe room, developing a long-lasting affection, fostered by his father, for handling the tools of his trade— the lathe, the chisel, the plane and the file. Then, he moved to London and started work at Michell and Thynne's.

For the first few months the two boys lived at a boarding-house in Finborough Road, Earls Court, but in the spring of 1892 the rest of the family joined them. The bank authorities had finally put their foot down and forced Mr. Casson to make a choice. Half thankfully he resigned, bringing his wife and the three younger girls, Esther, Elsie and Annie, up to London, where they took a house in Gunter Grove. There Will and Lewis joined them. Frances was a school-teacher by now, living in Derby. Randal was left in Wales to finish his schooling which he did with great success the following year, winning a scholarship to St. John's College, Cambridge to read Mathematics.

At first all went well and the family began to settle down. They retained their Welsh identity and Thomas and Laura were always "Taed-Taed" and "Naen-Naen" to their children, and later to their children's children. Their enormous enthusiasm for music, theatre and science was well-fed; they were never extravagant but there were always free lectures and recitals, cheap concerts and the galleries of theatres and the opera house, and of course organ concerts and recitals were part of business. The first play Lewis saw in London was *Henry VIII* at the Lyceum, with Henry Irving, Ellen Terry, Johnston Forbes-Robertson and William Terriss. He sat at the back of a very crowded gallery, impressed by everything— except Irving, whom he could not hear at all, though this improved on the next visit, to *Becket*. The first opera he saw was *Das Rheingold*.

At no point in those days did politics impinge on Lewis's life importantly. Much more important was the Church. Will had discovered St. Cuthbert's at Philbeach Gardens soon after his arrival. It was high Anglo-Catholic of startling flamboyancy. Thomas and Laura Ann had been brought up on High Church, Puseyite principles in which they both took great interest, but they were used to solemnity in the surroundings and the services. At St. Cuthbert's the family was flung into the brilliance of highly ritualistic cere-monial, richly ornamented decoration and magnificent and complex music. The parents were almost shocked at the festive atmosphere, but the children, especially Will and Lewis, were transported by it. Will joined the choir and sang Gregorian settings of the Mass, Palestrina and plainsong, for ordinary services and magnificent services by Gounod, Schubert, Cherubini and Beethoven for high festivals. It was a revelation to them. St. Cuthbert's depended upon its priests, chiefly Father Westall, under whose leadership it was erected, and the guilds he had founded to bring the congregation fully into the life of church and parish. The services were full of energy and vigour, the choir and clergy entering at great speed, their banners and vestments gleaming in the candlelight, the atmosphere heady with incense and the preaching both rhetorical and intellectually stimulating. To go there was to experience lavish ritual and spectacle, firmly centred in spiritual enthusiasm, a sense of fellowship and missionary zeal.

Hardly had the Cassons settled into their new London life before Annie, the youngest, caught scarlet fever. Despite the loving care the whole family devoted to her—for she remained at home throughout the illness, as was usual then—she died in June 1892 at the age of eight. The family was horribly grief-stricken. One of the very few family letters that have survived is from Fanny, miles away in Derby, to Lewis, and it tells of the closeness of these brothers and sisters:

> Our darling little sister; no one could be more ready to go away than she was; dear Lewis, what a comfort you must find it to think how you have always devoted yourself to those two little ones . . . Poor little Elsie, it is almost worst of all for her; Annie was to her what Will is to you . . .

They all suffered over this sudden loss, but Laura Ann was, for a while, quite inconsolable. It was as if all the pent-up fears and worry over her husband's career and the future of her children came pouring out in grief. In her pain she turned increasingly to the comfort of the Church, and through the ministrations of Father Westall, the compassionate and attentive priest of St. Cuthbert's, that comfort was provided. She recovered her strength and courage in time to face a more material disaster—the collapse of the organ business.

I have said that Thomas Casson wished to reform organ-building.

10

Like many reformers, he was an idealist, and had entered the business not to make money, or even, simply, because he liked building organs—which he did—but because he wanted to change much of the theory and practice of the craft. His attitude to the job was dismissive of anyone not motivated by the same reforming zeal. His particular interest was in the pedal organ, which he did not think had been sufficiently developed, especially since English organ-builders had adopted the shorter manual compass of German instruments, and his inventions often related to the pedal organ of the grand instruments suitable for large churches and cathedrals. To buy such an instrument of course required a huge outlay in any case, and yet Thomas Casson's designs often needed even more expenditure. Naturally many of the representatives of carefully-saved organ funds with whom he dealt, were cautious. All too often he was thwarted by what he called "the apathy of those whom I sought to benefit". Worse, financially speaking, was that when he did meet a purchaser whose musical sensitivity led him towards the new designs (for they were undoubtedly good and won him a very high reputation in the "organ world"), Thomas was so delighted that he undercharged and built the organ at little more than cost price. Inevitably, and with frightening speed, the firm collapsed.

For the Cassons, family solidarity held up most admirably. Thomas's younger brother Randal rallied round to rescue the beleaguered; Laura Ann blessed the foresight which had led her to hold back her own modest funds from the risky venture. Determined that this money would be used to educate her sons, she sent Lewis to the City and Guilds Central Technical where Will was now in his third year. The family moved from fashionable middle-class Earls Court to a set of rooms above an oil-shop in Willesden, where they lived in poverty, but not in squalor. Later they moved to Calcott Road, Kilburn, and then to Kentish Town. Thus, a year later than planned, Lewis began his scientific career. But somehow the spark had gone. To begin with, he chose the wrong subject. Will was studying Electrical Engineering and the friendly rivalry between them was such that Lewis decided to do Chemistry, although his natural bent was much more towards physics or engineering. Then, the teaching was not particularly good; the tutors were often too involved with their subject to take much notice of their students' needs, except a wonderful Danish Mathematics professor, Henrici, who became quite a hero of Lewis's. There was also a Chemistry professor with whom Lewis made a great success initially. He was deeply involved in a "heuristic" method of teaching, "under which you had to pretend you knew

11

nothing about things you knew perfectly well, and then do elaborate research to find out what you already knew". Lewis's dramatic instincts proved useful and he got 98 per cent for his first piece of work, but he never followed up this triumph and Professor Armstrong took little interest in any of the students, lecturing above their heads and occasionally inflicting on them a lecture he had given the night before at some learned society. Another real problem was the financial difficulties at home, which not only created worry and tension that affected Lewis intensely, but meant also that every day he walked the five miles or so from Kilburn to South Kensington and then back again. He found it very tiring to stand at a laboratory bench all day and had little energy for reading and study.

He entered the second year as one of a small group of chemists and the struggle to maintain interest grew, especially without the enthusiastic companionship of Will who had now graduated. He was by no means unhappy, but began to take more interest in the practical jokes he and some of his class got up to than in the work itself—such as the time they made bombs out of glass tubes and gun-cotton, which were laid on the ignition tube of the gas-engine ventilating the laboratory. A love of mischief was in fact a big trait in his character, which sometimes seemed incongruous to people who knew Lewis only slightly. Once he was relaxed in a social setting—and he was rarely shy but often reserved—he would take enormous delight in exploring its limits and testing its tolerance with ingenious jokes and a deadpan expression of innocence. But he needed to combine this humorous attitude with a complementary sense of commitment, and that was now lacking.

His ambitions were shifting radically. The family now attended St. Augustine's, Kilburn, one of the finest Anglo-Catholic churches in London. Father Henry Ross presided and under his guidance Lewis gradually came to believe that he could make a life for himself in the Church and become a priest. The most significant events of this last year or so had been the death of his sister, the swift sinking of the family fortunes and the effect of these on the family. He could see no way in which a career for himself in chemistry related to any of this, but priesthood showed him a path of pastoral and spiritual care which he wanted to follow. His parents were not against the idea. Thomas must have seen a reflection of himself in his son's discovery of a vocation and resolve to pursue it. His mother, herself something of a theologian, must have felt sympathetic to the whole idea, though concerned about the immediate problems. At any rate no family objections were raised, but the practical question—how

Lewis could possibly be educated towards ordination—was a large one. Fanny and Will were both independent and making their own way. Will would soon be involved in the building of the Glasgow tramway system. He may have contributed to the household expenses at this time. Randal was now up at Cambridge on a scholarship, but Esther's and Elsie's education was cut short and there was no money to send Lewis to university or college. Father Ross then offered a temporary solution. He took Lewis on as a kind of unpaid pupil-teacher at St. Augustine's. Lewis would run the children's services, teach in the elementary school, operate the magic lantern at illustrated lectures and generally make himself useful in the parish. He became a server and incense-bearer in the church and went back to his studies to try to qualify himself for some appropriate higher education. Much of it was humble work, but done in a lively community. Seeing the squalid conditions in some of the poorer parts of Kilburn he began to develop the mixture of sternness, kindness, humour and enthusiasm which characterised his pastoral work in later years.

It is not quite clear what income the Cassons did have at this time. Thomas picked up freelance work in organ-building and his brother Randal continued to help out occasionally. But his older brother William, a rakish character of whom Laura Ann disapproved, did little to help. These were years of painful scraping and pinching in which Lewis, of all the family, shared his mother's deep worries over money and sought all kinds of thrifty ways to keep the family clothed, fed and entertained. What he learned (or perhaps he always had it) was a complete lack of vanity on matters of expense. He never then, or in the future, attempted to live up to an external standard of living. He learned rather to admire a kind of Puritan, spartan attitude to material possessions. He did greatly appreciate objects of sentimental value, but even with those he would remind himself and others that they were "only things".

After two years, his persistence was rewarded by a Queen's Scholarship to St. Mark's College of Education, Chelsea; a personal triumph. He could now continue his education, cease to be a drain on the family purse and actually achieve an independent status. He was just twenty-one. The day he began he was given a big send-off from Kilburn by the family. ("The village all came forth to see him start," I hear his voice saying in *Carcassonne*, the poem he made his own.) It was a great moment, the drama not lost on him. But when he arrived in Chelsea to find nothing happening until the next day, he walked calmly back home again for supper.

Lewis studied at St. Mark's for two years, gaining a Board of

Education Certificate, Class II in the first year and Class I in the second year. His success, possibly helped by his greater maturity, gained him the post of Assistant Tutor at the College, at a salary of £60 per annum and residence. He was qualified to teach elementary English, French and Mathematics, and typically lent a hand in other subjects, including, surprisingly, Drawing. The whole experience was most liberating. He came under the influence of fine teachers, such as Owen Bredon, the Vice-Principal of the College and its organist, and Arthur Reed, a young English tutor, who introduced into the hitherto classical curriculum *The Oxford Book of English Verse*, Lamb, Thackeray, and Shakespeare. His main interest was drama, which drew Lewis to him in long discussions about Shakespeare, into which may have crept, quite early, the name of the Elizabethan scholar William Poel. Arthur Reed would later become an authority in the territory of Tudor drama, as yet unexplored, and this work brought him in touch with Poel. He and Lewis became fast friends. Arthur was soon introduced to the Casson household, where he met Esther Casson, later his wife.

Though Lewis had now veered towards the arts, he retained a lively interest in science, one that he rather preferred to indulge from the sidelines, often kept up to the mark through conversations with Will. But the greatest influence on his life at St. Mark's came through his Classics tutor, J. R. Thomas, who introduced him to the creed of Socialism to which he became a life-long convert.

Lewis had had two chances to look upon the world around him with fresh eyes, first when he left the gentle rural town of Denbigh and came to join his brother in the "great wen" of the metropolis, and secondly when the organ business collapsed and the family income disappeared. Until then life had been stable, and psychologically it remained so; the moral and emotional foundation of his life was strong and firm. The changes coincided with his growth into manhood. As Lewis was ready to reach out for new experiences, they came to him, and as he sought ways of explaining them and formulating a philosophy upon them, that philosophy was even then being moulded in all its newness. To be young and idealistic when the socialist movement itself was young and idealistic was a coincidence of personal and historical development which could only be uplifting.

In *Merrie England*, Lewis's first socialist bible, Robert Blatchford forcibly rejected the assocation of poverty with wilful vice. He did so by describing the sort of upbringing Lewis would recognise as his own: an education in "the principles of honesty, of industry, of virtue, of culture", an environment of "cleanliness and sobriety", a guarding of morals and a protection from "all that is vicious and indecent and unhealthy". From this Blatchford concluded that "even the children of educated, honest and virtuous parents need to be carefully trained and guarded to prevent them falling into idleness and vice". There followed the picture Lewis would also recognise of an upbringing deprived of all that: "Suppose it has inherited poor blood, dull spirits, enfeebled wits and stunted stature, from its ill-fed, untaught, overworked, miserable, ignorant and unhealthy parents, can you expect that child to be clean and moral and thrifty and clean and sober?" The comparison was too vivid for Lewis to miss. He began to make the shift "between trying to alleviate poverty and seeking to eliminate its causes". He saw that poverty could be moral, spiritual, cultural and intellectual as well as material. "My ideal," said Blatchford, "is frugality of body and opulence of mind." An ideal exactly suited to Lewis's disposition.

Although it was perfectly possible to be both a Christian and a Socialist, Lewis gradually found his ambition to be a priest declining. There was too much to be done in the world and too much to be thought about, to devote his life to Anglicanism. Socialism rejected the pessimism of original sin and he could not easily modify his beliefs or find an alternative to the firm adherence to Church doctrine and Church authority on which he had been brought up. And for him there was always a dichotomy between spiritual and political tasks. This would be a conflict he would long live with. From the first he was more practically minded than some theoretical Socialists, and supported Keir Hardie who was working towards Labour representation in Parliament as a means of spreading Socialism, as against the Fabian idea of "permeating" other parties.

Meanwhile there was his own career to be redirected: it seemed as if that would be settled for him by his filial loyalty. His father had at last managed to start his own firm and in 1899 Casson's Organ Building Company began business in Camden Town. After Lewis had been teaching at St. Mark's for two years and the company seemed actually to be a going concern, he was persuaded back to his first trade. The relative success of this venture was really Laura Ann's doing. As far back as 1887, Thomas had patented an invention which he called the Positive Organ. This term, borrowed from an earlier period, was used to describe an ingenious instrument designed for small churches. A small, almost portable, manual pipe organ, it incorporated devices by which the lowest note of each chord could be reinforced, giving the effect of pedalling, and also the highest note, giving the effect of the melody being played on a second manual. By some miraculous feat of tact and persuasiveness,

15

Laura Ann gradually convinced her husband that, in his own words, "instead of prosecuting organ reform generally, I should undertake the necessary, but less grandiose task of producing a small reel or pipe-organ to supplant the reed instruments". Once Thomas was won over, she had still the daunting task of converting his brother to the idea sufficiently to get him to put up the necessary capital. Somehow, Laura Ann managed both. The firm was launched, and since the Positive Organ filled a very real need, it prospered. For the next few years Casson's Positive Organs were built and sold to numerous churches in Britain and the Empire.

Lewis entered the firm, first installing much of the woodworking machinery, then working on the technical staff and actually taking out a patent of his own for some minor improvement. With the dawning of the twentieth century and the end of Lewis's quarter-century, his role in life looked clear. He was simply "the son of the organ-builder".

2

Enter an Actor
1900–1904

All this time Lewis had been acting. Attached to St. Augustine's was the Randolph Amateur Dramatic Society in which he made his first London public appearance, at the age of eighteen, playing, he remembered with relish, a very old French nobleman in a romantic mystery called *The Old Château*, at Kilburn Town Hall. This was followed by numerous other parts for the Society, which performed a standard repertoire of romances, melodramas and well-made plays. When working at the church he organised the production of plays by the Boys' Clubs, and they performed at the Bijou Theatre in Bayswater, where he appeared as Claude Melnotte in the ever-popular *The Lady of Lyons* and ventured into production for the first time, producing *The Merchant of Venice* and also playing Bassanio. While at St. Mark's he joined the Irving Dramatic Club which specialised in Shakespeare productions.

In a period before drama schools this experience was as valuable as any method of learning to act; he played a great range of parts and developed an eclecticism that would be useful in the future. But it gave him little guidance or training in techniques or style. His performances were based simply on instinct, modified by his considerable amateur experience, with the advantages of great enthusiasm, especially for Shakespeare, a naturally fine voice and a striking appearance. He could also learn from all the theatre he saw. At the Lyceum there were *Henry VIII*, Tennyson's *Becket*, Lytton's *Richelieu*, *King Lear*, *Cymbeline*, *The School for Scandal*, *The Bells*, *Richard III* and *Olivia*, but this was after the zenith of Irving's great reign. Melodrama occupied the Adelphi with William Terriss, until his untimely death. At the St. James's George Alexander produced Wilde's *The Importance of Being Earnest* and Pinero's *The Second Mrs. Tanqueray*. Johnston Forbes-Robertson, in a sense, inherited the mantle of Irving when he created his memorable Hamlet in 1897. In that year of the Queen's Diamond Jubilee theatrical offerings were rich: Bernhardt's Adelphi season included Alfred de Musset's *Lorenzaccio*, Sardou's *Spiritisme*, Gatti's *L'Etrangère* and Dumas's

17

La Dame aux Camélias. Cyril Maude at the Haymarket presented a
new Scottish play, J. M. Barrie's *The Little Minister*. Most excitingly,
Herbert Beerbohm Tree opened Her Majesty's Theatre with George
du Maurier's *Trilby*, playing Svengali. In that first season he also
presented his own version of *Hamlet* and Garrick's version of *The
Taming of the Shrew*, *Katherine and Petruchio*. It was more clearly he
who filled Irving's place; certainly he seemed to Lewis the most
dominant force in London theatre. The most vivid theatrical experiences of Lewis's twenties were Tree's lavish Shakespearian
productions: his *Julius Caesar* in 1898, with its magnificent setting
by Lawrence Alma-Tadema; *King John* in 1899; *A Midsummer Night's
Dream* in 1900, with its babbling stream of real water, its woods
"densely arboreal" and "well-rabbited", as J. C. Trewin described
it, and (in Maud Tree's words) "fortified by every available atom
of Mendelssohn's entrancing sounds". The most important new
plays Tree produced were Wilde's *A Woman of No Importance* and
Stephen Phillips's *Herod*. But Shakespeare was the centre of the
Cassons' theatre-going, and the romantic plays which had grown
up around the Shakespearian tradition, with its flamboyant school
of acting and its spectacular settings (not altogether unlike the
Anglo-Catholic services). In the 1890s Lewis was unaware of the
theatre of ideas.

The first important influence on his acting did not come through
the theatre at all, surprisingly. Thomas, building an organ for the
London Organ School (which later became the London Academy
of Dramatic Art), made friends with the professor of elocution,
Charles Fry, who edited the *Musical Times* and was a well-known
reciter. As with all his family, making friends for Thomas Casson
usually meant bringing the rest of the family into it, so when
Professor Fry needed some women's voices for a dramatic recital he
was planning, Esther and Elsie were quickly drawn in, and later,
Lewis.

It is surprising that the dramatic recital in the nineteenth century
has received so little attention. It was an important influence on the
serious theatre in several ways. To begin with it was a much more
respectable form of entertainment. "There is a magic in the term
'recital' which attracts many to whom the stage proper is anathema,"
The Times critic wrote in 1899. Then, when it developed into what
Charles Fry called "costume recitals", it became in effect an early
form of the simplified approach to producing the classics in their
authentic texts, so important a development in twentieth-century
theatre. "The only thing lacking," wrote the same critic, "is scenery,
and to the imaginative spectator this does not lack in the sense of

being needed. Graceful hangings supply the necessary background."
Public recitation was also superb training for a Shakespearian actor.
"No actor," said Lewis in later years, "who has been through it [this
training] will ever forget that the *audience* is the main object of his
attack and care, and the *words* offer the main interest of the art." The
open platform and the lighted audience made the experience something like performing on an Elizabethan stage. Recitations were
undoubtedly popular in Victorian society and there was quite a
group of semi-professionals who appeared for a fee at banquets,
society meetings and other functions, reciting poetry and drama.
Philanthropically they brought classics to the slums, as the Old Vic
would later.

Charles Fry came to this sort of work through music, which was
his first career; but during the 1890s he began presenting what were
really "concert versions" of Shakespeare, except that, from the
first, they were costumed. His casts were mainly taken from among
semi-professional reciters, and included a Mr. Patrick Munro, a
Miss Olive Kennett and the young Miss Elsie Fogerty. In the
summer of 1900 he decided to mount a dramatisation of Racine's
Athalie, never before presented in England as a stage play. Esther
and Elsie Casson were brought in as amateurs to supplement the
Chorus, and when the part of a Messenger fell vacant, recommended
their brother. Lewis met then for the first time both Charles Fry and
Elsie Fogerty, who was playing Josebeth, and who would become a
close ally in the theatre. The performance was at St. George's Hall,
pupils of the London Organ School played Mendelssohn's music,
and *The Times* music critic judged the whole event to be "historically
interesting even if it possessed few attractions to the student of
modern dramatic art".

For Lewis the performance was more decisive. His handling of
the Messenger impressed Fry, who offered him a place in the
Shakespeare series which had become an annual event. On the point
of joining the Casson firm, Lewis was able to accept, since he was in
a position to organise his own time and commitments rather more
than he could when confined to a teaching timetable. He always felt
that his father's musical influence gave him his love of phrasing and
rich sound in the theatre. Now he came under the tutelage of an
outstanding elocutionist whose approach to acting was to express
the emotions of the part through its musicality. Lewis found Fry
"a fine actor in the best and sincerest form of stylised rhetorical
playing". He learned from him how to harness his passions to the
medium of words and action, and how to exert the discipline of the
more rigorous art of music over dramatic training. It would be Elsie

19

Fogerty who developed the vocal techniques of such a training, and Lewis who helped bring it to productions.

The Shakespeare costume recitals were attended mainly by students, school-children and literary enthusiasts. This was partly because they were not publicised widely enough to attract a general audience, although the actors were of professional or near-professional standing. Sometimes such coverage as they were given was rather patronising:

> The habitual playgoer with no special feeling for the poetic drama at its zenith would perhaps demand something more remarkable in the way of acting to induce them to tolerate Shakespeare. But to the student, if he can forgive the inevitable 'cutting of the text' and to the child just beginning to be fascinated by the music of Shakespeare's verse, performances of this kind, especially when the less well-known plays are acted, are of distinct value.

Yet even within the same series *The Times* critic began to see the productions as something more important:

> Mr. Charles Fry has already a following, and his following assembled in full force for the last and most interesting of his series of performances [*Love's Labour's Lost*]. The size and character of the audience and the enthusiasm it showed awakened hope. It really looks as if the new century were to see a revival of interest in the Shakespearian drama—a genuine revival of the interest that loves the plays for themselves and not because they offer an opportunity for elaborate stage scenery.

In Lewis's first season with the company he played Sebastian in *Twelfth Night* and Dumain in *Love's Labour's Lost*; next year he played Hotspur among other parts; and his later parts included Posthumus in *Cymbeline*, Laertes, Cassius, Don Pedro in *Much Ado* and Polixenes in *The Winter's Tale*. He possessed sturdy good looks, a rich and naturally melodious voice—the musicality of Welsh speech had given him an advantage here—and a passionate intensity.

By 1902 Charles Fry's chief autumn venue had changed from St. George's Hall to the Royalty Theatre: a simple move which made the series a little more part of the theatrical scene. In fact the bulk of the performances took place in all sorts of halls and public places, often in the East End: workers' centres, such as Oxford House, and Excelsior Hall, both in Bethnal Green, the People's Palace at Mile End and even swimming baths. On Saturday nights through the winter they played in the huge Bethnal Green swimming bath, to crowded houses, at prices of twopence to a shilling. Lewis was fired with excitement to find himself playing in *Hamlet*, to an audience for whom the play was absolutely new.

Now he was able to implement the ideals of *Merrie England*, raising the cultural consciousness of the working classes. Filled with enthusiasm, he next joined the British Empire Shakespeare Society run by a Miss Greta Morritt, which did readings to all sorts of clubs. The professional in charge was usually the actor Acton Bond, from Irving's company, an experienced classical actor with a genuine love of Shakespeare. By the time Lewis became a professional he calculated he had played over a hundred parts.

As so often happens when the gods wish to propel us in a certain direction, fate began to twist some threads together. Lewis played Orlando for Elsie Fogerty in *As You Like It* at the Botanical Gardens, and again the two found much to share in their search for development of vocal expression. Acton Bond, impressed with Lewis's work, gave him two important introductions. The first was to John Highfield Leigh, barrister by profession and Shakespearian by inclination. Leigh, a considerable Shakespeare scholar, gave many readings and had a collection of theatre memorabilia. In 1898 he had married his ward, an actress called Thyrza Norman, many years younger than himself, and began to take a more entrepreneurial interest in the theatre, to keep up with his wife's ambitions. At various times he held the lease of the Savoy and of the Prince of Wales (where he presented Martin Harvey in the original and unsuccessful production of *The Only Way*); and he also staged several Shakespeare productions, using a mixture of professional and semi-professional actors, among whom Lewis would be one. In 1903, acquiring the lease of the Court Theatre, Leigh launched into a Shakespeare season, presenting *The Tempest* in which he played Caliban and his wife Miranda, with Acton Bond as Prospero. It was followed, early in 1904, by *Romeo and Juliet*. Mrs. Leigh now decided that the productions were old-fashioned and needed a younger and more exciting producer for the next one, *The Two Gentlemen of Verona*. They consulted the critic and scholar William Archer, who recommended the rising producer, Harley Granville Barker. When Barker accepted, on condition that he should also present some matinées of Shaw's *Candida*, Acton Bond gave Lewis an introduction, recommending him for the part of Sir Eglamour.

Before that meeting took place, other threads were being spun. One of the faithful followers of Charles Fry's work was William Poel of the Elizabethan Stage Society. Four years before, Lewis had taken a small part in Poel's production of *The Alchemist* at Apothecaries' Hall. This was before he met Charles Fry, so it was probably through Arthur Reed. In 1901 he saw Poel's production of *Everyman* which he found "moving and beautiful" and met him briefly. Late in 1903 Poel saw him play Don Pedro for Charles Fry just at the point when he was himself casting a production of *Much Ado About Nothing* organised by the London Schools Board and the London Shakespeare League. The production was to tour London town halls as part of the evening-class programme and Lewis was invited to play Don Pedro, his first professional engagement and his first important working association with Poel. He was ready to listen to Poel's ideas and to assimilate them in such a way that he could avoid the crankiness. Poel then was over fifty but this did not stop them striking up a great friendship as Poel often did with younger enthusiasts for his work, such as Granville Barker and Iden Payne.

Lewis recollected him as a tall, well-built man with the stoop of a scholar. "The head thrust forward enquiringly, little twinkling eyes half hidden by steel spectacles set well down his nose, over which he peered at you. An air of vague eagerness and the general aspect of a kindly old don. His speech was hesitant and almost stammering, interrupted at intervals by the queer interjection 'Ah rump tarrah'." At work he wore a long floppy grey alpaca coat and on their long walks on Wimbledon Common, a dilapidated green hat and an Inverness cape. Lewis found Poel "a charming, lovable, self-effacing character, but obstinate almost to fanaticism in carrying out the ideas and interpretations which continually sprang from him". The young actors in *Much Ado* spent as much time mocking him as learning from him, but Lewis found that both his ideas and his techniques made complete sense and turned Shakespearian representation into something much more truthful and exhilarating.

He took from Poel the belief that every play meant to be performed is designed by the dramatist with a particular form of theatre and style of production in mind. Poel thought that a play could have full justice done to it only in the sort of building and in the general style for which it was written. The foundation of his doctrine, as Lewis understood it, was "his intense belief that Shakespeare knew his job not only as a popular dramatist, but as a practical man of the theatre, and that we had only to find out what he *did* and follow it, to realise what he meant and make it manifest".

In later years Lewis spoke often about the importance of Poel's reforms, which he listed like this:

1) The full text in its proper order, without interpolations or re-arrangement.
2) Continuity of a speech from scene to scene without breaks between the acts.
3) A permanent architectural set with at least two levels, an inner stage covered by a traverse curtain.
4) A wide platform stage projecting into the audience.
5) Elizabethan dress (with a few period modifications).
6) Rapid, highly coloured, musical speech of great range and flexibility.

The first three principles, which he took to be interdependent, he accepted totally and his own productions would later contribute to their general adoption by Shakespearian directors. He was less enthusiastic about the platform stage and Elizabethan dress. He preferred to experiment more widely in finding suitable designs for Shakespearian productions. He liked the idea that the plays were never intended to be realistic, or to be spectacles to be gazed at, but were more like "games by the audience as on the nursery floor, in which they could make a ship or a battlefield at will, with soliloquies and asides talked to them with greater personal intimacy than those of George Robey or Danny Kaye". But, for most of Lewis's life, audiences would simply not accept such innovations, as he would find to his cost.

As far as the final principle, the vocal technique taught by Poel, he was in a strong position to learn from it without accepting all of Poel's idiosyncrasies. His long discussions with Poel led him to understand the basis of the method, and therefore not to be impatient with it in laborious practice. As Poel saw it, Elizabethans relied much more on the spoken word and therefore took a great interest in the sounds of words and the rhetoric of everyday speech; also Shakespeare's particular skill was to create magic by the mere sound of words, while charging those words with intense meaning.

What Poel required, as Lewis understood it, was the vocal imagination that could take a long view of perhaps a dozen lines of blank verse and compose one interesting melody to include them all; also the flexibility of voice to carry it through. He himself had considerable ability, through natural talent, musical sensitivity and Fry's training, but it was not possible for Poel to develop the ability in amateur actors, or professionals unused to it, in the rehearsal time at his disposal. This led to the use of a rehearsal method which many actors found cranky and stultifying. For Lewis it also led to a firm belief in the need for an acting school to train such skills.

Having cast the play, largely orchestrally, with the actors appropriate to each "vocal part" the play required, Poel then sat his actors round him for the first three weeks of a month's rehearsal; everybody "learnt the tunes" under his direction, and by endless repetition in a strongly marked exaggerated form, so that the play became as fixed in a musical pattern as if written in an orchestral score. He could justify every intonation by its rhetorical value and the thought and emotion to be expressed. One of the greatest values this work achieved was to reform the over-emphatic, loud style of speech which had developed in large theatres like Her Majesty's, blurring the subtleties of meaning. What he could not teach was the ability to combine the learning of "the tunes" with creating a character to whom such speaking sounds natural, and as if invented at the moment. To Lewis that seemed natural because of his vast knowledge, though indirect, of musical interpretation: learn the notes thoroughly and you are free to exercise spontaneous feeling and express emotion and mood *through* them.

Very late in life, Lewis gave a talk on Poel in which he explained the wider philosophy behind Poel's work. It was crucial in his own development. Poel was a humanist and a free thinker. He rejected any aesthetic justification of art, and believed instead in "art for life's sake". The theatre was "a laboratory for research into humanity", and it was the audience that must do the research. The dramatist, said Poel, provided a crisis, and characters who are involved in the crisis are shown in relation to each other and to the social setting. The actors impersonate and interpret the characters in what is virtually a series of crises. The audience should be so keyed up that they recognise each moment as a small crisis, anticipate it, then see it resolved and use their moral judgment on the outcome. This process works throughout the play, so that the audience, involved in creating the work of art, has thereby researched into humanity. Through the theatre, their imaginations are trained to look ahead at human problems, and perhaps be able to deal with them better. In accordance with this theory, the actor has a responsibility to arouse the attention, the emotion and the curiosity of the audience.

This turned the idea of theatre into something comparable in scope and significance to the Church and the political arena. It meant much to Lewis, placing what had always been his hobby in quite a different light. There began to revolve in his mind the very real possibility of a vocation in the theatre. Until then he had seen his first duty as the family. From his mother he inherited a conscience so strong that, like a sincere Puritan, he was suspicious of his own pleasure, fearing that it must spell selfishness or useless frivolity.

24

Since he also possessed an enormous capacity for enjoyment, a conflict was created with which he struggled all his life, often smitten with a heavy sense of guilt, a belief that he was failing in some way to fulfil some indefinable responsibility. Much of this struggle may have arisen from his double inheritance, for his father *had* perhaps failed in his responsibilities towards the family although he was never reproached. Lewis's mother seemed able to accept with no bitterness the considerable hardship which the organ-building ventures had imposed on her, supporting him with loyalty and, as we have seen, tactical skill. She taught her children this loyalty and Lewis was an able pupil.

Now he could see a vocation for himself in the theatre comparable with his father's in music. "Organ reform", his father had preached; "Social reform", preached Blatchford, Keir Hardie and the rest. Now "theatre reform" was what Poel preached. And Lewis began to see it was there, in the "laboratory for research into humanity", that he could find a glorious and selfless task. He confided at this time in a cousin on his mother's side and spent long hours with her, threshing out his thoughts and feelings about the theatre and the family. The fact that the family would make no demur and saw clearly that he had done more than his duty by them did not alter the case: he had to clear his own conscience.

One evening after the L.C.C. tour Lewis went to audition for Granville Barker, in a little old Adam house in the Adelphi. He met a tallish, slight young man of twenty-six with auburn hair parted in the middle and flowing back from his face. He had a lithe, mobile body which reminded Lewis of a panther, and a sensitive but not very mobile face. His voice was curiously vibrant, the higher harmonics too strong for the ground tone, giving an effect of higher pitch than it actually was. His personality had great charm and he showed a wonderful "bubbly" sense of humour. He made Lewis read the part, criticised his voice, made him read it again and eventually cast him as Sir Eglamour and the First Outlaw.

The production of *Two Gentlemen of Verona* turned out to be fairly conventional scenically with the usual transposition of scenes, but it was well received. What was remarkable for Lewis was the impression of youthful authority which Barker immediately made on a cast almost all older and more experienced. He showed immense bodily and vocal skill, and, recognising his brilliant imagination, the actors welcomed his help and his discipline and respected him for neither wasting time nor showing off. Lewis began to get some inkling of the qualities that he would later know so well: "a strong dramatic instinct, a keen intelligence and nobility of character, and the vocal and bodily skill to make full use of both."

During these weeks Lewis was able to watch a few of the rehearsals of *Candida*, his first experience of watching Shaw at work. Here too was a producer working with complete understanding of what he wanted from the actors, though he tended to leave the rest—scenery, costumes, lighting and grouping—as far as possible, to Barker. What his first impressions of *Candida* as a play were, Lewis did not record. It is surprising, in fact, that he said so little about his own discovery of modern drama. Had he read any Shaw at this time? Seen or read any Ibsen? I do not think he had. Although his chief passions were now for Socialism and for the theatre, I do not think he was part of the small group of the intelligentsia who already saw a future for the Theatre of Ideas. It was through working and living in the theatre that he learned more fully what the theatre could do. In that way he was, and would always remain, a doer in the theatre, not a scholar. His theories arose directly from his practice.

Whatever his response to *Candida*, he certainly did, like the poet Marchbanks, "fly out into the night". For now at last he made his final choice of a career, left the organ business and became a full-time professional actor. He had received enough encouragement from Poel, Acton Bond and Barker to believe that he could make a living as an actor. And he could see what sort of quality to aim at, even if it could not always be achieved.

This may suggest a very serious and dedicated approach to life and to the theatre, which Lewis did indeed have, but it would be as well to remember also his sense of fun and his ability to ride good-humouredly over all sorts of trivial difficulties. It was certainly necessary for him to remember, as he began to experience the indignities of small-time acting after the heady heights of Barker's directing. But then he was experienced; for he had been acting since the age of six.

The easiest way to get employment in the theatre in the early years of the century was to scan advertisements in *The Stage* to find what vacancies there were in the touring companies, and this Lewis proceeded to do. Before that he played for J. H. Leigh again, in some performances of *Timon of Athens*, and also for Barker in a Stage Society production of Yeats's *Where There Is Nothing*, his first performance for the Society which did more than any other to pioneer modern drama, and his introduction to the work of Yeats. Barker's meticulous and brilliant directing again impressed him and he began to see that Barker was applying to a modern play Poel's method of analysing the text and interpreting it "through definite stylised music, chosen to represent—to produce—the greatest emotional and intelligent interpretation of the actual thought and emotion".

This was the period when stock companies had completely died out. (Barker had worked in one of the last, Sarah Thorne's at Margate.) Repertory companies had not yet started, and the "bioscope" was a novelty not an entertainment industry. Middle-class provincial entertainment was provided largely by touring companies of which at one time there were 250. First in prestige and quality were Number One tours of current or recent London successes, or old star vehicles that audiences would not let go. Descending from these were various touring companies of second and third class standard, down to obscure little troupes barely subsisting, such as Mademoiselle Gratienne's which Iden Payne described so vividly in *A Life in a Wooden O* ("How little can you get out of the town with?"), picking up their bookings from week to week as they could. Shakespeare was represented at the top end of the scale by Frank Benson's company, in a class of its own, touring England for over thirty years and producing a whole school of actors, so that Old Bensonian became as much of a theatrical password as Old Etonian was a social one. Next came Richard Flanagan's spectacular productions in the style of Tree. (Lewis saw him in a production of *Richard III* in which he brought a live horse on to the stage and then appeared before the curtain to take a bow.) Then there were Ben Greet's "pastoral" tours, braving the English climate with open-air productions of Shakespeare, ramshackle, but reputable enough to attract some good young actors. At the bottom of that scale were imitations of Ben Greet, makeshift near-amateur companies often run by Shakespeare "enthusiasts" with absolutely no theatrical experience.

Lewis started near the lower end, in a tour of Robert Marshall's farcical romance *The Duke of Killiecrankie*, a recent West End success. The company was run by a well-intentioned actor, Leigh Lovell, who after trying, unsuccessfully, to tour Ibsen plays, had been reduced by necessity to the trivial. It was colourful and Scottish— whether or not Lewis had to supply his own kilt is unrecorded. He was more interested to recall that it was the first time he had earned a salary from acting, rather than fees. It was also his first experience of the strange social life of the English touring actor—Sunday special train calls at Crewe, where the tours converged and all the companies exchanged news, views, gossip and advice, while the carriages were shunted off and rehitched to carry them to their appropriate

27

destinations; and "theatrical digs", ranging from first-class home cooking and warm hospitality to cold, unpalatable meals and disgruntled landladies. Lewis was so utterly unfastidious that it is doubtful that he even noticed the difference. Lovell's production was not of the lowest standard. But was it also on this tour that Lewis played in a drama called *Alone* of which the hero was a blind colonel, and the actor, forgetting his lines, had to read them, including a memorable cry, "Oh God, give me back my sight for one instant!"? If Lewis laughed, revenge came soon, for on one occasion in *The Duke of Killiecrankie* he was so upset by the excruciating badness of the piano that he too forgot his lines and had to read them.

Next he joined an extraordinary pastoral tour, run by a couple from Bournemouth, the husband a chemist and the wife an ex-actress. The first performance took place on an asphalt path in the brand new Spa Gardens at Bridlington. *As You Like It* was the play; catcalls from an unofficial audience around the gardens suggested that the name was unfortunate. On one occasion, the Bournemouth lady, playing Rosalind, spoke the surprising line, "Worms have died and men have eaten them, but not for love", and once she tripped over a tree trunk at, "Thou canst not tell how many fathoms deep I am in love". Dressing-rooms were in the loos and the wardrobe arrangements were chaotic. The organisation was such that when they set off on the train it was said that nobody but the guard knew where they were going. Towards the end of the tour the company began to disintegrate. Hasty doubling occurred in *Twelfth Night*, for instance, in which H. F. Maltby played the Officer. "After fiercely accusing Antonio before the Duke," explained Lewis, "Maltby incontinently left his prisoner on the stage to reappear ten seconds later as the Priest, giving solemn testimony of Olivia's wedding, arrayed in a short cassock which plainly revealed the Officer's long thick boots." Such "coarse acting" stories are meat and drink to actors. Maltby wrote: "It was an engagement that called for a sense of humour and we all had that, and we were young, and I am sure that I never laughed so much before or since."

He and Lewis shared more than these absurdities. Maltby, who would later become a playwright and already knew Shaw's plays, hearing that Lewis had been involved in the *Candida* matinées, lent him *Plays Unpleasant* and then *Plays Pleasant* to read. It was a glorious revelation intellectually and artistically—characters actually discussing on the stage the deep concerns and values of life, and in language whose vividness and musicality he had already experienced in *Candida*.

28

When Lewis left the organ-building company he faced the prospect of a precarious career, with periods of unemployment (though less dismal than the prospects that face a modern actor). On the contrary, the next few years were packed with all sorts of different engagements, long and short; though salaries and fees were small, they were enough for a man of simple tastes to keep body and soul together. Lewis also seemed to be drawn, by some magnet, towards much of the most significant theatre of the time.

In the autumn of 1904 two theatrical partnerships began, between Otho Stuart and Oscar Asche at the Adelphi and between J. E. Vedrenne and Harley Granville Barker at the Court. The first has faded into the mists, the second is usually regarded as the beginning of the modern English theatre. Many playgoers of the time saw the first as the renaissance of romantic drama and the second as an intellectual minority cult. Lewis took part in both ventures with equal enthusiasm. When he returned to London after the summer he went again to Acton Bond, who obligingly gave him another recommendation, this time to the Adelphi management. Oscar Asche and his lovely wife, Lily Brayton, were both Old Bensonians and so were most of the company round them. The first production was a verse drama by the actor J. B. Fagan, *The Prayer of the Sword*, a romantic Italian drama in which Lewis played the small part of a precious dandy poet. There was quite a vogue for poetic drama during the Edwardian period, led by Stephen Phillips, hailed at the time as a major new playwright. Smooth-flowing verse and roman-tic settings seemed perfect "vehicles" for the fine rhetorical acting and beautifully painted scenes, then hallmarks of English theatre. *The Prayer of the Sword* was no better and no worse than Phillips's *Paolo and Francesca* or Comyns Carr's *Tristram and Iseult* (also done at the Adelphi by Oscar Asche) but, like them, it is now forgotten.

The Vedrenne-Barker season also began, experimentally and tentatively, with poetic drama, Gilbert Murray's translation of the *Hippolytus* of Euripides. It had first been done as a series of matinées for William Archer's New Century Theatre in May and was suc-cessful enough to interest a commercial manager, Arthur Bourchier, and William Poel. Barker, not wishing to let the play go, managed to interest J. H. Leigh in it for the Court venture. The autumn performances were also matinées, for the whole scheme at the Court was on a shoestring. The chief actors were paid a guinea a performance on the theory that they could continue their profes-sional careers elsewhere. A few young actors received a retaining fee to understudy and play small parts. Lewis was invited to be one of these. Knowing little of the background to the scheme or of its

29

aims, he was still delighted to accept, suspecting correctly that working with Barker and Shaw would be tremendously exciting.

The first excitement was *Hippolytus* itself in which Lewis understudied. Gilbert Murray had found a form of verse which retained the vividness of the original, but changed its metre to a surging rhythm which suited the English actors. Scholars criticised him for doing so, but audiences found themselves appreciating the Greek play as a living drama instead of an archaic curiosity. They were moved much more deeply than by the empty romantic platitudes of English poetic drama. Today Murray's translations are too lush and florid to many ears, but their vigour, passion and richness of description impressed Lewis deeply. The cast was a fine one: Edyth Olive's Phaedra was compared favourably with Bernhardt's Phèdre, Hippolytus was finely played by Ben Webster, and Barker himself created a sensation as the Henchman who brings news of the death of Hippolytus. Years later Lewis poured indignant scorn on a disparaging description of Barker as "no athlete". "Bah!" growled Lewis. "He did not play Rugby or even cricket. But few sprinters could have concentrated more physical energy into a few minutes than Barker in his terrific Messenger in *Hippolytus*." Barker was so eager to perfect the speech that on one occasion he rehearsed it with Murray thirteen times without stopping. When he came to do it, the passion and lyricism with which he spoke, and his careful pacing to bring the spectators to the same pitch of excitement as the character, made it the play's most memorable feature. Barker had produced it himself. "It has been good and satisfying work," he wrote to Murray, "to throw oneself at a big block of marble to chip, instead of putty as most plays are."

The next play was no piece of putty, being Shaw's *John Bull's Other Island*. His first play to be produced before publication, it caused great excitement because of its topicality. This was the time of the Irish Home Rule question. Shaw had persuaded Barker to postpone the opening until after Parliament opened in November, and this ruse was most successful. Tickets for the first performances were quite hard to get; Shaw exaggerated only slightly when he declared, "No words can express the impossibility of my getting three stalls for tomorrow. Tree has had to *buy* a box, Alexander having secured stalls by planking down solid gold." It was hoped that the Prime Minister, A. J. Balfour, would attend, but he could not come. When he did see the play a few days later with his friend Beatrice Webb, he was so delighted that he came again on separate occasions with leading members of the Liberal Party, first Campbell-Bannerman, Leader of the Opposition, and then Asquith.

It was exhilarating to find yourself flung into what was swiftly becoming an important theatrical and historical event. But for the small fry understudying and walking-on, all that was a little remote. However, the company was a happy one. The leading actors brought in for *John Bull's Other Island*, Louis Calvert, J. L. Shine, Nigel Playfair and Graham Browne among them, all worked as a magnificent team. Lewis had no idea then just how limited Shaw's directing experience was, so he was less surprised than he might have been to see these "old stalwarts" as he called them, "masters of their craft and directors of vast experience themselves, enthusiastically accepting Shaw's detailed direction". He did watch how it was done. It was partly because Shaw was himself "a mighty good actor" whom these good actors recognised and respected. He would give them a vivid half-minute sketch as a demonstration and so his suggestions on how a character would react were readily accepted; these actors' own tradition of good technical speech and movement did the rest. "They knew instinctively how to get lines over, hold attention and make points."

The small fry also got on well together and Lewis made particular friends with a young actor called Kenelm Foss. Later, no longer in awe of the company, they would indulge in great antics during their crowd scenes. In *John Bull*, for instance, they started making up as various well-known characters. Lewis experimented with Gladstone, The Oldest Inhabitant and Captain Hook.

Foss and Lewis saw André Antoine's production of *King Lear* when it came to London in December 1904. They were enthralled with its simplicity. A permanent setting with complete continuity of action—the characters moving forward and tabs closing behind them for transitional scenes, no act divisions—simply twenty-eight tableaux. During *Hippolytus* Lewis renewed acquaintance with Rosina Filippi, who had been in *Two Gentlemen* and now played the Nurse in the Greek play. She was an actress some years older than himself, the half-sister of Eleanora Duse. Educated in England and trained for the stage, she had played with Benson and with Tree. Her warm humanity and laughter made her most attractive; she was also a teacher of drama, and ran classes full of young ladies with too few men. Lewis was soon roped in to her Students' Display productions, where no doubt he cut a fine figure.

Before Christmas, Lewis created his first major role, the Statue of Love in *Prunella*. This play had a most inauspicious start, but for those who liked it, and Lewis did, it had a magic no other play could equal. Barker wanted a fairy play, "a play for grown-up children" (this was the first year of *Peter Pan*), and asked Laurence Housman

31

to write it. He and Housman had met just once, after a Shakespeare lecture of Barker's, and Housman's reputation as yet was scanty. Trained as a designer, he had already attained a little fame as a writer by a series of fairy-tale stories illustrated by himself. He was persuaded to try the theatre, but insisted that Barker should collaborate. It was the happiest of collaborations and Barker was excited with the result. Music—specially composed by Joseph Moorat—formed an essential part of the whole structure.

Prunella was a Pierrot play in which innocence found love, disillusionment, sorrow and ultimate reconciliation. Prunella, played by Thyrza Norman, was strictly brought up by her aunts in the discipline of the clipped hedges of the Dutch garden (the alternative title was *Love in a Dutch Garden*). She fell under the spell of Pierrot, played by Barker. With the magic of moonlight and love, the Statue of Love in the garden (Lewis) came to life and told her to run away with Pierrot and his troupe. Pierrot later abandoned her and when he wanted her back, could not find her. At last they returned separately, disillusioned and sorrowful, to the garden. The Statue spoke again and reconciled them.

The play opened on December 23rd but received lukewarm notices and business was very poor. Barker was disappointed and puzzled—"the people who come seem most enthusiastic, and yet so few come". The critic Desmond MacCarthy believed that it was alien to the North European mind: "For though the peculiar blend of human sentiment which . . . Pierrot engenders and embodies, contains both seriousness and tenderness, they are of a kind so inimical to ours, that we instinctively condemn them as hardness and frivolity." How hard it is, though, to make a judgment that will last. Desmond MacCarthy was proved wrong by countless revivals, and huge admiration for the play, which grew only gradually (proving the worth of a repertory system). It ran through fourteen impressions in twenty years and was played worldwide and filmed. Yet now it is in eclipse again.

Barker himself revived *Prunella* several times with ever greater success. Thyrza Norman never played it again. She soon disappeared from the Court scene. Later J. H. Leigh divorced her and she married a young actor. Lewis believed she gave Barker the beginning of an idea for the main character in *Waste*.

The play haunted Lewis for the rest of his life. "To me," he said once, in introducing a radio version of it, "it has a nostalgic fragrance quite untouched by time or by any other play that I have seen. It is delicate like old porcelain, saved from over-sweetness by a vein of fastidious sophistication—almost, but not quite of cynicism." Was the nostalgia increased by the loss of that "Pierrot" to the theatre? Perhaps. He particularly admired Barker's performance because, as he said, "Beyond all the beauty and fascination there was a touch of unconscious cruelty in the performance that gave a deeper pathos to the play." Forty years later he would write that Barker's voice and movements in the part remained with him "as vividly as yesterday".

3

Journeyman of Theatre
1905–1907

During the next three years Lewis worked harder than ever before. Now that he had at last found, or accepted, his vocation he devoted himself to it unswervingly. A sketch of him, done at this time by Ernest Jackson when he was playing Dante in a play for Rosina Filippi, is a profile, showing a striking and handsome face, the eyes intent and piercing, the mouth firm and purposeful. The artist found Lewis so serious that he got somebody to sit with him while the drawing was being done, in order to make him laugh. He *was* serious, because things mattered to him and he was not afraid to show it, but he was neither solemn nor stuffy; people who thought he might be were often disarmed when his smooth face suddenly broke into a joyful smile, his bright blue eyes gleamed with mirth, and his firm and upright posture rocked with laughter. Both expressions were equally typical—the surprise came because of the contrast.

Work at the Court continued in the New Year with the added prestige of a Command Performance of *John Bull's Other Island* for King Edward on March 11th, 1905. Lewis was also rehearsing a Brieux comedy for the Stage Society, performed the day after the Command Performance. Immediately afterwards he started rehearsals for another production at the Adelphi, playing Rosencrantz in Oscar Asche's production of *Hamlet* (H. B. Irving as Hamlet, Lily Brayton as Ophelia, Asche as Claudius). A glance at the programme tells us much about the production, played in thirteen scenes, requiring seven complete settings, of which six were by Joseph Harker. The entire Norwegian subplot was removed, for neither Fortinbras nor Voltimand and Cornelius appear on the cast list. It was, then, a conventional scenic revival of the time, and the emphasis was on Irving, a considerable star in his own right with his own following. The production was greeted with critical and public acclaim.

If ever Lewis was to feel he had entered a world of glamour and fame it would be now, and he did enjoy the grandeur of it all. But far more important to him was a letter, which he treasured for many years, until, like all the rest of his theatre collection, it disappeared in the flames of the blitz. It was from Shaw:

My dear Casson,
Do you know my play *Man and Superman*? The Stage Society are going to do it for a Sunday evening and two matinées in May and I would like you to play Tavy.
Henry Ainley was going to do it but now I want him to play Tanner and have you for Tavy.
G. Bernard Shaw.

So Lewis created Octavius Robinson in a performance which Desmond MacCarthy praised as being "finely insignificant", and shared in the greatest triumph Shaw had had so far. It was a choice due, Lewis thought, to the romance of his voice and looks at that time. Shaw had seen him only as Eglamour, the Statue of Love and a few small parts in other plays, and Octavius does stand for the romantic artist and poet, though, as Lewis remarked, "his lines fail entirely to justify it". Whatever the reason, Lewis felt honoured to be included in an illustrious company; he had read the play and privately thought it unplayable before he realised that Shaw's acting version cut some of Act I and omitted the Hell scene. But at once he loved the brilliant rhetoric, the characterisation, and the splendour of the philosophising.

Now he experienced Shaw's directing at first hand, appreciating the skill, the care and kindness, and the melodies of rhetoric which Shaw's Irish ear demanded from the actors. The great speeches, such as Tanner's on the artist in Act I and on mothers in Act III were like operatic arias; years later, Lewis felt he could almost have conducted them.

Meanwhile the *Hamlet* production continued until the early summer and Lewis was promoted to playing Laertes. Even before the Stage Society performances of *Man and Superman* took place, the Vedrenne-Barker management took over the production for the Court, and at the same time, began evening performances. They also started paying weekly salaries to all the company instead of fees. Lewis, who had received £3 a week as a general utility actor, was honoured with a rise of ten shillings in view of his increased importance, plus £5 to buy shirts for the Granada scene. (A fellow actor playing a small part and understudying in a melodrama at Drury Lane earned £6 a week, so this is an indication of the tiny salaries the Court could afford.) Lewis recalled with amazement in

35

after years that each Stage Society production was budgeted at no more than £250, including scenery, costumes and actors for three performances, and the early Vedrenne-Barker productions were budgeted at £200 for six matinées.

As Ainley now had other engagements, a new Tanner had to be found. At first it was planned to ask Robert Loraine, who already had the American rights to the play, but then it was decided to save money by using Barker himself. Ainley and Loraine were both powerful and heroic leading actors, yet Lewis preferred Barker's performance to any other, then or later. In some parts he found Barker's acting too analytical and a little detached from the rest of the cast, but in all that he played he was unforgettable, making a part so much his own that you never afterwards wanted to see anybody else play it. As Tanner he was much like Shaw in appearance and in manner, especially, Lewis suggested, "in his suggestion of genius, his impudence, his beautiful manners without which Tanner can easily become a cad". Shaw imposed a broader theatricality than Barker's own, and for *Man and Superman* the effect exhilarated. Opposite Barker as Ann Whitefield was the young Lillah McCarthy, with whom he had worked a few years before in Ben Greet's company. Shaw had seen her as Lady Macbeth for Poel and since then she had appeared mainly in melodramas. Now Shaw brought her charm, beauty and talent to enhance the company at the Court, and as he admitted later, almost threw Barker and her together.

Many people considered the production of *Man and Superman* to be the Court's meridian. Everything came together—play, company, public, even the critics. And the acting was most admired. Desmond MacCarthy extended Lewis's feelings about Barker's acting to the whole cast: "All reached that pitch of excellence in their part which makes a living person start up before the mind's eye afterwards, whenever the name of the character is mentioned."

What was actually happening was that the seeds of a new kind of acting and production had now begun to take root and blossom, largely through the efforts of Barker and Shaw. They held dear the ideals of establishing a national repertory theatre where dramatic art could receive the care and respect given to other arts, but, more important, they spread their enthusiasm through the company and their public so that the aims became a living force, not a theoretical outline. As Lewis had seen, the eminent actors at the Court respected their two producers enough to take direction from them, and work for small fees, and this meant that, from the first, the company was on a different social basis from the conventional actor-manager's hierarchical structure. Instead of a dominating figure directing operations, however benevolently, from a powerful position in centre stage, you had a group of fellow-workers with a lively audience of one giving directions, suggestions and responses decisively and constructively, all equally focused on an abstraction, the production itself. In rehearsal the most important thing was the dramatic impact of the particular moment being worked on; a single line in a minor part would get the same quality of care and attention as any of the great speeches. "General utility actors", like Lewis, felt themselves to be part of the whole creation and worked with a commitment and vivacity soon apparent to the audiences. It was the good acting at the Court, especially in the minor parts, that first established its fame. Once this artistic quality was established, its implications for the theatre of the future could be recognised. For Lewis, his firm footing in the company now blossoming meant that he began to be drawn a little closer into Barker's circle, and to see how the whole idea linked with a vision of a Socialist world, with no division between managers and workers, and with a national theatre, which was Barker's real aim. Lewis first admired Barker's work as an actor and producer; now he began to respect his mind and to share his goals.

Productions continued. During the summer break Lewis went off on another "pastoral" circuit and then rejoined the Court for the autumn season with its busy schedule of rehearsal and performance. *John Bull* was revived, and *Man and Superman*. Ibsen came into the repertoire for the first time with *The Wild Duck*, in which Barker gave another of his strangely memorable performances, as Hjalmar Ekdal. The new Shaw play was *Major Barbara*, which, for all its philosophical and literary value, Lewis found a little unsatisfying theatrically. It showed, he felt, Shaw's growing tendency "to overemphasise the polemical in his plays, at the expense of the character drawing and drama". The reason, he thought, was because Shaw was now "alas, sure of his pulpit". Some of the uneasiness may have been because the cast, for once, was not completely happy with things. Louis Calvert, burdened with Undershaft's huge moral speeches in the last act, felt he could make no dramatic sense of them, and found them almost impossible to learn and deliver. Yet under Shaw's coaching he gave an impressive performance. The play drew an interested audience, including Arthur Balfour, then Tory Prime Minister, and the Webbs, for whom it was most topical, as Beatrice Webb was on the Poor Law Commission. (Shaw's desire to be topical is shown by the fact that he actually set the play in January 1906, a month after the date of its first performance.) Barker played Adolphus Cusins, closely imitating Gilbert

37

Murray, on whom Shaw had based the part. Lewis took it over in January; whether he dared imitate Murray so closely himself I doubt, for he did not know him well yet.

There were two major new plays besides *Major Barbara*, St. John Hankin's *The Return of the Prodigal* and Barker's own *The Voysey Inheritance*. Lewis became particularly fond of the former and also enjoyed watching the rehearsals, for it was almost the first time Barker created a modern English realistic production. He began by reading the play to the company and had the movements sufficiently planned to start getting the actors going at once; no time spent in long preliminary discussion, though plenty of discussion took place as rehearsals proceeded. They all learned by doing, and Barker "moulded" (Lewis's usual word to describe what Barker actually did) as they went. In this way the actor contributed to the building. Lewis remembered that Dennis Eadie developed the part of Henry in *The Return of the Prodigal* along lines quite different from St. John Hankin's or Barker's original intentions. (Eadie had decided that Henry suffered from bad breath!) But Barker was so fascinated by the performance as it grew that he let it happen and helped to develop it. After a week of reading and movement in a rehearsal room, when the play began to move, he would always let each scene run, making voluminous notes, and then take it to pieces afterwards. In putting it together he would "mould directly—interrupting". But there was always the chance for an uninterrupted run afterwards. When they moved to the stage, he moved to the stalls and continued his note-taking, returning to the stage for "detailed analytical work". Generally he saw the first performance of each play, but seldom another. This was because, Lewis thought, he found the audience's reactions "too depressing"—a sad augury of the future.

Barker's method of production was naturalistic to the extent that the details were drawn from observation of life, and the scale of acting was smaller than the traditional declamatory style. As with Chekhov's mastery of detail, the effect was gained through the placing of the detail in the play as a whole. "By the time the performance came," wrote Lewis, "the whole piece was moulded into a musical and rhythmic pattern as definite as a symphony, where every word and phrase, every silence, every intonation, had been scrutinised and accepted as the best he could achieve with his material."

Lewis's own forte was his striking presence and voice; he had begun to learn how to control their effect. He had his first chance to play in one of the Greek plays, which he had been longing to do. His

Castor in *Electra* (for which Barker and Murray tried to get Mrs. Patrick Campbell), was full of gravity and beauty, showing his instinctive grasp of the material. Barker and Murray were impressed. He also acted in the production of *Captain Brassbound's Conversion* when Ellen Terry at last took the part Shaw had written for her, but alas, too near the end of her career to realise the part fully. The whole production was a little out of balance; Shaw criticised Lewis, in a letter to Barker, for "playing out" too much. Nevertheless Ellen Terry's stage jubilee which took place during the run of *Captain Brassbound* was a joyous occasion in which the whole company shared, as well as her public and the theatrical profession itself, including Duse who was in England at the time.

Another occasion which drew the company together was the marriage of the producer to the leading lady. Barker and Lillah McCarthy were married secretly in April 1906, just when the first successful run of *Prunella* was beginning. When permanent members of the company heard of it, they were all delighted, not just because it underlined the harmony and happiness within the company, but also because Lillah's warmth and devotion and her attractive elegance seemed so exactly what Barker needed to support him in his work. Under his direction her own work was blossoming, adding lustre to each production in which she appeared. The company clubbed together and presented the couple with a beautiful armchair, and in later years Lewis was convinced that this gift was the beginning of Barker's retirement from the theatre; for it pandered to the "streak of luxury" he had detected.

This was a happy time for Lewis. He had established himself in the professional theatre without difficulty and some of his work was gaining respect. He felt he had much to learn, especially about modern drama, and that was healthy too, for he hated to be standing still mentally. Though his salary was small it was quite enough and he decided it was time to set up an independent establishment. He had continued to live at home in North London, but socially and professionally it would be much better to have a place of his own in town. The household he left consisted of Thomas and Laura Ann and Elsie, for Esther had married Arthur Reed in 1904, much to Lewis's pleasure at bringing his friend into the family. So Lewis and young Kenelm Foss, with whom he had "made faces" in *John Bull*, and who was understudying in Hall Caine's *The Bondman*, found a top-floor flat at No. 16 Clifford's Inn, very near the Barkers, which they moved into and Lewis proceeded to "do up". For the next eighteen months or so, this was his bachelor home.

One would like to know much more about what he thought and

felt and did at this time. He had an abrupt manner which often frightened people at first, but once you got underneath it he was a most companionable person, interested in all manner of things, eager to hear about other people's concerns. He was not a great party-goer. What he liked best was long, informal conversation with one or two close friends, when they could put the world and the theatre to rights, argue fiercely without offending each other, share their plans and achievements. But who his close friends were at this time, we do not know. Nor his girl-friends. One of the advantages of having his own flat was, of course, the freedom to keep his private life private, and perhaps it was a romance that finally decided him to leave the family home. He was an attractive man, greatly attracted to women, but he was also a discreet and private person, and the names and descriptions of the girls he knew then are not known.

The flat in Clifford's Inn has been described by its other inhabitant, Kenelm Foss. At the top of three flights of old sunken stairs, it was entered through the traditional two doors—so that the "oak" could be sported when required. Inside was a long, low-roofed main apartment with panelled walls and casement windows extending the whole length of one side and looking out on a garden. The panelling, bilious green when they took over, was soon painted a more pleasing chocolate colour. There were two small bedrooms and a tiny kitchenette, hardly large enough to hold their charlady. There was no bathroom—a flat tin tub kept under one of the beds had to suffice ("failing which the Holborn Public Baths")—and no privy "save a communal six thrones across the cobbled courtyard". All improvements that could be made they undertook with alacrity, and Lewis's factory and domestic experience made him a first-class handyman, in this home as in every other that he lived in. They made a panelled window-seat, with thin cushions on top, to go the whole length of the casement. Once, after a late night, Lewis generously offered this seat as a bed to a friend, Harcourt Williams, who had missed the train, never thinking that anyone could be so soft-bodied as to find it too hard for comfort. The poor man lay in agony all night, hardly able to thank his host in the morning. They soon installed electric lights in lanterns that they found in the Caledonian Market, where they also found a gate-legged table, a wall-clock, a set of coffin-stools and the case of an elderly grand piano for which Lewis somehow found the innards. (Without a piano, a home was not really a home to him.)

Having got the flat organised as he wanted, as cheaply as possible, Lewis then took little interest in domesticity. He went out for his meals and had no particular delight in lavish entertainment. If friends or family happened to come round he was delighted, and enjoyed the talk and perhaps even some music. If alone, he was either reading, studying or doing a repair. He liked his own visits to be casual, whether to his parents in Kentish Town, or to the Reeds in Putney, or to see Will (when in London), or Frances, who was now teaching in London, or to friends. On one Sunday visit to see the Barkers in their house in Kent, he spent the time fixing up an electric bell for them, instead of enjoying a relaxed day in the country as they had intended. He played cricket a little, and golf a little, usually because a friend had asked him to, and he loved walking and swimming. He cycled when it was too far to walk and took a bus or train if it was too far to cycle. If a friend had a motor car he took the wheel with delight and that was the one luxury he longed and planned for: he saw it as one of the greatest of modern scientific achievements.

Theatrically, too, he seemed to see a new era dawning. The old era could be said to have ended when Irving died in October 1905. Lewis had met him once, after a dinner ("He was very gracious to me") and had seen him act many times with Ellen Terry. Now he himself had acted with her. Shaw created much offence by writing against Irving soon after his death. Lewis was at the dinner Shaw attended at the time, to raise money for Poel; Shaw was booed until some wit shouted out "Let us hear Bernardo speak of this!" and good humour was restored. Though Lewis shared the new ideals, he could not altogether share the rejection of the old, because he did find some theatrical satisfaction in the grandeur of the traditional, just as he liked Anglo-Catholic ritual better than low Protestant services.

The Court gave little attention to décor. Because of his "recital" background and his emphasis on vocal presentation, there was a danger that Lewis might have remained altogether too unaware of the visual needs of theatre to become a producer. But at this point he met a pioneer of stage design, Charles Ricketts, whose influence would be invaluable in his development.

Budgets at the Court were too limited to afford very much. Contemporary plays were staged with realistic sets, simple and adequate but not lavish, and some attention was given to modern lighting. The Greek plays, however, needed something more. The costumes were deliberately simple so as to give the actors no feeling of restriction and artificiality and the audience no sense of historical remoteness, but some sense of stage design was needed. Desmond MacCarthy wrote that in the *Hippolytus* the stage was "hardly

41

worth looking at". The whole concept of modern scene design had not yet received much attention in the English theatre. The greatest pioneer was Gordon Craig. But many of his beliefs and his almost choreographic view of theatre were incompatible with the school of theatre now developing at the Court, with its emphasis on words and its social and human scale of values. Some other approach was needed. It came through Charles Ricketts, whose interest in stage design was aroused by poetic drama, and whose style was decorative.

Ricketts lived with another artist, Charles Shannon, in the Vale, Chelsea, where they entertained, among others, James Whistler and Oscar Wilde and were in touch with William Morris and Edward Burne-Jones. Ricketts became interested in the idea of a theatre society for romantic drama and discussed the scheme as early as 1901 with a writer friend, T. Sturge Moore. Although Ricketts was primarily an illustrator and engraver at that time, he was already interested in reforming stage design and prophesied that in this society, "the scenery would be done on a new decorative and almost symbolic principle". He had many discussions with Craig; they shared a desire to find a more organic mode of stage design than the adaptation of large-scale oil painting, a style typified in Lawrence Alma-Tadema's splendid Rome-scape for Tree's *Julius Caesar*. But his methods and aims were very different from Craig's: "He [Craig] could not understand my advocacy of arbitrary colouring in scenery, absence of complicated lighting effects and general decorative treatment." What Ricketts aimed at was a combination of clean line and rich colour, both in costume and stage design, which would enhance the actors and relate to the language of the play. His understanding of form in language corresponded with his idea of artistic form and it was this understanding that made him sensitive to the needs of poetic drama and the work Barker and Shaw were doing. After seeing *Hippolytus* at the Court, he wrote: "Verse should be spoken as simply, that is more simply, than prose. Its beauty lies in its structure, texture and substance; to add a tremolo to it is as if you played music with a tremolo obbligato."

Ricketts and T. Sturge Moore founded the Literary Theatre Society on the proceeds of their Vale Press edition of Marlowe's *Dr. Faustus*. Interested in romantic and poetic drama, they were particularly concerned with plays which had been denied production by the Censor, such as Maeterlinck's *Monna Vanna*, and in the spring of 1906 they decided to present a production of Wilde's *Salome*. Lewis was cast as Jokanaan.

This was not the first production of *Salome*: Florence Farr, Shaw's ex-mistress, had directed two performances during the previous year, but she could not really rise to its tragic splendours. Barker had already had some difficulties with Miss Farr at the Court, easing her out of doing the Chorus for *Electra* after the "jejune harmonies" she had created for *Hippolytus* and the muddled coaching she had given to the actors. Ricketts's production of *Salome* had no connection with hers, though he used the same actor for Herod, Robert Farquharson, a romantic actor of saturnine mien and great flamboyance. Salome was played by an imposing actress called Miss Darragh. The design, very simple, was in fact the first in the decorative style. Ricketts had hoped to stage the play for twenty-five pounds, but there were "intolerable delays and mistakes", as he recorded in his journal, and "dreadful estimates from John Bull, the stage manager". John Bull in fact threw up the job, the scene painters did not turn up and new ones had to be found, and Ricketts, with his thin, high-pitched voice and slightly comic excited manner, had to take over the whole production at the dress rehearsal, which made the minor actors "restive and rebellious". At last a performance took place on June 10th at King's Hall, Covent Garden, which was very well received by the audience, with four curtain-calls at the end. Ricketts recorded his approval of the performances of Herod, Salome and Jokanaan, but not with the rest of the cast. A second performance took place a week later. There were very few records of the production because the scandal attached to the play and to its author made the press boycott it. Ricketts mentioned that "Shaw watched it intently" and that "Duse was so deeply veiled that I did not see her".

It was a small but significant start to an approach to modern scene design which would provide an alternative to Craig; an approach perhaps more suitable to English drama, with its emphasis on words. Lewis had two more opportunities of learning from Ricketts's work. He was asked to produce *The Persians* for the Literary Theatre Society, and Ricketts designed it for him. No records survive of this production, a cause for great regret because it was Lewis's first work as a professional producer, done with a one-act of Barker's, *The Miracle*, a symbolist play with two medieval characters, which Ricketts also designed. Robert Farquharson produced.

Other experimental productions in which Lewis took part in 1906 and 1907 all shared the same qualities of earnest endeavour, coupled with precarious finances and conditions, and displayed either eccentricity or brilliant innovation. There was a tour of Goldsmith's *The Good Natur'd Man* for William Poel, but the bookings were so poor that Poel offered a free place to every tenth

43

person entering—and was stopped by the police for running a lottery! On another occasion a concert was improvised which Lewis enlivened with a whistling solo. In a production by Elsie Fogerty of Swinburne's *Atalanta in Calydon*, in which Lewis played another of his Messenger parts, the lush flow of language was echoed in the movement, but the play came through indifferently and the style of the production survives only in comic imitations. Charles Fry produced the first revival of the original text of Shakespeare's *Troilus and Cressida*, with Lewis playing Troilus. It was not well-liked, yet it began the restoration of that play to the Shakespeare repertoire.

During one of these summers Lewis played with Ben Greet, father of all pastoral players. An eccentric pioneer with a voice like Eeyore, Ben Greet was an insatiable producer of the classics. He ran an Academy of Dramatic Art, founded two pastoral companies, toured America extensively, and started an open-air theatre in Regent's Park. His companies were nurseries of talent, the actors including Sybil and Russell Thorndike, Nigel Playfair, Harcourt Williams, Lillah McCarthy and Granville Barker. Greet's productions were simple and could be effective, especially the *Everyman* he did with Poel, but sometimes his lack of rehearsal, low budget and hectic touring led to hilarious, ramshackle productions as amateur as the numerous little companies his example inspired. Lewis had known of his work for some time and could have met him through any number of people: Poel, Barker, Nigel Playfair or Rosina Filippi. The strands of Edwardian theatre were closely interwoven as classical actors moved fluidly through the companies of Irving, Benson, Ben Greet, Tree and even Poel, and now the new generation began to create their patterns, Barker, Oscar Asche, Forbes-Robertson and so on. It was a period of infinite variety for audiences, who had no way of telling which styles of theatre were dying traditions, which would continue to flourish, which experiments would prove to be damp squibs and which would alter the pattern of theatre history.

A variety of responses awaited the major new plays of the Court season that began in the autumn of 1906: Galsworthy's *The Silver Box*, Shaw's *The Doctor's Dilemma*, Masefield's *The Campden Wonder* and Elizabeth Robins's *Votes for Women*. Lewis was in all of these except the Masefield, a macabre story of a seventeenth-century murder scandal, admired by a few and heartily disliked by many. *Votes for Women* was little more than a piece of topical dramatic journalism, its best scene, a brilliantly staged suffragette meeting in Trafalgar Square. *The Doctor's Dilemma*, Shaw's comedy of the medical profession, was much enjoyed, and as with so many of his plays, outlasted the topicality of its theme. But in 1906 it was *The Silver Box* that created the biggest success; Lewis found it the most memorable new play that Barker produced at the Court, the best kind of topical theatre, because it gave a portrait of Edwardian society which that society was just on the brink of recognising as itself. What Galsworthy did was to draw attention to social injustice by showing the different treatment of a petty criminal in the upper and lower classes of English society. In Barker's most skilful production, the realism seemed only part of a more transcendent pattern, raising it to the level of poetic tragedy. This would become Lewis's aim when he began to tackle modern prose drama himself.

The last Court Theatre season finally ended in June 1907 after nearly one thousand performances which had begun a revolution in English theatre. At a grand Criterion Restaurant dinner in honour of Barker and Vedrenne, to which the whole company was invited, Ricketts claimed he went just to discover if there really *was* a J. E. Vedrenne, or if he were "merely a smart impersonation of Barker's, done with a wig and a pair of blue spectacles". But there was indeed such a person; he made a speech in reply to Lord Lytton's to the guests of honour; and Barker made a speech, and Beerbohm Tree made a speech and Shaw made a speech, by which time it was too late for more speeches and all the guests departed. Lewis wandered back through the streets with his friend Harcourt Williams, and they went over the ground again, relishing the great moments of the last three years, praising Shaw for his plays and his producing and his vehement support of the project, eulogising Barker for his producing and his acting and his plays, and his inspiring vision of what theatre could be like if it were freed from the shackles of commercialism and allowed to develop as a fully-fledged art.

Among all lovers of theatre it was a time of enormous optimism. Lewis, proud at being part of a great movement, was yet humble in his desire to serve it. He threw himself into the work with all his Celtic fervour but, at the same time, because he had done so many things first, and had explored so many paths before finding this one, he was not blinkered. He saw the theatre in a wide context, thought deeply about its purpose in society, and sought constantly for ways in which it could best fulfil its purpose. It was this that made him respond so eagerly to the ideas of many who were behind the Court, but most of all, to Granville Barker.

He soon found another way, besides acting and producing, in which he could serve the theatre, and that was by strengthening the solidarity and organisation of the acting profession. During the time at the Court, led by Barker, he began to involve himself in the activities of the Actors' Association, founded in 1891 to further the best interests of actors and actor-managers. It was not at first political and not very demanding. Until the 1890s theatre had been, to a great extent, a family affair or financed among friends, but the development of the touring system and the growth of speculation in properties began to industrialise the theatre and bring it into the hands of financial syndicates. Barker's early career had shown him much injustice and exploitation of minor actors and he began to try to improve their lot. In 1904, at the Annual General Meeting of the Actors' Association, he proposed a revolutionary motion, requesting that all salaries should be paid on the weekly basis of six performances, with every additional performance paid for at the rate of one sixth of the weekly salary; that special salaries should be paid during rehearsals; and that no actor or actress should be employed in the West End in a speaking part, except as an understudy, who was not qualified to be a member of the Association. It says much for the established actors who made up the membership that they did not simply fling up their hands and shout "Socialist!" but gave his proposals some thought and elected him to the Council. However, many were managers, and therefore employers themselves, so that they were unwilling to make such large concessions to their employees, and those who were not managers did not wish to create a split in the profession. So the proposals were shelved. While at the Court, Barker was in the equivocal position of being a manager himself, but he continued to work for this cause and encouraged many of his company to join the Association and form a reform group in it. Lewis quickly became a keen supporter. In truth the need to protect performers in variety (where many of the syndicates operated) was more urgent than in legitimate theatre, and in 1906 this led to the setting up of the Variety Artists' Federation, the first real theatrical union, which actually staged a strike. Then, blessed by the General Federation of Trade Unions, the variety artists formed a National Alliance with musicians and theatre employees. In response to the National Alliance variety managers in London formed the London Entertainments Protective Association and the two sides of music-hall were lined up against each other.

Encouraged by this solidarity among variety artists, Barker and his reform group began to press harder. In February 1907 twelve members of the group were elected to the Council with a specific ticket: to put the Actors' Association on a sound financial footing and to obtain a minimum salary of £2 a week. Barker and Lewis were among them. But they soon saw that no real progress would be made unless the Association excluded the actor-managers and became a real trade union like the National Alliance, representing the interests of employed actors. So, rather precipitately, the Reform Group brought the whole issue to a head. Lewis presided at a meeting when Barker brought up the whole question of whether managers should be allowed to remain as members of the Association. With the cat out of the bag, they forced a special meeting which voted to exclude the managers, and it says much for their eloquence that they got their majority when the actor-managers were among the best-loved and most highly respected members of the profession. The majority was insufficient to change the constitution of the Association, but because it amounted to a vote of no confidence in the managers as associates, they all resigned, except Barker. So the Association suddenly found itself without many of its leaders: Squire Bancroft, George Alexander, Frank Benson, Arthur Bourchier, John Hare, H. B. Irving, Cyril Maude, Beerbohm Tree and Charles Wyndham. The loss of these prosperous actors was a disaster, leaving the Association so short of funds that in October it had to pass a resolution to liquidate. Appeals were made, and eventually sufficient money trickled in for the motion to be annulled and the managers rejoined. But much good will had been lost, mainly because the Reform Group was trying to marshal troops and set up battle lines for a war that did not yet exist in the legitimate theatre. Most of the managers in the Actors' Association were just as interested in good theatre as they were in making money, and as the Association had been formed to promote the best interests of the theatre as a whole, the Reform Group's attempt to turn it into a trade union was premature. Yet the theatrical business was changing, and, acknowledging this, managers themselves (not just actor-managers) formed the Theatre Managers' Association and the Society of West End Managers in 1908. An Actors' Union was also founded but turned out to be abortive. The Reform Group continued to be active and Lewis remained on the Council of the Association, but Barker, disappointed at its reactionary behaviour, turned away.

Barker was suffering another blow, the failure of his next attempt to establish some kind of repertory theatre in London. He and Vedrenne had leased the Savoy Theatre from Mrs. D'Oyly Carte to continue their work in a West End theatre. Vedrenne was also involved in building a new theatre, which became the Queen's, but it was not yet ready. The Savoy was much larger than the Court and not very comfortable, and somehow the season never quite got off the ground. Lewis had spent the summer touring in *John Bull's Other Island* and *You Never Can Tell*, including some time in Wales, where he visited all his relatives in and around Portmadoc and attended the Fabian summer school in Merionethshire. He returned for the start of the Savoy season, playing in *The Devil's Disciple*, and understudying in *You Never Can Tell* and John Galsworthy's *Joy*, a trite comedy and nothing like the success *The Silver Box* had been. The season seemed blighted. There was no new Shaw play, partly because he had not written one and partly because of his generous attitude to new playwrights. "Every night of Shaw is now time lost," he wrote to Barker. "I am not going to sit down in the way I have cleared and block it." The most interesting play was to be Barker's own *Waste*, which everyone who read it had found most impressive. But the Censor forbade it unless Barker made certain amendments, notably by cutting out the references to abortion. This he refused to do and so the production had to be abandoned, causing Barker great pain and frustration. At the same time he was trying to cast and rehearse *Medea*, Murray's new Euripides translation. There was some talk of getting Mrs. Patrick Campbell but Barker really wanted his wife to do it and she herself was very eager, knowing that she could bring out Medea's "barbarian savagery". Vedrenne, however, was so afraid of Barker's wife taking all the leading parts—Shaw had made an unfortunate joke about that at the time of the wedding—that he adamantly refused to allow her to play it, and Barker was forced to cast Edyth Olive, perfectly good, but not outstanding. As this was the first major production of the West End season he was anxious to do something quite spectacular. He and Shaw had thought of *Peer Gynt*, but there were too many practical difficulties. Barker was beginning to fuss endlessly over plays and casting, his relationship with Vedrenne was deteriorating, his disappointment over *Waste* was acute and he suffered bouts of moodiness and depression. Artistically and financially the season was not fulfilling expectations; morale began to sink a little. Though Barker had helped to change the face of English theatre in the last three years, the pace of development was still too slow for him, and at this period his stamina weakened and for a while he lost direction.

But Barker had forgotten the importance of disciples—men who could go out and speak with tongues of fire, even if, for a while, the original flame was quenched. One of the people impressed and inspired by the work at the Court was Ben Iden Payne, a young actor and producer now starting a company in Manchester under Miss Annie Horniman. Two years before, Payne had been to see Barker, who had then recommended him to Yeats and Miss Horniman at the Abbey. Now, in directing her new company, he wanted to follow many of Barker's ideas: produce Shaw, find other new playwrights, run plays in repertory and even get Poel up to direct. Barker was corresponding with Payne about making some of the Court plays available, including, perhaps, some of Gilbert Murray's. He immediately thought of the member of his own company most in tune with the Greek plays, Lewis, who was playing the Messenger in *Medea*. Payne had already considered engaging him, so this would be an admirable way of following through the methods of production used for *Hippolytus*, *The Trojan Women*, *Electra* and *Medea*. Therefore Barker urged Lewis to encourage Payne to do Greek tragedy, and recommended to Payne that Lewis should be engaged to produce one, as well as to act.

The manoeuvre worked well and they came to agreement. Lewis left the Vedrenne–Barker management only a couple of months before it finished and set off to join the Manchester company. He felt like a pioneer, going out to set the pattern of the whole world. He was determined it would be Barker's pattern.

4

Enter an Actress
1907–1908

The meeting between Lewis and Sybil Thorndike in Dublin Zoo is so much a part of family history that one of Sybil's biographers calls her equivalent chapter to this one, *The Lion House*. But if any person, rather than a lion, could be thought to have influenced their coming–together, it was, albeit unknowingly, Bernard Shaw, with his usual mixture of pigheadedness and generosity. Iden Payne and Miss Horniman wanted to do some of his plays in their new company, but he refused to let them. Eventually he agreed reluctantly that Payne should have his first play, *Widowers' Houses*, which he said was no good at all. He refused to let them do *Candida* but agreed to a separate tour of it, under Miss Horniman's management, with his own guidance and a chosen cast, including Nigel Playfair and the beautiful actress Ellen O'Malley, who had created Nora in *John Bull's Other Island*. When Lewis joined Miss Horniman's main company, on tour in Glasgow, in December 1907, he was soon cast as Harry Trench, the young hero of *Widowers' Houses*, and that is what he was playing when Sybil first saw him in Belfast where the two plays alternated. After she had impressed Shaw in a Sunday night performance for the Play Actors' Society, he sent for her through Nigel Playfair to read for the understudy of Candida. She knew nothing of Shaw or Granville Barker, but threw herself into the reading with huge energy and passion, causing him to shout with laughter and utter the prophetic words which also entered the family saga: "Splendid, my dear young lady. You go home and learn housekeeping and have four children, or six if you'd rather, and then come back and show me Candida." But he gave her the understudy, because she reminded him of his beloved actress Janet Achurch, who had created the part, and so Sybil watched his rehearsals eagerly and played an effective part in the curtain-raiser, Mrs. Havelock Ellis's *The Subjection of Kezia*.

Some credit could also go to Nigel Playfair, who had taken a benevolent interest in Sybil ever since her début with Ben Greet, and who knew Lewis from the Court. It was he who actually made the introduction, in a Belfast street, when Sybil had already been impressed by Lewis's photograph outside the theatre, and then by his lively, crisp performance in *Widowers' Houses*. There was something about his strong, determined face and manner, and his beautiful voice, that appealed to her immediately. Two days later she was out with Nigel and May Playfair when they met Lewis and the introduction was made. As usual, Lewis's greeting was rather gruff, "a sort of huffy how d'ye do", and his appearance shabby, but he always got on well with the Playfairs, and soon something Nigel said amused him and Sybil saw his face light up and the sternness disappear. Although they did not speak to each other, he did notice her lovely blue eyes and the meeting made an impression on him. It was the first of the series of pictures which made up his early memories of her. He saw her that night in the little curtain-raiser and was very much struck with her playing.

Next week the two companies were in tandem again in Dublin. Like many actors Lewis and Sybil were always drawn to zoos, where there were so many manners and life-styles to observe, so it was not surprising that they both made time to go to the one in Dublin. Again Sybil was with May Playfair, and they met Lewis as he was standing in front of a lioness, trying to tame it with a hypnotic gaze and a soothing voice. Again Sybil remained rather in the background as the other two talked the kind of theatrical "shop" she was only just hearing about for the first time. Being thrust so suddenly into the two companies of "highbrows" was actually quite a daunting experience; it was only her own combination of enthusiasm and humour, confidence and humility that kept her going. She had already tried to describe this slightly exclusive world to her brother: "The highbrows are led, or rather they follow, Shaw and Granville Barker, and people like John Galsworthy and Arnold Bennett are all highbrows, and people talk about them in an odd and very familiar voice and you feel when you listen that you are very cheap and that if you aren't careful you'll drop your aitches or giggle, but I keep a tight hold on myself." So she meandered along behind May Playfair and Lewis, through the monkey houses, past the zebras and giraffes, drinking in all that they said, until May called a halt, quite exhausted by Lewis's quick-march pace. Then Sybil decided she would go back to the lion house, where the wolves were as well, and Lewis, realising that he had not actually talked to her at all, went back too, and they had their first conversation, while he picked up a cat and stroked it—though he disliked cats—just to give her an impression of his sweet, gentle nature.

51

At this time Sybil was twenty-five years old, and had been an actress for three and a half years. She had enormous vitality and something of the inner glow that captivates an audience at once, a sharp sense of comedy and considerable powers of characterisation. She had trained at Ben Greet's academy and done two lengthy tours of America in his company. No one had as yet seen her potential as a tragic actress, though she felt it strongly herself. She was of medium height, slimmish, with wavy brown hair, vivacious movements, and that mobility of expression so valuable to an actress, so surprising in a woman, which could make her look radiant and serenely beautiful at one moment, and plain and homely at the next. Her voice was pleasant, though by no means so musical as it would become in later years. Lewis was very taken with her, and she soon found that in one-to-one conversation he was neither fierce nor terrifyingly intellectual. They discovered that they shared a common love of music, and that both had started out in other careers before going into the theatre. This did not surprise Sybil, who already thought Lewis looked like an engineer or a sailor or "something to do with real life" and not like an actor. And Lewis began to be aware of some of her determination when she told him how she had had to give up her piano career because of nerves and a strained wrist, and then had almost lost her acting career through vocal damage. Only six weeks of complete silence eighteen months before had saved her voice, and she had been struggling to get back into her career ever since.

The last few days in Dublin soon passed and the two companies went their separate ways. Lewis said goodbye to Sybil at the theatre, and carried away with him a clear picture of her, standing in the doorway of her dressing-room in a strong light, smiling her farewell. Then he plunged into his new work with added zeal.

One of the chief differences between working at the Court and working for Miss Horniman was that Lewis was a leading member of the new company, whereas he had been, even at the end, a junior member of Barker's. He soon established himself in the company as one of its keenest and most idealistic actors, utterly unresponsive to the cynicism of a few of the older actors who found the high-flown talk of repertory and the new drama rather hard to take. His immediate superior was Ben Iden Payne, to whom Miss Horniman had given a wonderfully free hand to develop the kind of theatre envisaged for the provinces by Barker himself. Payne was only twenty-six, a slight man with an almost chubby face and a rubicund complexion; a skilled actor who had worked in Benson's company and who was acquiring considerable skill as a producer. He was giving a memorable performance as the cringing Lickcheese in *Widowers' Houses*, while his fascinating and exotic-looking wife, Mona Limerick, was a suitably intense Blanche. Cokane was Charles Bibby, who had an amazing capacity for taking on the characteristics of his part quite intuitively, so that he seemed to become the role he was playing, a marked contrast to Lewis's style of acting in this play, which was much more alienated and indicated to the audience what they were to consider, through his brisk delivery and careful pointing of the lines. Others in the company were Clarence Derwent, an actor of urbanity and wit; Basil Dean, a promising and intelligent young man, enthusiastically committed to the whole enterprise, though sometimes reluctant to admit it, and Penelope Wheeler, a beautiful Rossetti-looking woman who had been with Barker (and whose husband, Christopher Wheeler, was his friend and doctor). Miss Horniman herself was, as yet, a remote figure to Lewis; she kept out of rehearsals and left most of the artistic decisions to Iden Payne. Lewis knew of her early support of Shaw's *Arms and the Man* and then of the Abbey Theatre. She was forty-seven at this time; slender, dignified, forceful and yet reticent, clad always in rich medieval-looking clothes, which added to her statuesque appearance, decorated, on special occasions, with an opal-studded dragon.

The other play on tour was *David Ballard*, by Charles McEvoy, which Payne and Yeats had seen together in a Stage Society performance. They were impressed with it and so was Miss Horniman. It struck what was then a new note in the theatre, the realistic depiction of life in a lower-middle-class family (here Cockney): a note which would become in some ways typical of the "Manchester school". At the same time, preparations were being made for the production with which Payne wished to open at the Gaiety Theatre on Easter Monday. Somehow he had persuaded Miss Horniman to let him open with Shakespeare, and to invite William Poel to direct it in the Elizabethan style.

This was a bold experiment. Not even Barker had attempted to bring Poel's innovative methods into a professional repertory company. Nor was Payne content with this. The play he chose was the dark and bitter *Measure for Measure*, almost as unusual a choice at that time as *Troilus and Cressida*. Moreover, he dared to do this against the popularity of Richard Flanagan's annual revivals in Manchester, spectacles beside which even Beerbohm Tree's were tame little productions. A description of Flanagan's style tells us that the moon habitually came out, not in one place, but six, and that everything that could possibly be real, was real: real deer, real horses, real goats, real waterfalls, real acrobats and, for any scene bordering on the religious, a great Roman orgy of incense and processions. This was Shakespeare as Manchester knew it.

Nevertheless, Payne was determined. Lewis was delighted. Poel, coming over to Dublin to sort out some of the casting and start rehearsals, was apprehensive on learning that the company would not be his own actors, but it encouraged him to find that Lewis and a small-part actor, Edward Landor, were already there, because (he said) they could "take the tones". At first he tried Lewis as the Duke, but found his voice not sprightly enough and eventually cast him as the Provost. He wanted instead to get James Hearn, who had played several big parts at the Court, and to have Sara Allgood, a foremost Irish National player, for Isabella. Payne was surprised and pleased to find that they were willing to come. Hearn played the Duke, Payne was Lucio and Charles Bibby Pompey, Basil Dean Claudio and Poel himself Angelo. But the rehearsals were by no means happy. Many of the cast were nervous of Poel's eccentricities. He sat them down and started by reading the play to demonstrate the "tones" and to give the cuts. These were surprisingly numerous. Although Poel wished, as usual, to restore the continuity of Shakespeare's playing text, he was also concerned with the amount of bawdiness in the play. He genuinely regarded much of Elizabethan frankness as quite unspeakable, which perhaps it was, to an Edwardian audience, but it is puzzling to think what point there is in a script of *Measure for Measure* which glosses over the exact nature of Claudio's crime, softens the crudeness of Angelo's desires, and cuts references to the bed-trick!

However, the "tones" caused the problem. Most of the company neither realised nor cared that Poel was revolutionising Shakespearian presentation. Older actors fumed at being treated like schoolboys and "tutored" in their parts. Clarence Derwent actually walked out. There was much loud dressing-room protest and noisy caricatures of the rehearsals, but no one ventured to contradict Poel face to face. In any event he was quite impervious to interruption or criticism. Some actors tried valiantly to imitate Poel's tones, with varying success. Some appeared to listen to his instructions and then went their own way. For Lewis it was a trying time. He grew angry alternately with the actors' dog-in-the-manger-ish and silly attitudes and with Poel's inflexibility. He had small difficulty in assimilating Poel's instructions into his own developing power of speech for the Provost's scenes.

Rather to everyone's surprise, when the production opened in the freshly-scoured Gaiety Theatre which Miss Horniman had bravely purchased, it was well-received by several critics and by many of the public. An approximation of an Elizabethan theatre, based on the Fortune, was set up within the proscenium arch, the costumes were specially tailored from Poel's specifications of Elizabethan dress, Elizabethan songs arranged by Arnold Dolmetsch were played in the interval, and at the end the company knelt in line on the stage and repeated the King's Prayer from *Ralph Roister Doister*, which, though not quite historically appropriate, created a great impression. The acting pleased too, to the amazement of the cast. Praise went to Charles Bibby and Iden Payne, who had been left to their own devices, rather to their relief; to Sara Allgood, and even to Poel's own somewhat eccentric performance. The fact was that Poel had never had such a fine team to work with, and despite the rehearsal dramas the combination of talents was fruitful. Then the new company was expected to sweep away some cobwebs, and so all those who were genuinely tired of the Flanagan approach came hopefully and were delighted. The production was toured for a couple of weeks and even performed at Stratford, home base of the Benson company, while the *Candida* company came into the Gaiety, a manoeuvre which postponed the next meeting between Lewis and Sybil.

One of the exciting things about coming North was that Lewis found himself much more in the thick of the Labour movement than he was in London. The last four years had given him the chance to observe life in all the major towns of Britain, while touring, and this had given more weight to his conviction that the whole social system needed reform. The Fabian movement spread and Robert Blatchford's followers formed themselves into the "Clarionettes". Lewis soon discovered that Basil Dean, thirteen years his junior, was an avid Socialist and *Clarion* reader. That year the Easter cycling "meet" of the Clarionettes was held at Shrewsbury, so the two men hurried over to participate in the Good Friday concert, where they performed the Tent scene from *Julius Caesar* to great applause. He was not quite so carried away as he would have been ten years before, because he was beginning to see (and his experience with the Actors' Association had helped him to see) that the strategies of social change were difficult and complex.

Back in Manchester there were only two more productions before the company took to the road again, while the Gaiety was re-modelled. Lewis was delighted to find that Sybil Thorndike had been engaged as an understudy in *Clothes and the Woman*. Hers was a longish part, which gave him a fine excuse to offer his services in helping her to learn it. They went up on to the roof of the theatre to talk and study. Sybil thoroughly enjoyed his performance as the stiff, humourless brother in *The Return of the Prodigal*. Later they began to go on walks together, with Hilda Bruce-Potter, a prominent member of the company with whom Sybil had made great friends, and Charles Bibby. A short train ride took them deep into the country where they walked the hills and talked, Lewis always contriving to walk with Sybil so that they could get to know each other better.

There were many things they already shared: knowledge and love of music, though Sybil's was the knowledge of the student and performer, Lewis's that of a discriminating audience; a strong Church background which allowed them to discuss religion with thoroughness and familiarity without being irreverent; unswerving devotion to their respective families. Although Sybil had travelled across America twice, her life had been rather a sheltered one so far, revolving round music, religion, the family and acting. She had fancied herself in love with various actors and suffered at least one quite deep infatuation, which made her rather nervous of her own feelings. So she adopted something of a pose, saying that she would never marry but would set up house with her brother Russell. She expressed delight when Lewis claimed that he did not wish to marry unless he could afford a valet and a secretary; while very attracted to him, she found their long talks much easier to handle than a direct challenge to her womanhood. For Lewis there was excitement in her openness and warm response to new ideas, lifting and expanding his thoughts and ideals into something exhilarating, instead of the intensity which was often in danger of overtaking him. He found himself pouring out to Sybil all his admiration of Barker, whose disciple he felt himself to be, eloquently explaining Barker's vision of theatre as a legitimate art to rival the best of literature, music and fine arts, trying to describe his breathtaking performances and inspiring direction, until Sybil began to feel that Barker was a god and that she was undergoing conversion. Though she loved acting, she had not, until then, considered theatre as seriously as music. It was the second string to her bow, which she had taken up when music was no longer possible. Like Lewis, she had turned a hobby into a profession, but unlike him she had spent many hard-working years dedicated to her first vocation. Now she began to glimpse the idea that theatre was as rich and rewarding an art as music for its artists and its audiences. This was important to her development, giving her the courage to continue in a career which had already brought her frustration and struggle as well as great happiness.

Sybil's religious thinking had brought her to philosophy, but not to politics, but now, before she knew it, she found herself swept into the Women's Suffrage movement under Lewis's instigations, taking the chair for Mrs. Pankhurst, unsure as yet whether she really believed in it all or was simply enjoying the part. And then the political meetings. There was great excitement in Manchester at that time over a by-election. Campbell-Bannerman had died in April and Asquith became Prime Minister. The by-election was in May and Winston Churchill was standing as a Liberal against the Tory, Joynson-Hicks, and a Socialist candidate. Lloyd George came up to support Churchill and Lewis and Sybil went to hear the Welshman, (whose brother had at one time worked as a clerk to Uncle Randal, the solicitor in Portmadoc). H. G. Wells put himself into disgrace with the Fabians by supporting Churchill instead of the Socialist. In any event, Joynson-Hicks was returned and excitement soon died down. At first, all this seemed to have no bearing on the theatre, but Sybil was soon convinced by Lewis's own belief that theatre had everything to do with living in the world, and that your acting would improve if you knew more about how society worked. Although she agreed, it was not so much by intellectual persuasion as by an intuitive grasp of the human values Lewis defined for her. For his part he began to look to her for a strength of moral intuition and a sort of spiritual enthusiasm which his own cautiousness denied him.

The end of the season and Sybil's three-week engagement came in May, and they travelled to London together. Finding she had time before catching the train to Aylesford, the quiet village in Kent where her father was vicar, Lewis invited her to tea at Clifford's Inn, where she actually sewed two buttons on his coat—the first and quite possibly the last, for she hated mending. He saw her off and, as far as she knew, that was that; but the yeast was beginning to work and Lewis quickly thought of a good ploy to see her again. He arranged to produce *As You Like It* at St. Mark's College and invited her to play Rosalind to his Orlando. In the same post, to her great delight, came a letter from Iden Payne offering her a place in the Gaiety company starting with a summer tour.

Lewis found it a great joy to play opposite Sybil, and took the opportunity to introduce her to some of his family who came to see *As You Like It*. She immediately took to his genial father and was enchanted with his pretty little Welsh mother, but his sisters were more alarming: Frances, now teaching in Southwark, Elsie, a social worker and rent-collector for Octavia Hill, Esther, with her gentle learned husband Arthur and their small children, all seemed very serious and clever to her and she felt she would have to mind her p's and q's. Soon however there were various other pastoral productions organised by Frederick Topham, Ben Greet's assistant and Sybil's old drama teacher, and Nigel Playfair, in which she and Lewis both appeared. This was a world they both knew and felt confident in, playing Shakespeare with the minimum of rehearsal and technical effects, throwing themselves into it wholeheartedly with no time to worry about their dignity.

For a few weeks, their ways parted as they played other summer engagements, but then at the end of July the Gaiety tour started and Sybil joined it in Brighton. Lewis and she met on the pier and immediately went off to see Doughty's Performing Dogs, swam off the pier and watched Marie Lloyd swimming as well. Then in Exeter Sybil had her first chance to play Candida. Lewis sat in a box with his old friend Jules Shaw, a wild, volcanic man whom he had known since the first L.C.C. tour with Poel, and who had just joined the company. He was thrilled with her performance, which even then captured much of Candida's radiant serenity, although she had too much bounce and jollity. (Basil Dean considered her later performances the finest Candida he ever saw.) He kept muttering his approval to Jules Shaw, but at the same time took copious notes, and when he met her with Hilda Bruce-Potter, in the fish-shop, he told her he had watched it and then said, to Hilda's indignation, "I've made notes and criticisms. Will you come and have some coffee with me and I'll go through the part with you." He then proceeded to tear her performance apart, but she accepted his criticisms gratefully. A more romantic encounter followed, with a trip on the river and tea in Lewis's and Jules's bankside rooms, when Lewis showed off by climbing a wrought-iron balcony. During this week he also introduced her to Barker who had come over to see Penelope Wheeler, and she found his dynamic manner quite matched the extraordinary accounts that Lewis had given her. Then on to Birmingham, and Lewis's mind was almost made up. A country walk, where Sybil lost a glove, so he kept the other and bought her a beautiful new pair; a morning call on Sybil in her digs with Hilda, bringing a little boy with him ("Just to see how you'd react," Hilda commented to Sybil); lunch together the next day; then a memorable evening walk in Edgbaston, still open country then, with a harvest moon, and two wonderful trees standing close together, which seemed to symbolise what was happening to the two of them. On the way back Lewis took her hand, and next day in the Kardomah Café he proposed. She was so surprised—here was a man still addressing her as "Miss Thorndike", who, she was still trying to convince herself, was just a wonderful friend with whom she was not in love—that she could not give him an answer. But she agreed to go to Early Service that Sunday morning, and that seemed to consecrate their union without her ever having actually said "yes".

Having skipped the formality of asking Sybil's father's permission, Lewis now had to face the ordeal of securing his approval. The Thorndikes were a little perturbed at what seemed to be their daughter's wild impetuosity, suddenly announcing to them that she was engaged. She had known Lewis only six months and hardly seemed to be sure of her own feelings for him, but her decision was based much more on intuitive knowledge that Lewis was the man she would marry than on rational judgment, or understanding of her own emotions. Lewis, however, was certain of his feelings and of his judgment. Sybil was the woman he loved and he knew that he wanted her as a life partner. Canon Thorndike came up to Carlisle, where the tour had taken them, to meet Lewis, who hid behind a milk churn at the station, to catch his first glimpse of his prospective father-in-law. But the meeting itself went off well and the two men liked and respected each other straight away. The engagement became official, and when the new Gaiety Theatre opened, the couple made their first appearance together in a little one-act play, the first by Basil Dean, and his first production, called, auspiciously enough, *Marriages Are Made in Heaven*.

The company now began to settle into Manchester and consolidate. It included the intelligent and distinctive Miss Darragh (who had played Salome in the Ricketts production), Louise Holbrook and Ada King who both became stalwart members of the Gaiety, Hilda Bruce-Potter and Charles Bibby, Jules Shaw, Basil Dean and the slightly remote, middle-aged figure, Henry Austin, as well as the Paynes and Sybil and Lewis. Later in the season they were joined by the romantic and flamboyant young Esmé Percy. Like most repertory companies they half belonged to Manchester and were half separated from it, living their own absorbing theatrical existence and often considered Bohemian. The theatre's public image benefited enormously from the high level of newspaper criticism by such writers as C. E. Montague, James Agate and Allan Monkhouse. Miss Horniman soon became a well-known and respected figure in the city, clad in her rich brocades, but living in very simple domestic surroundings with her cats.

In October came the opportunity Lewis had been waiting for, to produce Gilbert Murray's *Hippolytus*. Like Barker he combined this with playing the Henchman. Penelope Wheeler, from the original production, played Phaedra and designed costumes, Jules Shaw was Hippolytus, and Sybil, acting in her first Greek tragedy, was Artemis. Lewis kept in close touch with Barker while he was rehearsing, and as Barker was touring *Arms and the Man* in the North, he was able to slip, very discreetly, into a rehearsal. Then Murray arrived to give his assistance and coach some of the actors. By such co-operative methods between one company and another, Barker, Murray and Lewis felt that a kind of national repertoire of outstanding productions might be created, so every effort was made to imitate the quality of the Court production and build from it. Scenery was extremely simple; the music, specially composed by Granville Bantock, was unusual and effective, played by a hidden orchestra, to enhance some of the emotional moments. Instead of having his chorus chant as they had done, never quite satisfactorily, at the Court, Lewis had them recite, one at a time, and move in harmony with the changes of emotion, while stray notes of music set off the words. Though Murray did not find the chorus problem entirely solved, Lewis's method was an improvement and one critic commented that "the duty of the chorus to hold up a mirror to the play and catch the reflection of the actors' emotions, was performed far better than it would have been by elaborate chanting". Lewis's own performance of the Henchman's speech was highly praised except by those who found his pace too rapid, for his style of delivery was so much faster than the slow declamatory pace of traditional acting. C. E. Montague found it the finest individual performance, "so complete was the rescue from staginess, so urgent your sense of a higher power of reality than any but great acting gives". It was this universal quality which Sybil found difficult to achieve; Murray was asking her to cut out many of the lively individual traits with which she was used to characterising her performances. He insisted that he wanted Artemis to be "opalescent dawn", and added, for good measure, "Lewis will show you how." And indeed it was through Lewis's rigorous training and Murray's wise coaching that the company was brought to a fine achievement that established Lewis's reputation in the company and with the Manchester public.

There were seventeen actors in the permanent company and they were all kept very busy rehearsing and performing. Miss Horniman had abandoned the idea of presenting a varied repertoire during each week, so the productions ran for a week at a time, with frequent revivals of the most successful ones and occasional weeks in other towns while a different company performed at the Gaiety. The autumn season was a well-balanced mixture of new productions and revivals, and new and old plays. In what spare time they had, Lewis and Sybil made their wedding plans. Mrs. Thorndike came up, was taken to Blackpool and set about convincing her shabby-looking prospective son-in-law that it was to be a grand social occasion not a quick trip to a local church. There was a visit to London when Sybil received a warm welcome into the Casson home in Putney. Laura Ann took her aside to give her a special word of pleasure, "I'm so glad you're going to marry Lewis," she said. "He has always been *so* good to all the family." Sybil's brother Russell, just returned from a long American tour with Ben Greet, came up to Manchester with Eileen, Sybil's younger sister, to meet Lewis and see all the plays in this marvellous company they had heard so much about.

In December the company was in Dublin, where Lewis found Barker had been taken ill with typhoid. When he came out of hospital he visited them and Sybil played Bach to him and was impressed with his deep knowledge of music. Next week they were in Cork and had to rush through a final performance of *Candida*, in which Lewis was playing opposite her as Marchbanks, and get back to Dublin for the ferry. Then, straight down to Aylesford for a beautiful Christmas country wedding, with both the families gathered together, two bishops to officiate, a scarlet-clad choir and Mrs. Thorndike at the organ—not, unfortunately, one of Thomas Casson's. The villagers all watched Miss Sybil, dressed in a beautifully embroidered satin gown made in Manchester, as she drove to and from the church in an open carriage. Lewis had threatened to wear his first act *David Ballard* suit, but in the event he dressed in a style more appropriate to a solemn, joyous and emotional occasion. Sybil sobbed and Lewis wondered how he could take her away from such a loved and loving home. Then off they went to Derbyshire for two weeks of snowy walking, and driving in a borrowed Rolls Royce, and two weeks staying grandly and elegantly with Uncle Randal, Aunt Lucy and their son Alec, at Bron-y-garth, whence they could visit friends and relations in Portmadoc and all around, and where Sybil fell in love at once with Lewis's homeland.

So the series of pictures which formed Lewis's early memories of Sybil, stretched over ten months of 1908 and scattered over so many parts of Britain, came to an end as he embarked on married life and the establishment of his own family. Perhaps he was romantic enough to feel the future opening out for him as at the end of his favourite play, *Prunella*:

(Light begins to increase in the garden, and the singing of birds is heard.)

Prunella: Hush! Hush! The birds are waking in the night;
    They sing of thee and me, and our delight!
Pierrot: 'Tis not the birds: it is the stars that sing;
    Nay not the stars, nor any mortal thing,
    Either in earth beneath or heaven above;
    The song thou hearest is the song of Love!
    Hark! Look!

(They turn to the Statue, which is again flooded with light. Love's head is raised, and he plays upon his viol, while all the garden grows loud with song.)

Or perhaps he thought of *Man and Superman*, his other favourite play, and felt the Life Force pulsing through him.

5

The Irresistible Gaiety
1909–1912

In January 1909 the Cassons went eagerly back to work in what they soon found was a very rich season. Galsworthy came up to help produce *The Silver Box*. At first he struck them all as a little distant, but in rehearsal he would often say confidently, "I expect that line will get a laugh." Laugh? they all thought. How could he think this serious play would get laughs? But, sure enough, in performance the laughs came, even though the audience was deeply stirred as well. Payne outdid even Barker in the realism he brought to the scene in the police court. At his stage manager's suggestion he hired some unemployed men from the streets of Manchester to earn a few shillings as extras. Their weary, worn-out looks and manner added an inimitable pathos to the scene and sharpened the actors' responses. When Galsworthy, impressed by the accurate portrayals he took to be acted, heard the truth, he gave Payne a large sum of money to share between the men, over and above their payment, and walked sadly away.

Next came *The Feud* by Edward Garnett, a romantic drama set in twelfth-century Iceland, in which Lewis and Mona Limerick played a pair of star-crossed lovers. It suited her tragic fervour and Lewis drew on his Celtic powers to show the character's force, dignity and passion. The production was the most spectacular that Manchester had seen at the Gaiety, but when the play came to London, audiences and critics were cool and unmoved.

The Cassons settled in digs at Didsbury and came in each morning for the day's rehearsal, which ran from ten-thirty until four, with two quick breaks for coffee and lunch. They had just time to get home by train or tram and hurry back to the theatre for the evening performance. On Sundays they went for walks in the country. The company worked harmoniously together with great respect for their young producer who was clearly fulfilling almost all his aims in setting up the ideal provincial repertory theatre. The salaries were not large—Lewis earned seven pounds a week and Sybil five—but everyone had interesting and exciting work. Manchester audiences were responsive and good new plays were beginning to come forward as Miss Horniman had hoped.

The happiness of Lewis and Sybil was completed by the discovery that they would have their first child in the following October. They were on a two-week tour in Scotland when this was confirmed and, in celebration, Lewis bought a lovely plain blue vase which, over the years, stayed with them and somehow became a kind of symbol of family happiness. (When, years later, Sybil was asked what luxury she would like on a desert island, she decided to take the "blue vase".)

But still the theatre was not making money. Miss Horniman and Iden Payne decided that what would most increase the company's prestige and business would be a successful London season, if that could be managed. So they bravely engaged the Coronet Theatre in Notting Hill for a two-week season in May 1909. Turning out to be a triumph, this was extended for another week. Seven of their best productions, plus curtain-raisers, were performed, and critics and audiences, unanimous in their delight at the sense of ensemble and balance which the company created, felt they were seeing something quite new.

Despite the promising future that seemed to lie in Manchester, Lewis and Sybil rather unexpectedly decided to leave the company at this point and seek their fortunes in London. It was a risky decision, especially with a baby on the way and it was the first time either of them had voluntarily given up a good engagement. But Manchester was almost too safe and cosy; Lewis felt that he wanted to strike out for himself again. Iden Payne's position at the Gaiety was unassailable, his wife Mona Limerick clearly the leading lady. Charles Bibby and Hilda Bruce-Potter, soon to be married themselves, were also firmly established at the top of the company and perhaps it seemed that there was not much space for him and Sybil. Perhaps, too, he noticed the slight condescension of even the most favourable critics. "It is encouraging to know," William Archer had written, "that in a great provincial centre, a company of intelligent young actors is producing week by week, plays of a strongly progressive tendency, is winning high local appreciation and is, in the meantime, acquiring an invaluable variety of experience."

Lewis felt instinctively that they should stay in London and see what they could find, and in the end he was amply justified. He took Sybil down to Aylesford to await the baby, travelling rather boldly on a motor bicycle he had acquired for a few pounds, with Sybil tucked up in the side-car. He soon found himself a part in a Lewis Waller production and then in a Conan Doyle play at the

Haymarket. Further, he heard from Barker of some interesting plans for no less than two London repertory seasons, one at the Haymarket, which in fact never materialised, and one planned by the American manager Charles Frohman, a live-wire on both sides of the Atlantic. It was a question of sitting tight through the autumn and hoping. Meanwhile he managed to get a few parts in minor productions and in the suburbs. One Sunday night production was with Sybil's young brother Frank, just starting to make headway as an actor. When things were getting difficult financially, the family situation was altered by Canon Thorndike's appointment to the living of St. James the Less in Westminster (neighbouring parish to Father Olivier, whose son Laurence was just a few months old). This meant that the whole Thorndike family, including Sybil, moved up to the vicarage in St. George's Square and Lewis moved in too. In October, after a difficult and painful labour, Sybil gave birth to a fine son, John. Lewis's birthday on October 26th fell exactly between Sybil's on the 24th and John's on the 28th. The baby was christened by his grandfather with his uncles Randal and Russell as godfathers, and an old Rochester friend of Sybil's as godmother.

Thanks to Mrs. Thorndike ("Mother Don-Don" as she was called), they found a little flat only two doors away from the vicarage and Lewis began to furnish it. His idea of furnishing was the same as at Clifford's Inn. He would set off for the York or Caledonian Market and pick up various decrepit-looking, apparently useless objects which he would then restore, or adapt or use for mending other things. In this way he found for Sybil a dilapidated Queen Anne bureau which he bought for a few shillings and restored to a beautiful piece which she used till the end of her life. On one of these expeditions he persuaded Russell, who considered himself quite a man-about-town, to accompany him, and made a miscellany of purchases—a roll of red lino, an oak prayer-desk, the mahogany lid of a lavatory, and an ancient washstand with little holes of various sizes in it. He assembled all this in a heap on the pavement and, much to Russell's dismay, proposed that they should carry them to the Underground. Mortified by the spectacle he would be making of himself, Russell reluctantly agreed to carry the lino and then walked as inconspicuously as it is possible to do when carrying what looks like a large drainpipe, and as far away from Lewis as to pretend to disown him; Lewis, quite oblivious to his brother-in-law's embarrassment, strode briskly off with the prayer-desk and washstand clutched under each arm and the lavatory lid swung round his neck like a Hawaiian flower greeting.

Soon plans for Frohman's repertory season began to take shape

65

and in February 1910 it was launched, the first scheme of its kind in the West End. Charles Frohman was a successful and enterprising manager with great commercial flair and powers of critical judgment. He managed the Duke of York's Theatre for nineteen years and had worked closely with J. M. Barrie and the producer Dion Boucicault. Barrie had first suggested to him the possibility of presenting a repertory of modern plays with a first-rate acting company. Lewis thought that Barrie looked on Shaw as a sort of rival and wanted his own plays to have the kind of showing Shaw's had had at the Court. Frohman was attracted by the novelty of the idea; and, by now, quite a number of first-class actors, producers and writers were eager to join, some with much repertory experience. Boucicault and Barker, the two producers, immediately saw the venture as another step towards a national theatre. They engaged several actors from the Court, including Lewis; Sybil was invited to understudy and play small parts. But the only other Gaiety member was Mona Limerick, brought in for some performances in a Shaw play. This was something of a disappointment for young Manchester players like Basil Dean, who found that his success there was too provincial to impress Frohman. Indeed, apart from some actors from the newly-formed repertory theatre in Glasgow, most of the rest of the company were regular "stars", including Irene Vanbrugh, Lena Ashwell and Hilda Trevelyan. Each of these leading ladies had been specially engaged at the behest of one of the season's playwrights: a thoroughly "un-repertory" method of casting which did not bode well for the harmonious running of what was already a fairly heterogeneous company.

Lewis and Sybil were excited by the programme, starting with Galsworthy's *Justice*, Shaw's *Misalliance* and a triple bill of Barrie (two plays) and George Meredith, followed by Barker's *The Madras House*, all original work. *Justice* aroused most public interest; its moving scene of a prisoner in solitary confinement caused a public outcry about this treatment of criminals and influenced the Home Secretary, Winston Churchill, to modify the law. But though there was some critical acclaim for the first three productions, of a standard London had rarely seen, the alternation of plays and the intellectual demands they made did not attract a West End audience. Financially the season got off to a bad start, and when Barker's rather unwieldy new play was put on, it found very few admirers. Lewis remembered afterwards that Barker was not particularly surprised; he was not satisfied with the piece himself, but it cast a blight on a project which had not really taken root. Frohman was a commercial manager, but the season added enormously to his prestige, so,

66

rather against his businessman's feelings, he did not call a halt. He did, though, drop the repertory system of performances. It had been a great burden on the stage-management because each play had a complete elaborate set—there had even been talk of involving Gordon Craig—but the Duke of York's did not have space enough for storage, and all the scenery had to be left outside the theatre or carried across the river when another set came in. Barker and Shaw were horrified because to them the repertory system was the whole point of the scheme, allowing for variety and the gradual cultivation of an audience for each play. The next two plays, *Prunella* and Pinero's *Trelawny of the "Wells"*, were much more successful and played for several weeks, with a rather trifling piece by Anthony Hope, of *Prisoner of Zenda* fame. But at this point Edward VII's death badly affected the theatre. Another new play, *Chains* by Elizabeth Baker, was put on for a few weeks, until, in June, Frohman felt he could end the whole project without loss of face. Plays by John Masefield, Henry James, Gilbert Murray and Somerset Maugham, which had been announced at the beginning of the season, did not see the light.

Though the venture had been something of a fiasco and a great disappointment to Shaw and Barker, who felt that Frohman had let them down, it did create a big stir artistically and intellectually, and it was an inspiring experience for the company. Lewis played in *Justice*, *The Madras House* and Meredith's *The Sentimentalists* under Barker's direction, and re-created his performance of the Statue of Love in *Prunella*. Again he found Barker's approach a revelation in his ability to capture the emotional and intellectual spirit of a play through an accumulation of realistic and poetic details often quite brilliant in themselves. (Sybil commented on one of the gestures he invented for Charles Maude as Pierrot, "no one but God could have thought of"). Still, chiefly, Barker's personal qualities and charisma impressed Lewis. All through rehearsals or discussions he was "eager and tireless, blazing with an inner fire that yet remained always under the steely, flexible control of a keen calculating brain". His impish humour contributed; also his infectious belief in the importance of theatre in the world.

Lewis played, too, in *Trelawny of the "Wells"* and *Chains* under Dion Boucicault's direction. His was a more traditional authoritarian approach, very different from Barker's. Lewis had become aware of the tension and disagreements between the various men behind the scheme—Frohman and Boucicault who did not really understand the idea of repertory, Shaw and Barker who felt that their ideas were being trampled on, Barrie, the instigator of it all, whose own personal life was in tatters, trying to keep them in harmony. Nevertheless, he found Boucicault's meticulous and disciplined approach immensely satisfying and influential on his own style of producing.

For Sybil, the season was an inspiring experience. She played small parts, watched in awe these two producers at work, and saw the plays take shape. Then, at the end of the season, Boucicault gave her a big and rewarding part in *Chains*, playing opposite Dennis Eadie and Hilda Trevelyan, and this had an important consequence. Boucicault and Sybil worked hard on the performance, and he persuaded her of the value of restraint; Frohman, impressed at a rehearsal, offered her a season in America with John Drew, playing a showy part in Somerset Maugham's *Smith*. It was a strange climax to the repertory season and she was apprehensive, especially as it meant being separated from the baby. But the salaries offered herself and Lewis were extremely good, and Lewis was longing to see America, so they decided to go. They faced a thin period in between, for Lewis's seven pounds a week and Sybil's three pounds ten had not gone far in supporting a small household and they had not been able to save. Lewis did a few minor productions and some teaching and then they gave up their little flat, put John into the charge of his grandmother and a nurse, borrowed twenty pounds from the Actors' Day Fund to tide them over till the first salary, and were seen off to Liverpool, to catch the boat, by Thomas and Laura Ann. Sybil was upset at leaving the baby, and if Lewis had known that it was the last time he was to see his father, his own grief would have overtopped hers.

When they arrived in New York they received a typically warm American welcome and immediately fell in love with the city. They spent long hours with John Drew, making him talk about his days with the great actress Ada Rehan, and they made friends with many other artists, musicians and theatre people who formed a delightful little colony in downtown Manhattan.

All through the autumn they played at the Empire Theatre in New York, saw and did everything there was to be done, ate and talked with their new friends, wrote letters home and read the books they had had no time for over the last few years. It was the first time they had had so much leisure together, and for those few months it was enriching. Sundays could still be spent walking in the country by the Hudson River, and Sybil devoted much time to the piano. The only things to mar their joy were the separation from their son and then the sad news of Thomas Casson's death. He died quite suddenly, collapsing in the street with a heart attack, at the age of sixty-seven.

With his heart so firmly set on his ideal of a civic theatre it was hard for Lewis to be satisfied by a long commercial run. He felt he would soon have to make a choice about the kind of theatrical life he wanted for Sybil and himself. Just before the *Smith* company set off on a national tour, Charles Frohman came into the theatre with an amazing offer. He would, he said, make Sybil a star. She should play for three months a year in New York, and then go on the road. First, he offered a play opposite John Drew for the following season. Lewis's reaction was complicated. He knew that neither he nor Sybil could altogether enjoy a long run system, and that she had other aims besides being a "star". But it was nevertheless a wonderful offer, and if Sybil was destined to be a star, he felt she should be one. Also many financial worries would be solved, and such worries were always a very heavy burden for him, remembering those early years in London. There was also a strange quirk of conscience which made him think that if they preferred repertory theatre, that might be all the more reason why they should face the challenge of commercial theatre. The feeling was increased by his desire to serve an audience, not to impose on it. He had great respect for Frohman for giving his audiences the kind of theatre they enjoyed. Sybil's reaction was simpler: she was naturally tempted by the future career Frohman pictured for her, but she did not really care about the money, she knew she could not bear to lead a life that took her away from her child, and she missed the sheer hard work and challenge of a repertory company. They talked and talked and decided at first that they would accept Frohman's offer, so they signed a contract and set off on tour to the West.

Seeing California and all the other places Lewis had heard so much about from Sybil was exciting, and he found it all as breathtaking as she could have hoped. But soon, away from New York, the sheer boredom of doing one play began to tell on them, and they grew more and more apprehensive about their commitment to Frohman. Fortunately, or perhaps indeed by cunning design, Sybil found, within a few weeks that she was expecting another baby. She wrote regretfully to Frohman breaking her contract, but he immediately offered her a new contract starting when she had had the baby, and assured her that he could find her continuous work. The struggle of decision was repeated in Denver but this time they decided to follow their feelings and courageously refused Frohman's offer.

Within a week, they were amply rewarded for their courage. In Salt Lake City there came a letter from Miss Horniman inviting Lewis to take over from Iden Payne as producer at the Gaiety, with

69

the promise of parts for Sybil as well. The offer was completely out of the blue and they did not hesitate. They knew, without doubt, that this was what they wanted. The compass had swung round towards Manchester again. Lewis accepted the job at once and they began to look forward to the hard work that lay ahead. They finished the tour with twice the enjoyment, pocketed their savings and sailed back to England.

It was a wonderful homecoming. There were only a few days in London for reunions with the Thorndikes and John, now more than twenty months old, and the Reeds and Cassons, all in Putney, for Frances and Elsie had taken a little house with Laura Ann. Setting off for Manchester, and finding a semi-detached house in Heaton Park, they sent for their furniture, and then for John, with Alice, the girl from Aylesford who had always told Sybil she would come and be her maid, and had kept her promise, looking after John for all the months his parents had been away. Lewis was able to busy himself once again with building and repairing furniture, making toys for John and enjoying his fatherhood. To John he became the source of untold wisdom, skill and entertainment.

At the theatre he found a rather tense situation for the first few weeks. Iden Payne had handed in his resignation but it had not yet been made public; so the press gave Lewis a cordial welcome simply as a returning actor. Payne's decision had in fact been very long drawn out. As far as Lewis could make out, it was based partly on a quite understandable desire to captain his own ship. His wife, Mona Limerick, was particularly anxious that they should set up in management themselves. (This they did quite successfully for a time. Later Payne went on his own to America and remained there for the rest of his career, apart from a rather unhappy time at Stratford-upon-Avon in the 1930s.) The brilliant and volatile Mona Limerick and the dignified Miss Horniman did not see eye to eye at all, and as they were both quite forceful ladies and Payne was a man of gentle, unassuming demeanour, he had been party to some embarrassing scenes. Also Miss Horniman had started to take a much more active, not to say interfering, interest in the artistic side of her theatre. Sybil later said that "Hornibags", as she was irreverently nicknamed, "was taking such a hand in the productions that poor Iden had to leave", although Payne, in his own memoirs, did not make this accusation. He was certainly tired, both physically and mentally, from the strain of four years' almost continual effort.

There was also an unspoken conflict over his refusal to compromise his very high ideals for the theatre. During the last year his two best productions had both been financial disasters. Payne, writing on the Gaiety in its Christmas annual in 1909, had insisted, "When an art becomes a trade, the practitioner seeks the maximum of return with a minimum of effort". Miss Horniman stated her attitude differently: "The drama falls dead unless the public give their aid." Having financed the start of the enterprise, she was not prepared to run it as a business failure. In those days, when the costs of mounting a play, either for a commercial run or in a repertory season, could quite reasonably be expected to be met by the box-office takings, the argument was quite clear; the theatre as an art was either above and beyond money, or it was not. Barker's scheme for a national theatre assumed that productions would eventually pay their way. Lewis was nearer to Miss Horniman than to Payne over this. He believed that in a healthy cultural society good theatre could gradually win the respect and support of the public. His idea of "good theatre" did not rest on the high literary quality of the plays so much as on the standard of team-acting, and it included responsiveness to the audience's needs and desires. Consistently empty houses were an indication that a theatre had got badly out of touch with its public.

So Payne departed, under no cloud, but simply having recognised the end of his own task. The farewell was cordial on all sides and John Galsworthy presided at a dinner given in his honour. Everyone recognised the splendour of his achievement in creating so success-fully the first repertory theatre in Britain, (using the word "reper-tory" to indicate a series of plays in a season not, as Barker always intended, a variety of plays performed in the same week). Already the Scottish Repertory Theatre had been founded in Glasgow, inspired by the Gaiety, and Liverpool Playhouse, after an experi-mental season, was just about to open its doors under the direction of Basil Dean, late of the Gaiety.

Now it was up to Lewis to maintain this proud position. Soon he was being asked his plans and he spoke to the Manchester Playgoers, a lively club of theatre supporters, on "Strategy and Tactics at the Gaiety Theatre". He saw three purposes in its policy: to win over the more intelligent portion of the community; to entertain; and to make it pay. This was a cunning sequence of purposes, for if the first could be achieved, then the second and third might be fulfilled more easily without a lowering of artistic standards. Lewis did not propose to make any major changes in artistic tactics, but he hoped to introduce a repertory schedule instead of a weekly bill, because that served the purpose of the theatre better. The ideal arrangement was to have such a variety of plays each week that every taste would be satisfied. This would enable the Gaiety to keep its successes in the

71

bill for long periods and to cut its losses. Still, in the event, he was to find this repertory schedule unsuitable. (We should bear in mind that what he and others who favoured "repertory" had in mind was not just variety, but, more crucially, flexibility, for they intended that the exact programme should be arranged only two or three weeks ahead, not in the much longer periods of modern repertory scheduling.)

During the autumn Lewis began gently, sharing the production work, with Stanley Drewitt, a fine, sturdy actor who had joined the company after the Cassons left, though, as a close friend of Payne he had taken a great interest in the Gaiety from the start. Lewis's best performance was as Sigurd the Strong in Ibsen's *The Vikings at Helgeland*, significant because it turned out to be his farewell to the heroic romanticism of his youthful acting. Hotspur, Posthumus, Orlando, Troilus, Dante, Jokanaan, Marchbanks, Bue Asbirning in *The Feud* were all behind him; now, in Ibsen's Nordic saga he drew upon their poetic vigour and passion once more, before focusing his own force and power in the role of producer. C. E. Montague described the performance in terms which show us that the theatre may have lost a heroic actor of some importance, even though it gained an aspiring producer:

> His virile, eager voice, [Montague wrote], is as romantic in quality as a drawn rapier or a beaten drum; although it has not yet had its full chance, his art has a touch of the romantic power to alter for the moment the relative proportions of all sorts of things in your mind; it can flash out the fact or raise the illusion, that this or that action or end is the only thing supremely worth doing or gaining.

Lewis's first major production was in December, and with Miss Horniman's agreement, he wanted to follow Iden Payne's tradition of putting on something that would be festive, but not like a Christmas pantomime. He chose *Twelfth Night*, and decided he would try to make a fruitful compromise of new and old Shakespearian styles, with a real view to pleasing everyone. He seems to have succeeded. He was lucky in the designer, Hugh Fremantle. They used a mixture of curtaining and scenery; some scenes, like the street, and a room in Olivia's house, were played in front of decorative curtains, and others were given a full setting, the most lavish and beautiful being Olivia's garden. As Sybil was expecting the second baby she could not take a part, but she arranged some Beethoven sonatas as incidental music in keeping with the lyrical tone of the whole production. Lewis used the original text with minimal cuts—still something worthy of comment—but the spirit of the production was neither literary nor scholarly, but rollicking, boisterous good fun.

There had been changes in the company since 1909—Basil Dean had gone, and Miss Darragh, Henry Austin and Esmé Percy, as well as Mona Limerick and Iden Payne, but many stalwarts remained and some of the newcomers were well-established and very strong: a lively Lancastrian, Edyth Goodall, had come when Sybil left, there was Stanley Drewitt, and also another leading couple, Irene Rooke and Milton Rosmer, who were valuable members of the company individually and together. Lewis had worked with her, because she played in the original production of *The Silver Box*, and Sybil with him, because he had been on the second Ben Greet tour. Instead of trying to decide which of the two leading ladies should play Viola, Lewis decided to alternate Viola week by week. For Olivia he engaged Eileen Thorndike, his young sister-in-law. This casting was a great success. The two actresses proved to be equally good, Edyth Goodall stressing Viola's vivaciousness and wit, Irene Rooke the sadder, more serious side. On the domestic front this did nothing but good because it brought Eileen to Manchester in time to be with Sybil for her second labour. So when Christopher was born, in January 1912, Lewis could feel proud of both the families he was heading, at the theatre and at home.

Both families, however, were about to be split up for Miss Horniman's new expedition—to conquer the New World. A Montreal business man, David Walker, had put up a £2,000 guarantee for a six-week season of her company plus first-class travel expenses. Miss Horniman was delighted. With ever increasing confidence, she set off to do all the advance publicity herself—this would be cheaper than sending a man, she decided, for he would have to invite people to champagne lunches, while she could simply ask them out to tea. She pointed out that her grandfather had made his fortune by advertising his tea business himself, and keeping up its quality. (Her own wealth and the Gaiety Theatre backing were derived from Horniman's Tea.) She boldly announced that her aim was to make money and fame ("capital F please") and "to show that an English woman has the courage to do what New York businessmen tried to hire men to do". Before leaving she spoke from the stage of the Gaiety and told the enthusiastic audience that she was going to Canada to boast about it: "I am going to tell them it is not very big," she said in her forthright way, "and not always as crowded as it might be, but I am going to tell them I am very proud of it and of everyone connected with it." Then off she went, leaving Lewis with the mammoth task of organising the departure.

After much discussion they had selected a company of eighteen actors and four technicians who would present eight full-length plays and four one-acts chosen to show them at their best and most varied, (*Candida*, *The Tragedy of Nan*, Alfred Sutro's light comedy *Mollentrave on Women*, *The Silver Box*, *She Stoops to Conquer*, *The Return of the Prodigal*, *Cupid and the Styx* by a Manchester playwright, and *Man and Superman*). These were already in their repertoire, except *Man and Superman*, which Lewis produced specially for the tour, having wrested permission from Shaw. Sets, props and costumes, including real eighteenth-century furniture for the Goldsmith play, all had to be shipped over, fifty tons of it. Lewis was particularly pleased at the extensive repertoire which such a small company could present. "We are doing a thing which London could not do," he told an interviewer. "There is no single manager in London at the present time who could take eleven [twelve] plays representative of nearly every school of English drama, to the Dominion without months of preparation, but except for the business of removal we are doing no more than we do at any of our Manchester seasons."

The company had a great send-off and sailed from Liverpool on February 2nd. They had a rough crossing and were delayed in reaching Halifax. Then they met further delays on the railway and did not reach Montreal until seven in the morning of the day they were to open. Lewis was quite frantic with worry and frustration. He called a rehearsal at once and rushed down to look at the theatre, His Majesty's. It was much bigger than the Gaiety and he knew at once that the company would have to make considerable adjustments in its performances if it was to make any impression at all. But with all the splendid trumpet-blowing that Miss Horniman had been doing, expectations were already very high. Pushing and shoving the weary, keyed-up company through a rehearsal of *Candida* (in which he too was playing), he adjusted some of the stage business that was too subtle, and concentrated on extending the cast's voice production. He need not have feared; the months of co-operative work behind them paid off, and with no trouble at all Edyth Goodall portrayed Candida with a sincerity and sweetness totally unaffected by the harassing time. Milton Rosmer's Marchbanks did not please everyone, and the *Montreal Gazette* found Lewis's Morell "colourless"—perhaps not surprising after the drama he was already performing as producer. On the next night Irene Rooke made her début in *Nan*; within a few days, audiences and critics were bursting with admiration for the company's sheer versatility as production followed production, each performed with style and polish. At first people did not know if they ought to praise individual performances in this ensemble but they soon overcame their diffidence and began to enjoy picking out individual brilliance.

Although business was not quite as good as David Walker had hoped, the season was a great triumph, and its smooth running owed much to Lewis's efforts. He was immensely grateful to the actors who had rallied round to this exciting summons. But after such tension, and deprived of Sybil's warmth for the first time since their marriage, it was perhaps inevitable that his gratitude spilled over into a short but passionate affair with his new Candida, Edyth Goodall, the details of which were to remain private to himself and Sybil.

Miss Horniman was invited to extend the tour, but she refused, to Lewis's relief, for he realised that he needed to get back to Manchester to re-orientate himself personally and professionally. The company sailed back to England at the end of March, enjoying the hilarity of a newspaper announcement which stated that the distinguished passengers aboard the *Laconia* would include "Miss A. E. F. Horniman, leading soprano of an English opera company which has been touring the provinces". Looking at the dates, I am suddenly struck by the closeness in time of this voyage and a more fateful one: less than two weeks after the *Laconia* docked at Liverpool, the *Titanic* began its Atlantic passage.

Emotions were fairly high therefore as Lewis again took up residence in the little house in King's Road, Heaton Park, where Sybil had been enjoying her babies, but greatly missing Lewis and her acting, and getting bored with domesticity. But there was not much time to begin straightening things out before setting off for London for the longest season at the Coronet Miss Horniman had yet attempted. It included nine full-length plays and four one-acts from the repertoire; and again Lewis was very busy organising and rehearsing the company for these. At the same time he started rehearsing a new play which the company would do for the Stage Society before it was incorporated into Miss Horniman's season. This was *Hindle Wakes*, possibly the most famous new play the Gaiety ever did. At the end of April Lewis drove down to London in the battered 'Tin Lizzie' Ford he had bought and repaired, with Sybil beside him, for *Hindle Wakes* was to mark her return to the stage and it had to be rehearsed in London while the other plays were in repertory.

No modern discussion of pornography, violence or nudity in the theatre could be fiercer than the controversy that raged around *Hindle Wakes* and its examination of double standards of morality. Simple and firm in structure, accurate and sympathetic in character-drawing, it seems to have survived the years better than many Edwardian plays, especially considering that it was both local in scope and topical in its moral questions. It concerns a Lancashire mill-girl, Fanny Hawthorn, who goes off with her employer's son, Alan Jeffcote, for a weekend. When her "fall" and his "lark" are discovered, the families decide that the couple must marry despite their different class, but Fanny astounds everybody by firmly refusing to contemplate it. The weekend has been merely a "lark" to her, as to Alan, and he is not the sort of man she would ever marry: "You're not good enough for me," she tells him. "The chap Fanny Hawthorn weds has got to be made of different stuff from you, my lad. My husband, if ever I have one, will be a man, not a fellow who'll throw over his girl at his father's bidding." She leaves home and sets off to earn her own living and live her own life.

Lewis's sensitive and carefully-built production brought out beautifully the different standards, conventions, manners and surroundings in which the two families lived. For example, the scene where the two sets of parents meet became a brilliant detailed study of the English class system; the settings enhanced this realistic acting; individual characters stood out against a meticulously observed background in a way that was typical of the whole quality and tradition of the Gaiety. No better actors or production team could have been found anywhere to do justice to Stanley Houghton's script. There were three Lancastrians in the cast, Edyth Goodall, who played Fanny, Charles Bibby as her father, and Herbert Lomas, who, at the age of twenty-six, made a great success as the Jeffcote father. All their performances were highly praised. So were those of Ada King as Mrs. Hawthorn, J. D. Bryant as the "graceless cur" Alan, and Sybil as Beatrice, Alan's fiancée. The *Evening News* critic commented: "There are three dozen beautiful actresses who should come and hear her say 'I'll write to you, Alan,' as, giving up her lover, she goes out of the room without making an exit." Again with a Gaiety production, the best compliments, and those most acceptable to Lewis, were those that praised the ensemble as much as the individual performances.

After its two performances at the Coronet, Stanley Houghton wrote to Miss Horniman and suggested she might test its success by putting it on for a run in the West End during the summer months when the actors had nothing else to do. So she nosed around and persuaded Cyril Maude at the Playhouse to let her put on *Hindle*

Wakes there. Opening in July, it was again acclaimed. One critic, writing in the magazine, *John Bull*, said that it was in interpretation that this production excelled: "Seldom, save in the French theatre of the Antoine school, has an audience been awakened from its usually despondent lethargy by such enlightened art."

Lewis was delighted, but not thrown off balance, by the success of *Hindle Wakes*. He felt sure that it was not an isolated achievement, but the result of continuous painstaking work, and he wanted to get back to Manchester to consolidate his efforts.

Before he could do so, there were two sad family events. News came that Uncle Randal had died in Sicily. The youngest and most successful of the three brothers, Randal had established a fine life for his wife and son and himself in Portmadoc, but had somehow not been happy in it. Bron-y-garth, the beautiful house overlooking the Traeth, did not give him the pleasure it should have done. It had a powerful and brooding atmosphere, as many of the family would discover, which either enveloped you in a romantic attachment to the place, or drove you to black, despairing moods and melancholy. Uncle Randal found it a gloomy and depressing place and had taken to spending much of his time abroad. He was taken ill at his villa in Taormina where he died and was buried. Aunt Lucy came home and took up residence with their son Alec, now nineteen, on whom she lavished all her stern but caring devotion.

This event was soon overshadowed by another, closer still. No sooner had the news of Randal's death reached the family when Lewis's mother, Laura Ann, who had never really recovered her strength after her husband's death, sank quietly and died in her Putney home. She was sixty-eight and the years of fierce struggle to provide the home she felt her family should have, had sapped her vitality. Within a few months of Laura Ann's death, Elsie suddenly surprised her brothers and sisters by announcing, quietly and firmly, that she had decided to become a doctor, using the small legacy from her mother to pay for the training. At the age of thirty-one she set about taking matriculation, coached by her brother-in-law Arthur. The determination and persistent courage were inherited from her mother, but also the situation that necessitated it. For Laura Ann had always kept her daughters firmly subordinated to her sons, whose achievements were her chief pride.

Returning to Manchester in the late summer of 1912, Lewis experienced a surge of pride and love for his own family, together with some apprehension at the responsiblity he felt towards them. He and Sybil had established their marriage on a stronger footing than before, and he was keen for her to have much more chance to fulfil her own career. Against this background of questioning and decision-making about the women's roles in his own family, how strange it was to view from afar the outburst of publicity and protest that suddenly boiled up around the social and sexual mores depicted in *Hindle Wakes*.

Battle began when the theatre critic of *The Referee* condemned the scene in which Alan and Beatrice discussed his conduct with some candour, especially the possibility that he might have made Fanny pregnant:

> This, if the Censor will allow me to say so, is going a little too far. Believe me, I am not squeamish; and I recognise that such a play is not intended for the young and innocent or the vicious; still such a scene as this between Alan and Beatrice is out of place on the stage. Such discussion is no better suited to the theatre than to the drawing-room or to the family circle, and to talk of such things familiarly and without restraint, if persisted in on the stage, must inevitably tend to the degradation of public manners.

For the next six weeks the scandal of *Hindle Wakes* was discussed from every angle in articles and correspondence in all the leading newspapers and magazines. It was like a local English version of the outcries against Ibsen's *A Doll's House* and the hot defences of it. "It produced on me exactly the sensation that somebody had spat in my face deliberately," wrote Another Playgoer in the *Pall Mall Gazette* on August 7th. "It was in fact a nightmare without one moment of art or beauty." There were just as many to defend the play, including Michael Lykiardopoulos of the Moscow Art Theatre and even Gordon Craig. Stanley Houghton justified himself on the grounds of the realistic artist, that his aim was to present life as he saw it. It was all the more interesting given the importance of the whole question of censorship in Edwardian theatre. Barker and his friends had been trying to get the law changed ever since *Waste* was banned in 1907. The Joint Select Committee on Censorship was formed in 1909, after Shaw's *The Shewing-up of Blanco Posnet* was banned, and eventually it recommended that censorship should continue only on an optional basis. But the report was shelved and now the Examiner of Plays for the Lord Chamberlain was himself a dramatist, Charles Brookfield, with very firmly held views of his own. He may well have regretted giving a licence to *Hindle Wakes* and it is very likely that if it had been submitted as a commercial London play in the first instance he would have refused it. It was left to the Vice-Chancellor of Oxford University to take action, placing the theatre out of bounds to undergraduates while it was on in the city. Miss Horniman, delighted at the publicity, sarcastically praised the Vice-Chancellor's loyalty to "the passing tradition that the lords of creation are to be allowed a lower morality than the unenfranchised helots", and his protection of the male undergraduates from hearing "the horrible fact that it is as reprehensible for them to go for a gay week-end as for a woman from Newnham or Girton".

On a more popular level, many magazines took up the moral question, "Should Fanny marry Alan?" and the long discussion of this also made good publicity. The question was soon plastered across the posters of the London Underground and Edwardian playgoers of a robust moral constitution rushed to see the play and form their own opinions. It is a tribute to the tightness of the play that the question can still bear discussion, because the two double standards, of class, as in Galsworthy's *The Silver Box*, and sex, as in Pinero's *The Second Mrs. Tanqueray*, are so carefully intertwined. A third argument tossed back and forth was the actress's moral position in all this. If it was granted that Fanny's behaviour was indecent, where did Edyth Goodall stand? If an actress disagrees with the morality of a character, can she "honourably undertake to voice it across the footlights for the sake of her salary"? And if she does, will not her own virtue be corrupted? These questions too led to a mass of protest and defence. (Gordon Craig suggested that playing a drunken man night after night would be likely to make you a teetotaller for the rest of your life!)

It was one of the achievements of the whole theatre movement of which Lewis was a part, that it was bringing audiences to an awareness of just how close theatre, morality and politics might be. Had he not told Sybil that her acting would be better if she knew more about life? And was he not trying to attract an intelligent and questioning audience to the Gaiety? And looking for plays that had something interesting and moving to say about the human and social condition of his audience? The whole art/morality controversy over *Hindle Wakes* should rather be seen as a sign of true success for progressive theatre; it had succeeded in establishing a real dialogue, metaphorically, between stage and audience, instead of a clear division into entertainers and entertained. It was this dialogue that was important to Lewis, not whether an actor or dramatist was right or wrong. This was the joint "research into humanity" which he wanted the theatre to undertake.

6

The Producer's Scene
1912–1914

When the Gaiety Theatre began its autumn season of 1912, Lewis was starting his second year as a producer, but with Payne's slow departure, the Canadian and London tours, and *Hindle Wakes*, he had hardly had a chance to settle in. He was eager now to establish a pattern and actually to do many of the things he had talked about so often. To begin with, there was the question of his own description. The idea of being paid to "produce" plays was still fairly recent. He must work out for himself what it actually meant, artistically and personally, and whether he liked it and was good at it.

First there was Miss Horniman to deal with, and his sessions with her became an important part of his work. He would visit her in her rooms by appointment, and find her, sitting in solitary brocaded splendour, among her cats, her books on astrology, feminism, travel, politics and anything else that had caught her eclectic interest, and the numerous play scripts she received from authors and agents. There they discussed and exchanged the scripts that interested them, and considered matters of policy. She held decided but rather naive views of her own, and had acquired theatrical tastes based on her youthful experiences of German theatre. She read copiously. It was said she must have spent half her time in Manchester simply reading scripts, and many young playwrights were flattered to receive an informed acknowledgment of their offering within a few days of sending it. Her judgments were sometimes maddeningly eccentric and irrelevant. "Oh no," she once told Iden Payne, "that play would never do. When they did it in London they used a green grass mat to cover the stage for a scene set in Italy in October! Everyone knows that in Italy grass is burnt brown in the autumn." Lewis, on the other hand, did not have time to read very widely in drama. Most of the plays he wanted were either because he had actually seen them or been in them, or were recommended by a friend, or because the script had landed on his desk, asking to be read and produced in the coming season. They both liked the idea of doing Shakespeare, Galsworthy, Shaw, Masefield and so on, and

Miss Horniman was usually open to some suggestions outside her own liking, such as *Prunella*, which Lewis persuaded her to take into the repertoire despite her low opinion of it.

At first Lewis found her method of making decisions rather disconcerting. If a suggestion was to be discussed she would talk about it for a few minutes, then veer off on to some quite different topic, as if unable to concentrate. A few minutes later she would suddenly return to the original point with a decision made, not by common sense or reason, but by some kind of intuition. She took an immense interest in astrology and psychic prediction, and Lewis could not help wondering if it influenced even her theatrical decisions. Once she had made up her mind there was no shifting her, although, strangely, it seems to have been easier for Yeats and Iden Payne, her two earlier associates, to persuade her, with their soft, gentle manners, than for the more forthright Lewis. His relationship with her was respectful, often argumentative, never intimate. No one seemed able to penetrate to her real feelings and motives, but perhaps her Quaker upbringing brought her an inner quietness that did not need to be shared. Her generosity came out more often in action than in speech. For instance, during that summer, Lewis was amazed to learn that she had given the provincial rights of *Hindle Wakes* to her faithful business-manager Edward Heys, as a wedding gift—thereby losing both his services and the profits that were made. Sybil once tried, later, to explain her character: "Well, she was a feminist, a family rebel. One of the first women to ride a bicycle over the Alps. That sort of person. Oh, and so highly cultured too. You could never love her but you couldn't help liking and admiring her for her taste, the standards she demanded. She was a sort of Queen Elizabeth of the theatre. She was—she was—, oh, I don't know, she was—grim!" In a way Miss Horniman and Lewis were rather alike, with their disinterested approach to the theatre, and their outspokenness on matters of art and politics. But Lewis was warm, passionate and accessible beneath his outward reserve, whereas hers was an inner reserve; and where he felt himself to be no better or worse that any other ordinary man, she set herself slightly apart, with her unusual dress and manner, and rather traded on her eccentricity.

The production team Lewis worked with at the Gaiety was a fine one. The stage designer, Hugh Fremantle, was an enthusiastic, good-humoured pillar of the establishment and Lewis felt lucky to have such talent and versatility to draw on. Costume design was not as firmly established as stage décor in those days, and provincial actors were expected to provide all modern clothes themselves, with perhaps an allowance for some special need (like the shirt allowance Lewis had received at the Court for *Man and Superman*). But for historical plays, costumes were often specially designed and much admired. Scenery, props and costumes were all made at the theatre, in the scene and costume shops which Miss Horniman had had built, and so the company was completely self-contained technically, with a sympathetic and efficient stage-manager, Edward Broadley, co-ordinating everything. The first innovation Lewis wanted was to make the music as much an integral part of the company's work as the visual aspects. He put this to Miss Horniman, and as it was very much in line with her own liking for a self-contained artistic unit like the German theatres, she agreed. Pleased with his success, he then wrote to the violinist Nicolai Sokoloff, whom he and Sybil had met in New York and much liked, inviting him to become musical director. To their delight, Sokoloff came, and a small permanent orchestra was employed to play music especially written or adapted for each play, no longer "incidental" but a part of the whole production concept.

Then there were the actors, to be considered as a team as much as individuals. Some were lost to the commercial success of *Hindle Wakes*, including two of the finest, Edyth Goodall and Charles Bibby, but the company was a strong one, with Irene Rooke and Milton Rosmer still staunch members, Sybil able now to take major roles, and a fine new leading actor, Brember Wills. There were still many old hands like Edward Landor, Frank Darch, Leonard Mudie, Jules Shaw and Muriel Pratt, and some new enthusiastic recruits like Lewis's brother-in-law Russell, fresh from a world tour with Matheson Lang, Percy Foster and Christie Laws, all of whom made valuable contributions. At the older end he included the formidable Mrs. Albert Barker, Harley's mother, a grand old lady of imposing presence and immense experience. Eileen Thorndike now joined the company at the Liverpool Playhouse, run by Basil Dean, who kept in close touch with Lewis so that they were able to exchange scripts and ideas and play in each other's theatres. The whole company was almost twice as big as the original seventeen and could handle a wide range of material. All this boded well and Lewis felt proud of the social and artistic cohesiveness of the group. He liked the idea that his actors were, as he said, "normal human citizens who do a day's work and go home at night, instead of a troupe of wandering mountebanks whose life is the play they are acting". It was a pity that the *Hindle Wakes* cast had in fact been the ones most deeply rooted in Lancashire, but there were still several who were local people, and Lewis and Sybil were beginning to feel quite settled in the city they had been fond of for over four years. Though some Northerners still regarded the theatre folk as strange and alien people, they were naturally warm and hospitable and could not help feeling proud of the national and international reputation their repertory company was gaining. Lewis just wished their pride would sometimes take a more demonstrable form of buying tickets for the theatre! Within the company his and Sybil's particular friends were Jules Shaw, Frank Darch, who had been with Sybil on the first Ben Greet tour, and had once made her a mock proposal of marriage, and Russell of course, and they were often to be found gathered for Sunday night supper at Heaton Park.

The first important job and the most critical for a Gaiety producer was selecting the plays. During the autumn of 1912 eight full-length new productions were mounted and three one-acts. There were also two revivals. Three of these eight were original plays, *Elaine* and *Wonderful Grandmamma* by Harold Chapin, and *Revolt* by George Calderon; two had recently been done in London, *The Pigeon* by John Galsworthy and *The Polygon* by Harold Brighouse; two were modern plays which had not been acted before in Manchester, *Prunella* and Shaw's *The Devil's Disciple*; and one from an earlier period, Sheridan's *The Rivals*. The two revivals were *The Silver Box* and St. John Hankin's *The Charity That Began At Home*, both of which had been done originally at the Court and later entered the Gaiety repertoire. Most of the plays have entirely disappeared from the modern repertoire, and only the Shaw, the Sheridan and perhaps the Galsworthy would be likely to appear on a reading list of dramatic literature, but that is not really a criticism. For one thing, until quite recently, there has been a surprising lack of interest in this fruitful era of British drama, so that the two Galsworthys, the St. John Hankin and the Housman, all major plays of their time, are still mere relics of a bygone age, but might, at any moment, be taken up by a major company and brought into the public eye again. The other plays, by Chapin, Brighouse and Calderon, are perhaps less likely to be seen again. But looking at the season from this point of view, nearly seventy years later, and asking "Would I enjoy seeing these plays *now*?" is irrelevant. It was a season designed for 1912, and when we look at it as such, the choice of plays begins to seem a great deal more interesting and exciting.

Theatre was still the only medium of dramatic entertainment and the sheer variety of the material to fill so many imaginative needs is impressive. There is, first of all, a group of plays on the level of good television drama—taking serious and relevant modern topics and dramatising them in an interesting way: *The Silver Box*; *Polygon*, which was a study of housing problems; *Revolt*, a most exciting play of its time, which centred, prophetically, on a scientist who was looking for alternative sources of energy and discovered how to split the atom; the St. John Hankin play, a light-hearted demonstration of the impracticability of practising Christian principles in Edwardian society; and *Elaine*, a witty, gently satirical comedy on the contradictions contained in current attitudes to love and money in marriage. Like many of the most interesting plays of the period, it was centred on a neatly provocative idea, that of an unmarried couple, who have been living together for years in order to avoid a situation where the woman has "married for money". Manchester audiences were also able to see Miss Horniman's other company in *Hindle Wakes*, which falls into the same category. The Gaiety was sometimes criticised for doing too many plays that were gloomy, realistic social tracts, but this was not a just complaint because, for one thing, the best and most successful of the realistic genre were often comedies, and for another, social topics were of enormous interest in these years of Liberal reform and feminist propaganda, and Manchester was itself a socially progressive town and enjoyed the thinking, talking and planning which these plays might provoke. Galsworthy's *The Pigeon* was rather a disappointment of that season because it was not focused on a social problem, but was mainly a character study and a kind of fantasy based on the futility of human charity. Other plays of less topical interest were the successful revivals of *The Devil's Disciple* and *Prunella*. Lastly, there were the two Christmas plays, *The Rivals*, which followed what had become a Gaiety tradition of reviving an old English comedy in a warm, glowing, festive production, and *Wonderful Grandmamma*, a children's play which Lewis, already a masterly story-teller himself, made enthralling for Manchester's young audiences.

This catholic season did not suit the intellectual minority, and the editor of the *Manchester Playgoer*, a lively magazine on the theatre, wrote a damning article on "The Failure of our Repertory Theatre", accusing Miss Horniman of losing her sense of mission and pandering to "business". The Gaiety was now smug, mediocre and dull, he insisted, and not in advance of its times. The last phrase is a give-away, because there can hardly be such a thing as theatre "in advance of its time". Theatre is an event and therefore always contemporaneous. But he was hankering for the heydays of Iden Payne's reign, with its Poel production, its *Hippolytus*, its Ibsen and its *The Cloister*, all productions which explored the whole art of theatre a little further, but, the writer omitted to mention, played to very sparse houses. The problem was to find the right balance between the "avant garde" and popular success, and for this season, certainly, Miss Horniman had tried to go for what might appeal to a general, intelligent audience more than to a theatrically sophisticated minority. Lewis was pragmatic and felt reasonably satisfied with her approach, seeing the problem clearly. "If you are pioneering, you appeal only to a minority," he said in later years, when asked to assess Miss Horniman's achievements. "If you set your standard too high, your faithful minority is too small to make the theatre pay. If you popularise your standard too far, your minority is disgruntled and you compete too directly with the ordinary theatre. If you proportion the length of the run to the popularity of the play, the minority gets less than their share of intellectual food. The only valid solution is real repertory . . . where the popular plays subsidise the unpopular, without depriving the minority of regular food . . . The only other solution is heavy subsidy." How familiar the theme sounds! What seems amazing is not that they found no permanent solution at the Gaiety, but that they were arguing and experimenting with problems so very similar to those of arts administrators two generations later.

Some features of the problem were more particular to 1912. One was the general attitude to theatre-going. The Victorians had raised the social tone of the event, but this was the infancy of the movement to develop its intellectual potential, and those who encouraged its growth were rarely those with money. We can picture a typical audience at the Gaiety: in the gallery and pit (sixpence or a shilling) is squashed an enthusiastic heterogeneous collection of students and young working people eager to have their horizons extended. Going home on the tram they will discuss what they have seen, and, if Lewis has succeeded in his purpose, get quite heated, or perhaps sit silently, moved by what they have seen, to ponder on their own lives. In later years Sybil often heard from some of the mill-girls who had enjoyed her performances and remembered them. In the pit stalls and the upper circle (one and sixpence to half a crown) is that small section of the reasonably paid Edwardian middle-class that takes an intelligent interest in the arts: professional people, tradesmen, more prosperous factory workers, other artists, perhaps members of the Manchester Playgoers Club, or from further afield; and they may have more experience of life and art to compare these productions with. Possibly they are the ones who would most enjoy a repertory schedule at the Gaiety, allowing them to pick and choose and yet still attend regularly. But the stalls and dress circle (three to five shillings) and the boxes (twelve and sixpence to two guineas) are too often almost empty. On first nights and special occasions the critics sit there, with perhaps a few civic dignitaries, all in complimentary seats provided by Miss Horniman. Slowly, very slowly, critics and company are educating a wider public to expect plays which speak of the issues being debated in Parliament and city councils, plays which examine the philosophies of human existence, or probe into the inner depths of human experiences. But for most theatre-goers these are quite unacceptable uses of drama. They do not expect the theatre to reflect what goes on in their council chambers, their studies and in the intimate corners of their homes, but to be an entertaining extension of the drawing-room, where they will be delighted but not provoked, and where the actors they have come to see will speak and act with decorum. So they read with pride of the great reputation their local theatre is gaining among the intelligentsia, and most of the time they stay away from the Gaiety in droves. To make a profit, Miss Horniman's theatre had to be three-quarters full, and the expensive seats, still cheaper than in other theatres, had to be regularly filled. Ironically, the financial situation was made worse because it never became a centre for merely fashionable people to be seen, and because all the seats were comfortable with good sightlines. Two incentives to buy the expensive seats were much lessened.

Still, Miss Horniman had not set out to make a profit, she simply wanted enough support to keep a theatre of high artistic and intellectual standards in business. Looking at the quality of the programme, we find another problem peculiar to this period. Many of the plays you would expect to find in such a theatre were simply not available. The provincial rights of many Ibsen plays were already disposed of (to Leigh Lovell, for instance, with whom Lewis had toured), and so *The Vikings at Helgeland* was the only one they were able to do. It would please theatre historians to find that Miss Horniman pioneered productions of Strindberg or Chekhov, but alas, those of their plays which had been translated were still too obscure for a general audience. English playwrights were often reluctant to let their works go to provincial companies because they earned such tiny sums from them. A week's run of *Mary Broome*, a Gaiety success, brought its author, Allan Monkhouse, under eighteen pounds. Barrie withheld his plays from Miss Horniman, so did Shaw, as we have seen, though he gradually allowed her several. He and Barker were reluctant at first because of the artistic risk as well, but that fear, they soon found, was groundless. Galsworthy, more generous, took great interest in the Gaiety. Many minor playwrights offered their work, usually hoping, like

Stanley Houghton with *Hindle Wakes*, to get a London production as well. So, making the selection of plays was far more difficult than simply designing the perfect repertoire, though that did not frustrate Lewis, who liked the challenge.

The plays are chosen then, and the producer must set to work. There is still a lot to be done before he can start rehearsals. First the plays must be cast and the schedule of rehearsals and performances worked out. Much was talked in repertory theatres of getting rid of the "star" system, but this did not mean complete equality in the company. Leading actors, like Charles Bibby in the early days, Irene Rooke and Milton Rosmer at this time, were paid more and expected to carry a heavier burden of the acting than the supporting actors. Egalitarians, romancing about the Saxe-Meiningen troupe in Germany, might praise the way you could see an actor playing Hamlet one night and speaking one line the next, but Barker had shown that this casting method was sadly uneconomical of talent and salaries. At the Gaiety, as at the Court, there were differentials, but they were smaller and more gradual: the top salary (twelve pounds a week) was far less than conventional "stars" would be likely to receive, and the lowest (about three pounds) was enough to feed, clothe and house the actor, who also had the security of a forty-week contract. Some actors at the Gaiety acquired large and faithful followings, perpetuating a kind of "star" system by natural demand, but the welcome change from an older tradition was that such actors might be playing supporting parts, as the character actress, Ada King, did, and they were praised for their versatility and skill rather than their personality.

So, during this autumn season Lewis cast the plays with the main parts carried by Brember Wills, Jules Shaw, Milton Rosmer, Irene Rooke and, increasingly, Sybil; and the rest of the company, including himself, played a wide range of parts. Once the plays were in rehearsal the "ensemble" character of the company came out strongly, because, like Barker, he treated all the parts as equally significant. For instance, a young actress, Doris Bateman, played no fewer than three small parts in *Revolt*, and each became a complete cameo and received as careful attention as Milton Rosmer's leading part.

The number of new and old productions presented at the Gaiety in one season was so great that when you look at the schedule you realise that no play could have had more than two weeks' rehearsal; often that calculation does not include one-act plays and revived productions. (Miss Horniman was willing to pay rehearsal salaries, but in fact she and Lewis were careful to begin their new seasons with revivals, so that only a couple of days would be needed before opening, when full salaries started.) Technically, such a full schedule relied heavily on Hugh Fremantle, who steadily produced set after set, which then had to be stored against future revivals. The stage-manager, Edward Broadley, ran his stage crew with true shipboard efficiency. Two weeks seems to us now woefully inadequate to mount a full production. (Barker had rehearsed for three weeks at the Court.) But we need to bear in mind that some aspects of production, most notably lighting design, were much simpler than in modern theatres: Lewis expected to co-ordinate the lighting, set-changes, costume changes, music and other technical effects in one mammoth (usually nightmarish), dress rehearsal, which, with no union regulations, might go on well into the night.

There are also important differences in the whole approach to theatre production which help to account for the apparently mira-culous achievement of presenting, week after week, performances worthy of critical notice. Unquestionably, Edwardian productions lacked the finish and polish which television and cinema techniques have trained an audience to expect from first-class theatre nowadays. The change is like that in music, where high-fidelity recordings have placed a much greater emphasis on technical perfection. Wrong notes, which are corrected in the recording studio, are corres-pondingly less acceptable in the concert hall. Similarly, a shoddy-looking costume, a makeshift prop, or an obvious piece of doubling, can entirely destroy theatrical illusion for many modern audiences. It was this later trend towards technical perfection which made Lewis proclaim, in later years, a lack of interest in décor, not just for himself, but also on behalf of Shaw and Barker. At the Gaiety he was meticulous and progressive in his staging methods by the standards of the day, but he was still able to make other things his priority and yet mount a production in two weeks.

When Lewis spoke of his own work, or Barker's or Poel's, and compared it, as he often did, to conducting an orchestra and making a complete pattern of interpretation, he was comparing it with the tradition of theatre which preceded his, something that, with the exception of the great geniuses like Irving, and perhaps Tree, presented a gallimaufry of unrelated pictorial, musical and histrionic delights. There was no such thing as a single guiding concept. And although this has been said many times before, it is usually without acknowledging the compensating factor; you had a large number of people in the theatre pursuing their own crafts with dedication and individuality. When Henry Ford invented mass production for his motor cars, Lewis, among thousands, benefited from it, but also continued in the technically inventive attitude bred in him by his father, tinkering with his "Tin Lizzie", adapting it, "improving" it, till it bore little resemblance to any other machine that came off the same conveyor belt. Similarly, Barker and his followers were very gradually evolving patterns of interpretation and administration that would co-ordinate theatre into a more consistent, coherent and unified corporate art; their new method, mingling with the much more individualised approach of Victorian theatre, was tremendously invigorating. People spoke with excitement about the Gaiety "style" because they could not remember ever seeing an entire company co-ordinated in this way, but the company itself brought to rehearsal all their previous knowledge, and experience of a more self-sufficient tradition. They were confident and competent in their individual styles, created through apprenticeships in the dressing-room ("Now, my boy, I'll tell you what you need to play that scene"), rehearsal ("Watch how I make this entrance, young lad, and then you'll know what to do"), and frequent testing of their craft against an audience. They presented to the "producer" all the various brightly-coloured and contrasting pieces for a patchwork, and he simply arranged them and sewed them together.

So, with the plays chosen and cast, and the sets and costumes under way, the producer starts his rehearsals, and at once the final reason for the sufficiency of two weeks' rehearsal becomes clear. Most of the actors are completely at ease with each other and with the theatre, like a class that has come up the school together. There is none of that embarrassment and suspicion which makes some early rehearsals so awkward. Comfortably chatting, they arrive at the theatre in good time for a ten-thirty start and soon hear the ringing tones of the producer's wife as she breezes in with a warm greeting for everyone, followed by Lewis himself, whose salutations, less effusive, are just as sincere. Then they start.

If it is the first rehearsal of a new play, he reads it to the assembled cast, unless the author is present to do the job himself, putting in all the contrasts of expression, moments of suspense, the climaxes, the significant pauses and the variations of pace he sees fit, not to mention any necessary sound effects, dogs barking, trumpets blowing. Then briskly he sets to work, and plunges the cast into action, giving moves and positions which he has worked out in advance (just like the stage-manager of earlier times), making the set clear as he goes along. Now he can get on with the real business in hand, working on the actors' interpretations, and it is then that the fireworks start. Writing or speaking about acting, Lewis expressed himself with philosophic lucidity, giving an impression of

89

wisdom, sincerity and tranquillity. Well, the first two qualities were there in rehearsal, but not the third, because Lewis's rehearsals were violent, storm-tossed affairs during which he barked and growled and roared at his actors, while they seethed or yelled back or quaked in their shoes, according to temperament. The loudest retaliation usually came from Sybil. Preparing to start a speech for perhaps the sixth time, she would summon up the approximate emotion, draw breath, open her mouth and get as far as, for instance, "Now I—" "No!" shouts Lewis. "But I haven't *started* yet," expostulates Sybil. "But you were doing it wrong." "Well, how can I get it right if you don't let me *do* the speech. What I was trying to—" "If you start the speech wrong, it will be wrong all through—" "But you didn't even *let* me start. How could it be wrong?" "The way you took your breath." "Lewis! What does it matter how I take my breath? The important thing is for me to know what she feels like." "Rubbish! The important thing is that you say it so that the *audience* knows what she's feeling, and if you can't do that, we might as well pack up and go home!" And so on. By the end of the morning everyone is quite exhausted. If tempers have been only lightly ruffled, then a few calming and good-humoured words all round soon soothe everybody down; if Lewis is still brooding over the total incompetence of his cast, his wife included, Sybil has to sit out his glowering at lunch-time, or cajole him back to cheerfulness; if the insults still rankle with some of his victims, then she does a little mollification herself, but if he has been abominably rude, then she faces him with it squarely, and before long he has gone round to every member of the cast and humbly apologised. When the afternoon rehearsal starts, everything has blown over, it is clear that a great deal of valuable work was actually done during the morning and Lewis starts calmly and quietly working out an improvement to a piece of business that will make the actor feel more comfortable and the audience more involved. This, with variations, is the rehearsal pattern. What becomes abundantly clear is that Lewis's eloquent Welsh fury is never intended to be taken personally, it is simply his way of expressing his whole-hearted dedication to the task of interpreting the dramatist to the audience.

Lewis's methods, quite apart from the exciting rows he provoked, were a rich amalgamation of all the producers he had worked with, for he had admired and learnt from each. From Charles Fry and Poel he had developed a musical understanding of language which was extended into a greater understanding of theatrical language through working with Barker. Despite his dogmatic manner he liked "as far as possible"—note the reservation—to get the idea from the actors themselves and mould them into what he was trying to do. (A little reminiscent of Lady Britomart in *Major Barbara* perhaps, "I have always allowed you to think and feel exactly as you wished, so long as you thought and did what I could approve of.") Musically it was often a question of making the actor's way of saying something more vivid, by increasing the pitch and range of his speech, and extending his phrasing. Like Shaw, once the play had been chosen he was no longer concerned with its message or literary merit, but focused entirely on the craft of bringing the dramatist and the audience together. "For," Lewis once explained, "the audience is the string on which the actor is playing the dramatist's music, and the responsibility for keeping that string taut is his. All the actors share it, though the main responsibility passes continually from actor to actor, like a tossed ball." As the producer he guided the path of that tossed ball.

From Iden Payne Lewis learnt as much through the contrast between them as through imitation. Payne worked intuitively. He did not bother very much about technique. Indeed, as Basil Dean once commented, his vagueness, "almost an affectation of ignorance upon some matters of stage-management", aroused criticism and laughter among some of his company. But he had a flair for letting people have their heads, and yet, through his own instinctive grasp of the general atmosphere of the play and his power of communicating that to his actors, somehow guiding them into "a kind of emotional unity that was a complete expression of the play's purpose". He despised any form of analysis and liked to rely on the actors' spontaneity. That method is fine if either the producer or the actors has the spark of genius that will bring it off, and Lewis had experienced that with Barker even more than with Payne. But he did not feel that one should rely on this creative inspiration. Rather, he preferred to build a firm structure of technique for the actor to operate in, and to analyse a role in detail. Complete mastery of his craft, he felt, would give the actor the freedom to use inspiration, if it came, not to alter the broad effects of his performance, "but in the minutest details and shading that is the difference between a fine performance and a great one, but this difference ought to be imperceptible to the senses of the audience, however much they may feel the difference in the emotional effect". So he made Boucicault his own blueprint as a producer, not Payne or Barker, for Boucicault's rehearsal approach was clear, workmanlike, authoritarian and understandable.

So rehearsals proceeded in their squally way. Few had the heart to

91

bear Lewis any grudges for his outbursts, because his utter selflessness would keep shining through and melting their sense of griev-
ance. Despite the sparks of impatience, he showed, over a longer
stretch of time, a steady, patient determination to get every show as
good as it could possibly be. He had a greater sense of practical detail
than Payne and was better at co-ordinating the whole machinery of
a production.

After that first half of the season, Lewis had a challenge to face,
because Miss Horniman had accepted another tour of Canada with
several weeks in the United States as well. Lewis was reluctant to go
again, and also very concerned that Manchester should not be left
high and dry as in the previous year. Continuity was all important
for the audience as well as the company. So they split the company
in two, sending eighteen to Canada, under Milton Rosmer's leadership, and keeping the other half at the Gaiety. For the tour, six
full-length productions were revived (*Candida*, *Nan*, Arnold
Bennett's *What the Public Wants*, *The School for Scandal*, *The Silver
Box*, *She Stoops to Conquer*), all prepared while the Christmas shows
were on, plus *The Rivals*, which they were then playing, and two
one-acts. It was an amazing achievement for half a company, with
Miss Horniman's production of *Hindle Wakes* still touring as well.
Remaining in Manchester, Lewis and Sybil, with Russell, Brember
Wills, Jules Shaw and the rest of their troupe, including a wonderful
character actress Clare Greet, who had been at the Court, set about
continuing the season. Both Manchester and America complained
that they were being fobbed off with the second-best half of the
company, but in fact the honours were fairly evenly divided, with
one leading lady apiece, two or three first-class actors and the rest
carefully chosen for their response to the plays selected. Although
Sybil's reputation was not nearly as high as Irene Rooke's, she had
played the vigorous and idealistic young heroine of *Revolt* with
great success, and this season would bring her to the forefront of the
company.

The second half of the season opened in February 1913, with only
a one-week gap after the Christmas shows. In ten weeks, five new
full-length productions were mounted, and there were three
revivals. Again the balance was very good: there were two
premières, Frank Rose's *The Whispering Well* and St. John Ervine's
Jane Clegg, and three plays new to Manchester. The best revival was
Prunella, still a favourite of Lewis's; and because Milton Rosmer,
who had played Pierrot, was away, Lewis engaged Denis Neilson-
Terry, the brilliant and charming nephew of Ellen Terry, to play it.
He captivated the entire company with his warmth and ebullience,

as well as making a success of the part. Sybil was larking around in that play as "Romp" and incidentally frightening the life out of three-year-old John. The two new plays were a great contrast and both impressive. *The Whispering Well* by Frank Rose was a sort of morality play about avarice, set in eighteenth-century Lancashire. Rose was a Socialist journalist whose contributions to the *Labour Leader* Lewis had often enjoyed. No one quite knew what to compare it with—it was like *Faust*, it was like *A Christmas Carol*—if they knew, it could have been compared to *Peer Gynt*, for it was, as the *Morning Post* described it, "a queer jumble of fairy-tale, folklore, symbolic morality and realistic irony". Hugh Fremantle went to town on the settings, which had to move, with most complicated stage-managing, from scenes of homely, rustic comfort, to eerie glimpses into a land of "boggarts". Jules Shaw, as the hero Robin O'Tums, and Sybil, as his wife Malkin, both gave fine, sharply characterised performances, and John Foulds had composed wonderful haunting music. *The Whispering Well* was operatic in its scope, but Lewis blended all the elements together and everybody found the staging impressive. He was proud of this production, which he afterwards considered one of his finest for the Gaiety and he was pleased when it was successful enough to be repeated within the season. But though Manchester audiences loved it, it did not travel well beyond the boundaries of Lancashire, and the play itself has now vanished into the misty land of the boggarts.

The other new play, *Jane Clegg*, was an achievement of a different sort. It was a grim, realistic study of an unhappy marriage, mainly focused on the wife, played by Sybil, who endures the selfishness of her "absolute rotter" of a husband (as Sybil termed him) until he drives her past all possibility of love or forgiveness. The challenges here were to get the same kind of authenticity as *Hindle Wakes* had needed, and a strong emotional effect on the audience from Sybil's performance, and through these to raise what, at a later period, would be labelled "kitchen-sink drama" to a poetic level of experience, as in *The Silver Box*. With his now customary mixture of bullying and guidance, Lewis moulded Sybil's performance, never, with her, needing to extend her range, but to contain and discipline her power. Just like Galsworthy and Gilbert Murray, he tried to tell her to do less, but unlike them, he had her indignant protests to contend with. So they continued their argument about the place of emotion in acting, in rehearsal battles, over the breakfast table, the bath or the bed. She worked through a strong emotional identification with the character she was playing, and while Lewis agreed with this as an approach to acting, he thought it was a stage in rehearsing a part which the actor should eventually get beyond. Emotional response was really the result of technical imperfection. Putting it on paper, calmly, he maintained that "the more skilled the artist, the less he is dominated by his emotions when he is playing". With the number of violent arguments they had, he was lucky she was not simply dominated by the emotion of anger. Instead, her harrowing performance was a complete triumph for both of them. Allan Monkhouse wrote in the *Manchester Guardian*:

> The interest of the play is almost wholly in the woman, and the stern logic of her character with its underlying and repressed emotion was given with perfect understanding and discretion by Miss Thorndike. She never stressed a note unduly, she maintained the type with unfailing fidelity: it would not be easy to recall a piece of acting at the Gaiety more austerely right in its expression.

Jane Clegg was the season's most unqualified success.

They now descended on London for Miss Horniman's fourth season there. Courageously, she took the Court Theatre, with all its lofty associations, and it was there that the two halves of the company were jubilantly reunited, after the successful American tour. The most popular productions were *The Tragedy of Nan* in which Irene Rooke was, as usual, much admired, and *Jane Clegg*, Sybil's first real conquest of London and the first hint that she had the makings of a tragic actress. Desmond MacCarthy wrote in the *New Statesman*, the weekly newspaper recently founded by the Webbs: "She hardly raises her eyes during the three acts, but when she does it is with tremendous effect." St. John Ervine, delighted with the success of the play, acknowledged in his stage speech at the Court that most of the credit was Sybil's.

Lewis and Sybil decided to stay in London for a few weeks after the season. The boys could go to stay at Dymchurch, the little seaside town on the Romney Marsh where Mother Don–Don had bought two cottages. For themselves they could see some plays and some friends and catch up a bit with what was going on in the South. The most exciting thing they saw was the Diaghilev Ballet. This was on its third tour to London, but they had been in America the first time, and too busy with *Hindle Wakes* the previous year. Going to *Sacre du Printemps*, they were completely astounded by Stravinsky's primitive, strident, atonal score, the strange, unlyrical, passionate dancing, and the wild, garish décor. Sitting there, breathless with excitement, Sybil felt as if an entirely new world of experience was opening, sending violent thoughts and feelings, sensations she could never have imagined, rushing through her whole body. Suddenly, she thought, "If Lewis doesn't go for this, it's the end for us. It's too important to disagree about." But when it was over and the applause broke out, she jumped at the sound of his voice beside her roaring approval, his body tense as a tiger and his face aglow with exhilaration.

Talking with friends, visiting theatres, concerts and art galleries, they realised that although much seemed unchanged, new artistic horizons were opening up all over Europe. From the Barkers they heard about Max Reinhardt's *Oedipus Rex*, adapted from his huge German arena production and done at Covent Garden the previous year in Gilbert Murray's translation with Lillah McCarthy as Jocasta and Martin Harvey as Oedipus. Basil Dean at Liverpool had already praised to them Reinhardt's spectacular productions, which explored stage space in a new choreographic and architectural way. News of Gordon Craig's *Hamlet* designs in Moscow were seeping through. Though it would be many years before Stanislavsky's work was read or seen at first hand, yet something of it was known and seemed to correspond with, and extend, some ideas in progressive English theatre. Most exciting of all were the reports from every side about Barker's innovative Shakespeare productions at the Savoy. He had done *The Winter's Tale*, still not a popular play, on an open apron-stage, with swift and passionate performances from Henry Ainley and Lillah McCarthy, and all the rest of a carefully chosen team coached and coerced and inspired to great heights of acting. It was Poel's method, made more dynamic and sophisticated, with a starkly impressive set by Norman Wilkinson, and brilliant, lavish but uncluttered costumes by Albert Rutherston. This was followed by an exquisite black-and-silver *Twelfth Night*, entirely designed by Norman Wilkinson, played continuously in an intimate but boldly poetic atmosphere, which suddenly made all previous productions seem stale and conventional, including, Lewis felt, his own. *The Winter's Tale* had confused many and it had not done good business; but, as if the way had been prepared, *Twelfth Night* delighted everyone and sealed Barker's reputation. Lewis was thrilled to hear about these productions though he did not quite approve of what he heard about the designs; they seemed to have been so exciting that they distracted from the play itself. He began to brood on other methods of achieving the same swiftness and directness. Barker agreed that perhaps some focus had been lost through the use of designs which were really works of art in themselves (though his *A Midsummer Night's Dream*, with its strange oriental fairies, was even more outlandish). Lillah was now in prosperous management at the Kingsway Theatre and they were on the point of leasing the St. James's to put on Shaw's new play, *Androcles and the Lion*. All seemed to be going well for them and, with several rich lords persuaded by Lillah's determination to back them, the prospect of a more permanent London repertory theatre again looked good. Lewis felt unexpectedly encouraged and warmed by the idea that though Manchester was so far away, he too, as director of the first repertory company in England, was part of a national and international movement forward in the theatre. He began to feel that perhaps it was time at the Gaiety, too, to introduce some artistic changes. So he returned to the North, refreshed and eager, in the new season, to press a little harder on the established ideas of theatrical taste.

For the autumn season of 1913 Irene Rooke and Milton Rosmer were no longer in the company. This was sad but inevitable; they had devoted several years to the company, and it was time for them, just as Lewis, as producer, wished for himself, to explore other spheres. Though he missed their talents, Lewis was nevertheless most satisfied with the team he took into the new season, led by Jules Shaw, Brember Wills and Sybil. Percy Foster, Muriel Pratt, Christie Laws, and newcomers Horace Braham, Lucy Beaumont and Douglas Vigors were strong members of a company smaller and less experienced, but loyal, eager and co-operative. When he started conferences with Miss Horniman she struck a sadder blow by deciding that, after all, a permanent orchestra and conductor was a luxury the theatre could not really afford. So the little group was disbanded and Sokoloff returned to America (where he too established a successful career and remained a good friend of Lewis and Sybil). They settled down to plan the new season and Lewis broached the idea of doing some Shakespeare. There had been no Shakespeare during the previous season, and in the past, except for Poel's *Measure for Measure*, only Christmas productions. He proposed, in two stages, to break Manchester audiences into the new production methods he was planning—by mounting *Julius Caesar* for two weeks in October, followed by a Christmas production of *The Tempest*. Miss Horniman who had always hoped the Gaiety would establish a Shakespeare tradition, was quite pleased with the idea. Round these two major productions they planned a season which started better than it ended. Lewis found that, once more, Miss Horniman had planned a simultaneous tour, this time to London and other towns, to try to keep finances healthy, so for several weeks there would be two companies again, as well as the *Hindle Wakes* production. Even so, for the fifteen-week period, there were to be six full-length productions, of which three were new plays, plus three revivals.

The first new play, *The Apostle*, by the French dramatist Paul Hyacinthe Loyson, a tautly-written dialectical study of conscience and duty, pleased the critics but failed at the box-office. The second, *The Price of Thomas Scott*, a family drama by Elizabeth Baker, whose *Chains* had been popular in two previous seasons, prompted an accusation in the *Manchester Courier* that the Gaiety had fallen into "rather a dreary realistic rut". Lewis was furious because it was not true, and because so-called "realistic" plays were the only ones everyone rushed to see. He immediately dashed off a vehement defence of the Gaiety's policy and programme, enclosing a list of work done in the previous year and pointing out, somewhat acidly, that the "realistic" *Hindle Wakes* and *The Silver Box*, just being revived yet again, did by far the best business. For the moment, any ill will was dispelled with that revival, accompanied by a hilarious one-act by Allan Monkhouse, *Nothing Like Leather*, which satirised the Gaiety and everybody connected with it. Lewis took up the idea of this theatrical romp with huge enthusiasm and made everyone take great pains to get their portrayals accurate. Percy Foster played the critic "Topaz" (James Agate, to whom the piece was dedicated), casually dropping references to Sarah Bernhardt, and he was coached by Agate himself, who lent him his distinguished overcoat. Horace Braham played Lewis, who was "Mr. Push", described by the real Agate as "the incisive Napoleonic producer, that hand of iron weighing upon the actors in playful unlikeness to a velvet glove". Lewis did the make-up for Braham, and achieved a startling similarity to himself. Mr. Push's idea of producing, it seemed, was to manipulate a table and chair through various brilliantly imaginative permutations of position. The most difficult part to cast was Miss Horniman, but at the last moment Lewis boldly wired to London, inviting her to come and play herself. To the company's delight she accepted and, as Agate described it, "walked on in her habit as she lives to the immense delight and applause of a greatly amused house". She later confessed it was one of the great moments in her life.

Meanwhile, two important productions approached. The third new play of the season was Eden Phillpotts' *The Shadow*, a strong, hot-blooded drama set among Dartmoor villagers, and acted with sly humour as well as tragic pathos by Sybil and Jules Shaw. Phillpotts' *The Secret Woman* had been banned the previous year, so there was much interest in the play. It was very well reviewed as another triumph of beautifully structured realism, with powerful co-ordinated acting from the whole cast. Lewis gnashed his teeth over some reviews which indicated, in complete contradiction of the *Courier* attack, that this was the sort of play the Gaiety Theatre should be doing.

At last, on October 13th, 1913, *Julius Caesar* opened, the production which, of all others, Lewis felt he "ought to be doing", and had worked towards for a long time. It was ten years since he had met Poel and begun to think seriously about modern Shakespearian production. With *Twelfth Night* in the previous year he had trodden warily, making few innovations, but now he pushed much further ahead towards his own vision of Shakespearian theatre. The set, which Hugh Fremantle designed and built under his close supervision, was partly influenced by the simple unity of the Antoine *King Lear* which he had seen in 1904, and partly by the clean lines of Ricketts's *Salome*, but it had evolved into an idea that was entirely his own. It was skilfully constructed so as to be manoeuvrable in various pieces. It consisted of a symmetrical group of pillared arches and several steps, all mounted on castors. The stage jutted forward, making an apron, and appropriate front, wing and back cloths were flown in. The varied use of curtains, furniture and lighting, and the changes in positioning of the main set, including its complete removal for the final part, made it possible to differentiate between each location, as in a conventional Beerbohm Tree type of production, and yet eliminate all scene-change pauses. When you consider that this was before the much later innovation which allowed changes to be made with the scene shifters in full view, it was a remarkably ingenious feat. What it achieved artistically was a unified impression of Rome conveyed by the "columnar grandeur" of the setting, as Cecil Chisholm of the *Courier* described it—and therefore, conversely and appropriately, the loss of that grandeur on the plains of Philippi. The effect was gained with almost no perspective painting. The set was later shown in the *Stage Year Book* for 1914 and Lewis gave a fairly complete idea of how the various scenes worked.

The setting of the play consisted of one built set only. In the first scene the centre arch closed by grey velvet curtains running in a panorama groove stood for the entrance to the circus.

The night street scene was a front cloth, painted without perspective on a wall of grey squared stones. The cloth was dropped immediately behind the two small permanent arches in the P and OP corners. For Brutus's orchard the central arch (mounted on castors for easy movement) was run down to the side of the stage and formed the entrance to Brutus's palace. A few very dark tree wings completed the scene, which was lit by a single shaft of light from the flies. Caesar's house was a front scene, used like all the front scenes in connection with the apron, backed by a loose drapery of old gold, with a bold blue stencilled border. The street scene which followed was the same towering wall used for the night scene.

The Senate scene was a rearrangement of the original set, the panorama curtains backed the recesses thus formed, and the steps were set in a different formation. At the exit of the conspirators a black drapery fell behind Anthony, and during the "havoc" speech and the scene with Octavius's servant this interior was instantaneously converted to the Forum scene by the striking of the various curtains and rearranging the steps. The pulpit stood on one of the bastions of the central arch. The absolute continuity from the murder scene to the end of the Forum scene was a great gain. The Cinna-poet scene was played on the apron with the curtain down, and Lepidus's house scene on the main stage before the same cloth as Caesar's house, with different lighting and furniture. This scene finished the second half.

For the third part the main set was the Plains of Philippi. For the tent scene the panorama curtains were closed. A few short scenes were played on the apron in front of the curtain, but except for these and for changes of lighting this set stood for the whole of the battle scenes. The production was designed for absolute continuity of voice and action throughout the play but as a concession to the wishes of the modern audience, there were two intervals.

The costumes, designed by the actress Muriel Pratt, were extremely simple versions of Roman draperies, with leather armour, making it possible for the actors to move quickly and naturally without any statuesque posing usual for "classical" productions. The lighting was very modern. Here, too, Lewis had the advantage of his accepted "masters", for he knew and understood far more about the technical management of his effects. Instead of pictorial lighting from the battens, he lit from the front and used some directional lighting, so as to create half-light and relief effects against the sombre draperies and enhance the solid architectural set by a new three-dimensional sculptured effect. In all these ways his design was a much more integrated part of his production concept than Barker's, although, of course, less lavish. "In time," said a *Courier* leader "[this new staging] may teach us a proper contempt for pasteboard palaces and gilded spires as arch-cumberers of the mind and the worst sort of dramatic deadweights." John Foulds composed the music, which was sparing, limited to ceremonial trumpets, and, in marked contrast, an authentic Pythian ode for the boy Lucius to sing. The acting was swift, vivid and poetic, with many original interpretations. Caesar (Brember Wills) was not the conventional all-conquering hero, the great Colossus, but a war-weary figure, well on the way to his dotage. And in restoring the full text, Lewis resurrected the forgotten scene of Cinna the poet, the key for an extraordinary volcanic crowd which poured through the auditorium for the Forum scene and "erupted emotion in volumes", turned on Cinna, when the moment came, and tore him down on the apron stage only a few feet from the stalls. Jules Shaw played Cassius with "sustained fire, choleric gustiness and stupendous energy", contrasted with Lewis's interpretation of Brutus as a milky sentimentalist.

On that first night, nerves strung high, the performance started coldly, the audience clearly nonplussed by what they were seeing and hearing, but soon the clarity and thought-filled passion began to work on them; they were drawn into the relentless tragic thrust of Shakespeare's full text, continuously played with all its rush and hustle, and the actors responded to this and relaxed, till by the end there was warm acclaim from the whole house and wild enthusiasm from the gallery.

On the morning of October 14th Lewis was gratified to find, over the breakfast table, that the critics of both the *Guardian* (C. E. Montague) and the *Courier* (Cecil Chisholm) had been thrilled by the production. "This is one of the greatest things the Gaiety has done," Chisholm summed up. "For it gives us the whole of the seething fury of mean passions, shot with stray sparks of an out-grown idea that was Shakespeare's vision of the grandeur that was Rome." Later he would read a whole range of criticism, most of it favourable, but also including a thorough condemnation in the *Evening Chronicle*, whose critic was not to be shaken from the conviction he had long held "that Miss Horniman's company do not shine in Shakespeare". He heartily disliked the auditorium entrances, the tableau curtains and the gabbled, over-realistic speech. He criticised the "immoderate eulogies poured upon the production from a quarter prone to over-praise everything done by Miss Horniman's company", and ended, "If the actors of the future are all to be repertory-trained and we are to have our Shakespeare dosed out to us in this nerveless way, then the sooner we start to kill the repertory movement the better."

For such a mixed reception Lewis was prepared. Indeed he was delighted to find just how many critics and playgoers had enjoyed and understood what he was trying to do. But he was entirely unprepared for the scene that took place with Miss Horniman later that morning. She had sat in on several rehearsals and technical sessions—it had become her habit to do this quite frequently lately—but not offered any comments, and that too was usual. Now she appeared suddenly in Lewis's office to tell him, without beating about the bush, that the production was "freakish". He was, quite simply, astounded by her reaction, and at once blazed out in his own defence. The only thing she would say clearly, in tones of great indignation, was that the production was "Gordon Craigish" (which it was, as several critics had pointed out, though his influence was only indirect). Lewis was still in the dark. What on earth had she got against Craig? Why had she not spoken before? What right had she to interfere in the production side, entirely his province? Why take any notice of critics anyway? And how dare she call it "freakish" of all things? There was no discussion. Tempers and feelings grew higher and higher to explosion point. Miss Horniman cancelled there and then the plans for *The Tempest* and Lewis countered with his resignation. They stormed away from each other, while members of the company, flattened by this vocal tempest, stood by as they passed and waited hopefully for calm to be restored.

But there was to be no going back, no reconciliation. When tempers had cooled, Lewis realised that far more lay beneath Miss Horniman's fury than simple dislike of his experimental production. (He did discover that her abhorrence of Craig stemmed from an attack he had once made on her work at the Abbey, in *The Mask*.) Years later he wondered if she was responding to some dimly-felt premonition of the Great War, for she seemed, over the next few months, almost to be inviting disaster. She had ceased to speak frankly about the finances of the theatre, or of her policies, which were obviously causing her great concern. Bookings for *Julius Caesar* were predictably low, because the enthusiastic minority was small, and he felt he must take full responsibility for this, but it had been a crucial step in his creative development, and *The Tempest* was to have been also. He could not, with integrity, remain to follow a different artistic policy; in any event, she was not prepared to draw it up with him. So his resignation stood. When it was announced it released a swarm of argument about the Gaiety, which turned his anger away from Miss Horniman towards the Manchester public itself.

Correspondents and critics agreed that something was wrong,

but disagreed about what it was, so they busied themselves diagnosing, prescribing and generally telling each other what Miss Horniman ought to be doing, with scarcely a thought for what supporters of her theatre ought to be doing. They suggested bringing back the orchestra, doing more comedies, doing fewer comedies, bringing back old Gaiety actors like Charles Bibby, Milton Rosmer, Irene Rooke, doing more revivals, doing more Shaw, doing less Shaw, with a few staunch advocates like St. John Ervine and Allan Monkhouse declaring that it was not so much the company that was failing as the public. Lewis, too, felt that there would be no need for all this pessimistic talk about failure if the public would only support their theatre more warmly. Except, he said, for the most obvious successes, Manchester's response to Miss Horniman had been "grudging and barely adequate".

Lewis had agreed to stay until Christmas. He put on a couple of comedies and tried to keep things going even when the cream of the company was performing *The Shadow* and *Jane Clegg* in London. So much of his time as director had been spent taking successful productions from Manchester, and recasting when actors left the company to gain the benefit of their enhanced reputations, that he could not help remembering Tree's wry witticism. "When is a repertory theatre not a repertory theatre? Answer: When it's a success!" Lewis felt few regrets now and began to think about his own plans. Yet again, a professional change was coinciding with family development; Sybil was expecting another baby in the following May. So they planned to go to London and set up house at 40, Bessborough Street in Westminster which his mother-in-law had bought in one of her frequent property-buying ventures. Then, he and Sybil decided it might be the moment to invest some of their American savings in some valuable travel. He felt the need to expand his own ideas with a visit to Berlin, Munich, Moscow and other centres of the new art theatre movement of which he was now so integrally a part. However, plans for a theatrical exploration of Europe early in 1914 were soon dropped when he was invited to direct a season in Glasgow, where the Scottish Repertory Company was launching an eight-week season after a two-year lull. At once he felt a familiar stir of excitement and for the moment gave up the cultural holiday. As usual, when he had a choice, enthusiasm for the practice of his craft far outpaced a desire to pursue its theory.

Before he left Manchester, one more event brought his career there to a suitably dramatic conclusion. A splendid dinner was organised in honour of Sybil and himself, where everybody smiled and congratulated everyone else, and a good time seemed to be had by all until Lewis rose to reply to the lovely things that had been said, and, with thunder in his brow, lashed out at the complacency of the Manchester public. It was, he said, just like the elderly Mrs. Clegg—it wanted to be mindlessly "let alone and be happy" instead of responding to the new, exciting possibilities offered to it by its servants in the arts. Gathering in eloquence, he said that Manchester liked to call the Gaiety its "own" theatre, but it "hadn't founded it, didn't work for it, and didn't pay for it"! After this outburst, delivered with all Lewis's rhetorical punch, there was an embarrassed pause which Sybil tactfully ended by bursting into laughter and thus restoring good humour to the evening. What she said to Lewis afterwards in the privacy of the bedroom she did not record; I dare say it was fairly scathing.

They now packed up the household in Heaton Park and resettled it in Westminster. Then Lewis left for Glasgow in mid-January and spent the next three months or so up there, with occasional weekend trips to see the family in London.

The repertory company in Glasgow, founded in 1909 by the Scottish Playgoers Ltd., was financed by £3,000 capital from local shareholders and directors, raised mainly through the initiative of its promoter, Alfred Wareing. A theatre-manager and producer of great enthusiasm and vision, he saw no reason why Scotland should not follow Manchester's example and have its own repertory theatre. He pioneered the whole scheme and led the company for three years. There were some excellent productions, including the first English version of Chekhov's *The Seagull*. Over thirty original plays were done and over fifty established ones, representing all the leading dramatists whose work had been seen at the Court and other modern theatres. Barker had been up as a guest producer and the whole venture, greatly approved, was hampered only by its theatre, the Royalty, a huge, uncomfortable barn of a place, enormously expensive to rent, especially for short periods. Glasgow, with its dour asceticism and suspicion of too much wit or mirth, did not have a rich theatrical tradition. For three years the company ran at a loss and then, reluctantly, Wareing's contract was terminated. Now the Royalty had become available for a short season and the directors were willing to chance their arm again. Clearly, it was not the moment for progressive experiment but for carefully building up the audience for a good company. After the public battles in Manchester, it was a test of Lewis's patience and persistence to start again the slow nurturing of the art of theatre as he understood it—a joint artistic growth of both actors and audience. Yet he managed it, making an artistic success and a profit of several hundred pounds for the Scottish Playgoers, which greatly reduced their deficit.

At first Lewis was apprehensive about being responsible to a board of directors. How could one talk art with ten businessmen, or would it be like dealing with ten Miss Hornimans? He soon discovered that the chairman, Colonel Morrison and the board member who had first approached him, Major Jowitt, were, like the rest of the Board, deeply cultured men anxious about both the theatre and the welfare of their city. For the first time, he felt the difference between a civic theatre planned, financed and administered by Glaswegians, and the Gaiety, with its unavoidable tinge of patronage. "We have chosen Manchester," Miss Horniman and Iden Payne had announced in their very first press release, and her apprehension was that perhaps they had chosen wrongly. As he sat down to plan the Glasgow programme, Lewis reflected on the impossibility of running any reasonable-sized theatre solely on "sincere works of art", another phrase from the Manchester announcement. Even if you could, he thought, such a theatre is not doing its job as a "city" theatre for a reasonably large proportion of the townsfolk. He began to put his whole Manchester experience into perspective. Frankly, it was a relief not to have to cope with Miss Horniman's prickly feminism. Typical of her female chauvinism had been her comment on the appointment of Lewis's successor, Douglas Gordon: "You can add," she told the press, "that I would rather have had a woman, because they have more sense."

He assembled an excellent company at the Royalty, including Brember Wills and Frank Darch from the Gaiety; several former members of Wareing's company, among them Franklin Dyall; Eliot Makeham and Beatrice Smith, both players of much experience and ability; and Nicholas Hannen, a strikingly handsome and fiery actor with whom he would have a long and happy association. He then proceeded to discipline and bully them into a fine team who worked incredibly hard for that short season. Every week a new play was put on, and at the beginning there were matinées as well. The schedule, planned only about three weeks ahead, began with a series of comedies attractively produced to offset the prevalent idea that repertory theatre was "grim". After an auspicious opening, all parts of the theatre well filled, the support remained steady and he began to branch out a little. *The Devil's Disciple* was revived, with "Beau" Hannen a charming and dashing Dick Dudgeon. Lewis launched some new full-length plays, including Miles Malleson's *The Threshold*, and more daring material, such as a dialogue from Schnitzler's *Anatol*, translated by Barker. The eight weeks ended with Henry Arthur Jones's *The Liars*. The author himself, well known for his support of the repertory movement, attended with the Lord Provost, making quite a grand civic and theatrical occasion of it. The directors, delighted at the appreciative response, and finding that audiences were actually growing, leased the theatre for another five weeks, with two revivals from early in the season, another full-length new play and, at the end, *Man and Superman*, becoming Lewis's typical crowning of a repertory season. Playing Tanner himself for the first and only time, he was proud to be praised for a magnificent performance, "vigorous, intellectual, polished".

The whole season was a great success, with only a few caveats from a "Humble Pittite", who asked, in the *Glasgow Herald*, for fewer comedies; one or two critics who confidently encouraged the recognition of plays "of stronger and more exacting quality"; and Lewis himself, who hoped that in future the directors would not neglect "the very finest class of plays", which could only attract a small audience, but which it was the theatre's vital task to present. One thing that helped was Lewis's choice of several Scottish plays, especially a one-act tragedy, *Campbell of Kilmohr*, and *Marigold*, a comedy later adapted to become a London success in the 1920s. He could really feel that he had made another small but significant contribution to civic theatre, and, on a personal level, worked through the anger of the last weeks at the Gaiety.

At a farewell reception he was presented with a laurel wreath and warmly thanked; and as he caught the night train back to London, he reflected with some smugness that he had behaved with a graciousness of which Sybil would have felt proud.

7

Enter a Soldier
1914–1919

The long all-too memorable summer of 1914 began. Lewis returned from Glasgow refreshed and invigorated despite the hectic schedule he had imposed on himself and the company. Sybil was well and happy, settled into the house in Bessborough Street. Her third childbirth was so trouble-free and quick that Lewis was able to assist her, when, on a beautiful May morning, his first daughter, Mary, came gently into the world, before the midwife could arrive. John and Christopher had caught whooping cough, so after a brief introduction to their sister, he bundled them into the car, down to Dymchurch, to whoop their way back to health on the sands. As soon as they were well, he brought Sybil and the baby and there they stayed, getting tanned and glowing, in and out of the sea, while he went back and forth from London, and, at another time, Blackpool, keeping them afloat financially. He did various minor productions which left him plenty of long weekends with the family. There were afternoons of bathing, teaching the boys to swim and helping them to build sandcastles; and when they ran off to buy their sticky buns, he and Sybil sat on the sea wall having long talks, and building their own castles in the air as they gazed out to sea. They went on long walks and explored the little churches scattered over the marsh, and several times, when Lewis was drawn inevitably to the organ loft, he found the familiar shape of a Casson organ welcoming him like an old friend.

All the Thorndikes were down there, and it was during this holiday that he again shamed Russell with his total disregard for appearances. After a bathe one afternoon he proposed a short car ride to test some repair he had just done, so he, Russell and Sybil climbed in, dressed in their beach gear, and rattled off along the Kent lanes. The repair was quite successful and they soon found themselves near Canterbury, still bounding merrily along. Sybil just happened to say that she had never been inside the Cathedral.

"We'll go in then, while the car cools," said Lewis.

"But we can't go in dressed like this," Sybil objected. "We look awful."

"People will be far too interested in Becket to notice us," answered Lewis. "Don't be conceited."

So in they marched, the respectable daughter of a minor canon of Rochester Cathedral, with her collarless husband, and brother, ex-chorister of St. George's, Windsor, lagging behind fully aware of their sartorial inadequacies. According to him, they actually overheard two American visitors mistake them for gipsy hop-pickers, and when they emerged, they saw some well-known dignitary of the Cathedral approaching whom Sybil and Russell had known since childhood. As his face lit up with recognition, Sybil saved his imminent embarrassment by nudging Russell and saying in a loud voice, "'urry up, George. Me and 'enry wants to get 'ome," and hurrying past him, to hide her blushes in the car. Thus did Lewis's most un-Edwardian lack of class reveal itself.

In the evenings, when all the family gathered and the children were in bed, Russell was called on to read to them; for he was spending that summer almost literally tied down to a desk, writing the story which he had planned ten years before with Sybil, when they were touring together with Ben Greet—the first enthralling tale of *Dr. Syn*, the clergyman-smuggler of Romney Marsh, whom he made so famous that tourists in later years came to look at the rogue's old haunts, and even a waiter at the Mermaid Inn at Rye once assured a party, in my hearing, that Dr. Syn was, in truth, an eighteenth-century resident of the place.

We can picture Lewis then, among his family. Thirty-eight years old and in the prime of life. Slim and vigorous, with a very upright posture. Those clear blue eyes, which looked so hard at the immediate view that they seemed to see right past it towards some distant horizon. A serious brow, and firmly pressed lips, expressive of his steadfastness. You might not pick him out of a crowd unless you heard his voice—vibrant, with rich harmonics, making everything he said almost more impressive that it was, you might think, with its resonance, its rhythmic sense and its clear intonations, except that through it came the deep conviction behind his words. So that, in his speech and in his stories, the words, the meaning and the music were all inextricable.

Long before they met the conceitedness of Toad in *The Wind in the Willows*, his children and later some of his grandchildren, knew, for instance, the sad cautionary tale of "the grandest motor car in London", who always tooted at the other vehicles: "*Getout* o' the way! Don'cha know—I'm the GRRRANDEST MOTOR CAR IN LONDON!"

until he met a tram, who could not get out of the way, and he was smashed to smithereens! Most children on their way to the seaside try to see the sea first, but for Casson children this ritual was caught in a tune as definite as the response in Church:

Who can see the see............a?

There was also a ridiculous game when Lewis looked at you with mock horror, sitting up in your bed after your bath and said, "Whatever are you doing in bed at this time 'o the mornin'? Don'cha know it's *ten minutes to eleven!*" Then, when you leapt out of bed, his horror increased. "Wot*ever* are ya doin' out of bed at *this* time o' the night? Don'cha know it's *ten minutes to eleven!*" And so on. Once, at a grand dinner at St. John's College, Cambridge, which his brother Randal invited Lewis to, he was trapped by his own sense of speech patterns. The waiter asked his neighbour, "Chicken or beef, sir?" and the man replied, "Chicken." This was then quite a luxury, but then the waiter asked Lewis "Beef or chicken, sir?" and Lewis had to forego the poultry because he felt bound to keep the vocal symmetry and said "Beef!" His greatest achievement along these lines was the immortal lullaby he invented for John, which started as the story of the Twenty Trees, then became Thirty Trees and finally the Fifty Trees. It was about a man who was very tired one night and arrived at the railway station with a long walk ahead before he would be home. And he said to himself—in a lovely, soothing, chanting kind of voice, as he passed the first tree on the road:

'Fifty more trees and then I shall be home, and I'll go to bed and I'll go to sleep and I'll sleep all night 'cos I'm so tired and so sleepy I don't know what to do.' So he went walking and walking and walking and walking, up the hill and down the hill and up the hill and down the hill until he came to another tree. 'Forty-nine more trees and then I shall be home and I'll go to bed and I'll go to sleep and I'll sleep all night 'cos I'm so tired and so sleepy I don't know what to do.' So he went walking and walking . . .

He was happier at times like this, in simple domestic surroundings with hard work to do, than in sophisticated circles or with too much leisure—he liked the routine of family meals, odd jobs around the house, reading and walking, relaxed and informal entertaining, talking and arguing about his two passions, politics and the theatre, with religion and ethics thrown in too. He had taken easily to the authoritative roles of father in the family and producer in the theatre. He was able to speak and act as vigorously as he wanted, because Sybil's vitality was always a match for his. The two of them expanded and enriched each other's minds and hearts, and the children thrived in an atmosphere of love, challenge and self-discipline.

Now more of a city dweller than a rural Welshman—at home in Manchester and New York, Glasgow and London—he seemed still a man of the hills when he was walking with that rapid stride that left his companions breathless; in life, too, it was as if he were always climbing Snowdon, intent on each step but spurred by the knowledge of a glorious prospect ahead. So they talked, he and Sybil, of what they might do if Barker started a repertory theatre, or if they risked their savings and found someone to back them in some management venture of their own. And what either of these might lead to. And what might be the future for the children. And whether they would grow up in a better world. They still wondered if Lewis should stick to his earlier plan and explore the theatres of Europe, but meanwhile another good offer came for the autumn, from J. E. Vedrenne, to direct the well-known actor Matheson Lang in a new play at the Royalty. He was known to the family because Russell had been on a world tour with him and Frank Thorndike, now well embarked on his own career, had acted with him the previous year. And all the time, Lewis kept his eye on the newspapers, but did not always speak his thoughts and fears aloud. He was in Dymchurch on June 28th when the Archduke Franz Ferdinand of Austria was assassinated at Sarajevo, and it was on his next trip down, early in July, as Russell recollected later, that he stood on the beach and voiced his conviction, "There's going to be a war in Europe," and Sybil said, "Thank God you're not a soldier then."

As the news grew worse, Lewis decided they must go back to London, so they all packed up and left the little seaside town. They did it in two trips. On the day war was declared, Lewis was driving the boys and their nursemaid Alice back. As John remembered in later years, the day acquired a quite different significance for the children, when the front tie-rod broke and they ran into a wall on Maidstone Hill and tumbled out into the road, shaken but not hurt—it was always the day of "The Accident" to him.

109

Back in London, all was in a flurry of patriotic fervour. His brother Will, a keen Territorial for many years now, was called up immediately with his battalion, the 7th City of London, which was to be sent to France. His response was to commit himself at last to the girlfriend he had known for some years. He married her and went into intensive training. Russell was in the Westminster Dragoons and his regiment was put under orders for Egypt. Twenty-year-old Frank immediately enlisted in the same regiment, and the two of them could be seen training at Vincent Square in Westminster. Soon came the day they were to sail, and Lewis, determined that they should have a good send-off, drove Sybil and the boys and her father to their departure point. As the Brigade rode proudly off, eager to do battle, tears poured down Lewis's cheeks. Arriving home, he walked into the house with a set face, and told Sybil, "Put the children in the pram and let John walk and come out with me." So, with Christopher and Mary in the pram and John trotting beside them, they set off down the Vauxhall Bridge Road and watched a long column of soldiers march over the bridge, with a brass band playing and crowds cheering and waving them off. Then Lewis made up his mind. "I've got to be in this, you know," he said. "It's the biggest thing that's happened in our lives—one can't stand apart—."

Like so many Socialists, he had strongly resisted the idea of war. In a world where there was so much work to be done, so many human needs to attend to, what place was there for military expense and national aggression? He sympathised with the Labour demonstration of August 2nd, which Keir Hardie had addressed, together with H. M. Hyndman, George Lansbury and Arthur Henderson, Secretary of the Labour Party. He admired the Neutrality Committee, which included one of his own mentors, Gilbert Murray, and Ramsay MacDonald. He felt torn between the straightforward and courageous patriotism of his brother and the pacific idealism of the neutralists. But, like all except the small cluster of Britons who remained unflinchingly anti-war, he felt compelled by the German invasion of Belgium to accept the inevitability of the war, and then experienced to the full the extraordinary fever of euphoria and relief that overtook the country when at last its splendid isolation ended. As the Labour party and the trades unions swung behind the war movement, it began to look as if this war might be an opportunity to make a clean sweep. First, the war became a matter of honour; and, accepting that he would, like most other citizens, rather die than see his country submit to oppression, Lewis recognised his commitment, then came the more hopeful prospect that this war might help not hinder the creation of a new order. Lastly, he found, for the first time since he had entered the theatre ten years before, that it could not satisfy his present aims. While Barker, his other shining light, prepared to make the best effort he could to fulfil his ideals through theatre work, and set off for America to do so, Lewis felt a passionate need to play a more active part in this world epic.

Within a few months Gilbert Murray himself had shifted from his neutral position and with his Oxford Pamphlet, *How Can War Ever Be Right?* brought comfort to Lewis and to many other thinking men by his articulate expression of the force of "honour" and the emotional justification of war. At the end of August, Lord Kitchener raised the age-limit for recruitment to thirty-five, and made a special appeal to married men. Lewis was still too old, and had to falsify his date of birth to be accepted, but he had no qualms about that. He went to the Duke of York's Barracks in Chelsea and joined the Army Service Corps. Money was going to be very tight, and those cherished American savings might have to be put towards financing a rather different European trip from the one he and Sybil had imagined. But they had great hopes she would find work herself before long.

So Lewis dropped the role of actor and producer and became a private soldier, like so many thousands of others. He was sent to the camp at St. Albans where he met the playwright Harold Chapin, a Manchester friend also in the R.A.S.C. Things were not very organised at the camp, and after several years of running a theatre efficiently, Lewis found the first few weeks irksome and frustrating. He soon reacted in his usual irascible and forthright way by telling his Commanding Officer, "The only thing I've learnt since I've been in the army, sir, is how to loaf." The colonel then put him in charge of the cook-house and he soon had that running like clock-work. Then he was transferred to Mechanical Transport to drive lorries, which he much preferred. Meanwhile he was relieved to find that Sybil had landed herself a job in what appeared at the time to be an eccentric scheme doing Shakespeare down in Waterloo. Ben Greet had got her into it, and they were paying her ten shillings a show.

Lewis managed to get home for Christmas and was to leave for France in January in the 47th Division, the same as Will's. Ironically, Sybil was at last to make her first appearance in tragedy, playing Lady Macbeth to Fisher White's Macbeth at the Old Vic. How familiar it sounded! The years with Charles Fry doing Shakespeare in the East End came rushing back to Lewis as he heard of the rough-and-ready productions presented to enthusiastic working-class audiences in a shabby and ill-equipped building. The extraordinary woman running the theatre, Lilian Baylis, was a niece of Emma Cons, with whom his sister Elsie had worked before their mother's death, doing social work and collecting rents as she had for Octavia Hill. And it was his old friend Rosina Filippi who had first suggested doing Shakespeare at the Vic. Then Matheson Lang came in for a few months and now Ben Greet was in charge of productions, while Miss Baylis herself hovered around, keeping her theatre happy and holy. "Your father's a priest, isn't he?" she said to Sybil. "Church and stage—same thing—should be!" As she prepared to play Lady Macbeth, throwing herself into it with a gusto which would help her to get through the pain and fear of Lewis's departure for France, Miss Baylis gave her a few acting hints. "I think Lady Macbeth is a very easy part for you—she loved her husband and wanted him to get to the top of the tree, and I expect you feel that way too, and if it wasn't that you go to Communion I dare say you'd do all sorts of wicked things to help Lewis." But Sybil did not find it quite so simple. "I simply love Lady Macbeth," she wrote to Russell, "though my performance so far is nothing like her."

Lewis's last few days at home soon passed and he set off at the end of January 1915, eager to join the fray, more fearful for Sybil and the children than for himself, comforted by the knowledge that she was energetically involved in work they both loved, his loneliness eased by the old comradeship with Will. Over the last few years his marriage and career had led him in a very different direction from his conservative and scientific brother. This was no bad thing, because he had escaped the early danger of becoming Will's rival, and established their friendship on the basis of equal and quite different skills. They had not always seen much of each other, perhaps because the Cassons were all quieter and more retiring people than the extrovert and effusive Thorndike family, into whose bosom Lewis had been swept. But his love and admiration for his brother had never wavered.

From France he wrote to Sybil every day, and she wrote too. She kept these letters all through her life, a sad and moving record of one man's experience in that long holocaust. When she died, and the neat package came to light among her papers, the family could not at first bring themselves to read them—it seemed still, over sixty years later, an intrusion of their privacy. Now, somehow, the letters have quietly vanished. If they have gone for ever, that loss must be sustained like any other, but perhaps they will find their own moment to surface again, and take us back to those almost unremembered days.

He soon heard the news, somewhat ruefully, that exactly nine months after his departure, she was to have another baby! But, as so often in his family, news of a birth was matched by that of a death. In the spring, his sister Frances died of cancer at the age of forty-two. Fulfilled in her career, but frustrated and often unhappy in her personal life, she had always been a very caring sister, was godmother to Mary and to one of Esther's daughters, and Lewis would greatly miss her intelligent concern.

The war which everyone had hoped would be over quickly was already dragging into its second year when Lewis came home for a few blessed days of leave in August 1915. Again they were at Dymchurch, where they sat on the sea-wall just as they had the year before, and he and Sybil told each other all the things they had written in letters, but, as Sybil said, "face to face was better telling". Her stories were of the children, of Russell and Frank, now at Gallipoli, and of the Vic, where Shakespeare was still playing to packed houses at rock-bottom prices, and Miss Baylis was cooking steaks and sausages in the wings. His were of the debilitating and dispiriting life he was seeing on the Western Front, the horror and ugliness of trench warfare and the sudden moments of fellowship, courage and self-sacrifice. They did not dare talk much about the future.

Back in France, Sir John French, commander of the British Force, launched an offensive at Loos which cost him 50,000 casualties but did not break up the German line. On the morning of September 24th Lewis managed for about the third time since they had both been on leave, to see Will, who was to go into battle. So disastrous was the attack, and so chaotic the British line after it that it was a couple of days before Lewis heard that Will had been killed. It was a dreadful blow, the first and the worst loss he could have suffered. His first reaction was to send word home, to his sisters and to Sybil, and then to find out exactly what had happened. As soon as possible, he found his way to Will's Commanding Officer, waking him up to speak with him and hear the full story. It turned out that Will had been leading a flank on the extreme right of the British attack; when some of the main attack veered too far to the left, he had to try to keep communications open over the gap as he saw it form, cover it, and at the same time rally his men during the furious counter-attacks. Twice they were actually driven out of the trenches they had taken, and as Will was having some difficulty in controlling his confused and frightened men from the trench itself, he got out on the parapet and strolled about smoking a pipe, "bucking the men up". The position was held till the advance could continue but meanwhile a sniper had shot Will. The C.O. described Will's work as magnificent and assured Lewis that it would have won him the D.S.O. The whole battalion had lost heavily. Every single officer in the first three companies was either killed or wounded. Lewis stayed to speak a few words to some of Will's men and was cheered by their pride in him. Then he took his father's signet ring which was the only thing recovered from the body, and went bleakly back to his own base to write to Esther and Elsie, to Sybil, and to Will's widow, Gertrude, whose marriage had been so terribly short-lived. Trying to look at the thing as positively as he could, Lewis wrote: "The big thing I feel about it is that I am glad his life wasn't just thrown away worthlessly as so many fine men and good soldiers are. He died because nothing but the bravery and skill that brought his death would have saved the position." Yet the whole battle, he realised later, had achieved almost nothing, except the recognition of French's inadequacy as a commander. Harold Chapin, whose warm heart and wit Lewis had admired in the man and in his plays, was killed at the same time.

There was no cure for his grief. Until the end of his life Lewis missed Will quite actively. The only panacea was a fiercer effort on his own part. He felt suddenly that his contribution to the war was not serious enough—he, too, should be risking his life to bring men through this frightful and decisive ordeal. Impulsively, without even waiting to hear from Sybil, he applied for a commission. And while his application was being considered, he stirred himself to make a characteristic contribution of his own, founding the first army concert party, at Lillers in the Pas de Calais area. It was a pierrot troupe called "The Follies"—a far cry from the Pierrot of the Dutch garden in *Prunella* or Chapin's affectionate *Marriage of Columbine*, but its plucky and enthusiastic members began the arduous task of entertaining their audiences and momentarily distracting them from their dismal surroundings.

News from London was less cheerful than before. Zeppelin raids had started, and although they were wonderfully exciting, Sybil's mother soon persuaded her that the children should be out of the way, and found a little cottage for them at Kingsdown in Kent, about twenty miles from London. Ann was born in November 1915, and Sybil returned to work immediately to play Ophelia at the Old Vic. It was a frantic time for her, rushing back and forth to the vicarage to feed Ann; then to Kingsdown to see the other children, usually walking the long miles to and from the station (she must have felt she was acting out the Fifty Trees herself); giving John, Christopher and Mary enough love and attention to make up for having only one part-time parent around, and worrying endlessly about Lewis, Russell and Frank. Early in 1916 both her brothers were home. Frank had been ill with dysentery, and then Russell suffered a severe injury when a machine-gun fell on his back, fracturing and dislocating his spine. For months he had to lie on his back, and was finally invalided out of the army, still stooped and bent like an old man. But somehow, they all three kept each other's spirits up. When he was well enough, Russell joined the Old Vic company, and he and Sybil began an extraordinary partnership which lasted almost to the end of the war.

In the spring, Lewis's commission came through, and he came home on leave before taking it up, seeing his daughter Ann for the first time, visiting the Vic and having tense, emotional reunions with the rest of the family. Then he returned to France. The "serious" work he sought had been given to him in a form more vile and grim than he had dreamed of. For this was the period when gas warfare had begun; and when his half-finished Chemistry degree came to light he was given a commission in the Royal Engineers (Special Brigade) to work on poison gas. It was a loathsome form of war for which he had to summon up considerable stoic fortitude. He was commissioned as second lieutenant, quickly became a full lieutenant and within six months was promoted to captain with his own company, carrying out the deadly work of preparing and placing cylinders and projectors of poison gas along the line. He was heavily involved in this right through the Battle of the Somme. It was like an awful parody of the days at the City and Guild Institute, when he and his classmates had contrived their ingenious weapons with no worse intention than to play up the professor. Nothing could have expressed more clearly the mood of grim determination to win the war, which had now gripped the country, than Lewis's disciplined concentration on his lethal task.

He managed to get home for a three-day leave in the late summer and found that Barker was in London. It was a strange meeting, because Barker was in the middle of a personal crisis over his marriage. In America he had fallen in love with Helen Huntington, and was now trying to get Lillah to divorce him. His attitude to the war was bitter and disillusioned. He had worked for the Red Cross in France, producing an uninspired book about its work, but the Military Services Act had made his return to England a moral imperative, even though his name was not on the official register for conscription. He was now in training at the R.G.A. Cadet

115

School, which he hated. Within a few months he would manage to get into the Intelligence, which suited him more. Lewis had to be influenced by Barker's deep dissatisfaction with the war and with the triviality of London wartime theatre. He tried to suppress his own disillusionment to concentrate on the job of finishing the war. He bore Barker off to the Old Vic, where they saw Russell playing Lear, and Sybil playing his Fool, a piece of casting she rejoiced in, made necessary by the lack of young actors. (Their relationship on stage, with Sybil like a shadow, blankly reflecting Lear's moods, made an extraordinarily poignant performance; she was delighted to find that Barker had not even recognised her.)

On the same leave Lewis too was roped in to perform for Miss Baylis, playing Fortinbras in *Hamlet* under the pseudonym of Christopher Holland (taken from the names of his mother and his son) since it was quite against King's Regulations for a soldier to act, even the part of a soldier. It was the right part to express his firm and warlike purposes, in contrast to Barker's Hamlet-like philosophical vacillations. For all the Old Vic actors and audiences it was a comfort to grapple with the huge tragedies, the epic histories and the rumbustious comedies of Shakespeare, drama so full-blooded that it alone could give them the catharsis they needed. *King Lear* had opened on the night Waterloo Station was bombed. Russell played the storm scene against the thunderous raging of the air raid, and took advantage of it to stride downstage at one point—with Sybil at his heels—shouting "Crack Nature's moulds, all Germans [germens] spill at once," to a huge round of applause as he shook his fist towards the guns. Clapping had hardly died away, and the guns had started up again when Sybil capped this with "Here's a night that pities neither wise man nor fool," and once again the audiences roared their delight as the actors expressed the brave defiance shared by the whole house. Such experiences made Sybil wish suddenly that she could tackle the Greeks, and with Lewis she began to explore the idea of telling the war story of Europe through *The Trojan Women* of Euripides.

Meanwhile, playing such demanding parts was putting a tremendous strain on Sybil's voice, and Lewis found himself just as concerned about that as about the ghastliness round him in France. He wrote from there to Elsie Fogerty, to ask her to work with Sybil. It was comforting to know that creative tasks still presented themselves, and from this time on, Sybil did work steadily on freeing and supporting her voice.

Still the war on the Western Front continued. By 1917 Sir Douglas Haig had replaced Sir John French as commander of the British troops there. Lord Kitchener was dead. The Tsar was overthrown. Lloyd George had become Prime Minister. The Americans were about to join the Allies. But trench warfare continued unchanged, with its appalling casualties and sickening conditions. In May, Frank Thorndike, still fighting fit, joined the Royal Flying Corps. Like Lewis he found the disastrous situation in France a spur to greater activity. After only four hours of solo flying, he was sent out to an airfield just outside Arras, in the middle of the Allied Nivelle offensive. He was quite near Lewis, but they did not meet. Lewis was heavily involved in his own company. By this time his cousin Alec Casson was also in uniform. The same age as Frank, but much less healthy, he had been declared unfit and gone up to Christ Church, Oxford. Aunt Lucy, however, could not bear to have him left out and started pulling strings herself, as a result of which he was at last accepted in the army and sent to France.

Of these three, Lewis was the first casualty. He was sent on a mission to lay cylinders of phosgene with a party of Australians. For some reason the Australians did not turn up, so Lewis set off with just his sergeant and a few privates. We can picture his surly impatience at the inefficiency of the organisation, and his angry resolve to get the job done. He succeeded, but at the cost of a shrapnel wound in his shoulder. After a short spell in hospital in France, he was sent home to the immense joy and relief of his family. In August, while on leave, he learnt that this exploit had won him a Military Cross. But this was small comfort, when, in the same month, news came that Frank had been injured in an aeroplane crash. Not badly hurt, he was expected to make a good recovery. Then, two days later, when everyone had begun to look forward to his homecoming, he died in a French hospital. It was like Will's death all over again, but this time Sybil's family suffered the dreadful loss. The shock and grief suffered by her parents at the news was so overwhelming that Lewis must have felt some relief, in retrospect, to think his own parents had been dead by the time Will was killed. On the day they heard—Sybil would later recall—her mother was quite unable to play in church, and she herself sat at the organ and accompanied her father while he bravely conducted the service as usual. Russell was badly shaken, having been even closer to his brother than Lewis was to Will. Frank had joked about the Roll of Honour at St. James's on his last leave. "I've been on every list in the parish—choirboy, sidesman, bell-ringer—and sure as anything I'll be on that one too. I don't care a bit, really, but if any of you start being melancholy about me, or wearing black, I'll just haunt you all and make your lives a nightmare." He was buried in France and

117

there was a memorial service for him at home. His father, who had once meant to be a soldier himself, had the church decorated as for a festival, filled it with glorious, rousing music, and spoke valiantly of the great cause for which Frank had died. No doubt he included the hymn which, over the years, came to express the hopes and fears of Sybil and Lewis and their family at all significant moments in their lives:

> Now thank we all our God
> With hearts and hand and voices,
> Who wondrous things hath done
> In whom his world rejoices.

On the family grave at Aylesford was inscribed the moving soldier's epitaph on Young Siward in *Macbeth*:

> He only liv'd but till he was a man;
> The which no sooner had his prowess confirm'd
> In the unshrinking station where he fought,
> But like a man he died
> Why then, God's soldier be he!

Yet again Shakespeare shed an ironic light on the event, for Frank had played the part at the Vic on his last leave. The family suffered no more and no less than thousands and thousands of other families; like so many others, their response was not to criticise the generals and statesmen, but to muster up their remaining courage and resolution to see the war to its end, comfort each other, and live as the dead would have wished.

Because of his wound, Lewis was on "light duties" until Christmas, and could undertake more heartening work. He joined the Army Camp Theatres, which his old friend Basil Dean was running. These had developed from Dean's initiative in providing garrison entertainment, in the same way that Lewis had started "The Follies" in 1915. They were put on an official footing with the formation of the Naval and Army Canteen Board, and much valuable, morale-raising work was done in camps throughout England as well as in France and elsewhere. Lewis was glad of the break from military routine and a few months of productive work.

In October, yet another family loss. Lewis's cousin Alec was reported missing at Passchendaele Ridge, the latest futile battle of the Western Front. He was presumed dead, though this was not confirmed until 1920, when a skeleton was found, bearing a

Lewis aged about four.

The Casson family about 1888. Standing, left to right: Lewis, Will, Frances, Randal; sitting: Thomas, Laura Ann, Esther; in front: Elsie, Annie.

Lewis and Sybil about 1908.

The family at Dymchurch about 1921. Left to right: Sybil, Ann, Mary, John, Lewis, Christopher.

Lewis as Dante in *Beatrice*, 1905; a drawing by Ernest Jackson.

Lewis with Russell Thorndike in *Latitude 15° S* from the fourth *Grand Guignol Annual Review*, 1921.

The tent scene from *Saint Joan*, New Theatre, 1924, with Lewis as Chaplain De Stogumber (far left), Eugene Leahy as Cauchon, Lyall Swete as Warwick.

Lewis as Shylock, 1927 (above left), Socrates, 1930 (above right), and
Professor Linden, 1947 (below).

The French court in Lewis's production of *Henry V* at Drury Lane, 1938, with Ivor Novello as Henry, Dorothy Dickson as Catherine, Gwen Ffrangcon-Davies as Chorus.

Lewis as Macbeth, Sybil as Lady Macbeth, Old Vic tour in Wales, 1940.

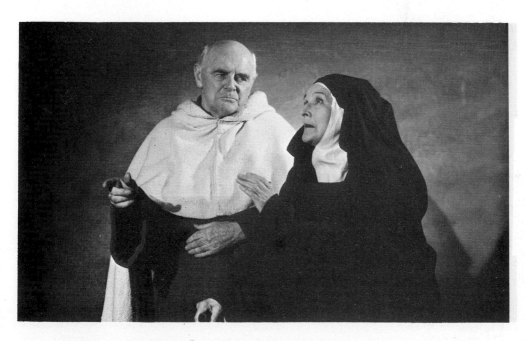

Lewis as Father-General, Sybil as Teresa in *Teresa of Avila*, Vaudeville, 1961.

Lewis about 1955.

ring with the Casson crest, a macabre reminder of the slaughter. Yet more loss and suffering would follow. In December, with Lewis away at a camp in Cornwall, there was a much more unexpected blow. In the middle of conducting a Sunday evening service Sybil's father collapsed and died. The pain of Frank's death, kept firmly suppressed, had done untold damage to his body and spirit. Lewis was given a few days' compassionate leave and came to London to find his mother-in-law quite incapable with grief. Never separated from her husband for a single day, she could not imagine any kind of life without him by her side. Sybil, Russell and Eileen tried to rally her and were a warm support to each other, feeling severely the loss of a saintly father who had commanded their entire love and respect. The three of them went down to Aylesford with Lewis for the funeral, and Canon Thorndike was buried beside his son's memorial and mourned by his old parishioners. Russell and Sybil refused to stop working and went on with the ridiculous Christmas revue they had planned at the Old Vic. Very gradually their mother began to recover her spirits. To Aunt Lucy, mourning her son in the sombre and solitary splendour of Bron-y-garth, Lewis could only write, and it was hard to break through her aristocratic pride. But it was now, he realised, very much his responsibility to try. Suddenly, he had become the head of both the families. With Will gone and Alec presumed dead, he became chief heir to Uncle Randal's property, and with Canon Thorndike dead, he became the natural head of Sybil's family. It was a double responsibility which sat heavily upon a man who had been fighting for three years. But his term of light duty ended and early in 1918 he was summoned back to France, now Major Casson, to continue the hated gas work, still leading a company of the R. E. Special Brigade.

During the first months of 1918, Lewis invented a more efficient mechanism for gas missiles, something that in later years caused him much mental anguish, even though he tried to reason that no weapon or tactic designed to kill was morally better or worse than another. He continued, when appropriate, to hearten his men with entertainments. A member of his company once sent me the programme of a concert given by volunteers, which Lewis organised after a particularly fierce raid at Pacaut Wood. Items offered by "M" company on this occasion included musical sketches by Captain E. Makeham, the actor Eliot Makeham who had been with Lewis in Glasgow. There were recitations, songs and musical items, and Lewis himself contributed impromptu recitations of "Once more unto the breach", from *Henry V* and Kipling's "If". My correspondent scribbled "Damn fine" on his programme, and against his own recitation, modestly, "I was not satisfied myself". The awful contrast between this jolly community affair and the destructive work they were engaged on had to be put firmly to the back of their minds. These were the fearful months of the German offensive, after Lenin had capitulated on the Russian front and American intervention had only just begun. The time when Haig issued his now famous order, "With our backs to the wall and believing in the justice of our cause each of us must fight to the end."

In the autumn, when Foch and Haig were beginning to drive the Germans back and regain the ground lost in the spring, Lewis was suddenly recalled to London to take up an appointment as Secretary of the Chemical Warfare Commission, working at the Ministry of Munitions. It was a great relief to be away from France, but his new post only increased his sense of oppression about the work he was doing, because he must now become involved in the whole policy of gas warfare. There might still be long months, or even years, of work that sat hard upon his conscience.

"Home" during this time, though an improvement on the trenches, was far from luxurious. The St. James Vicarage had gone to the next incumbent, and Bessborough Street had long ago been let. A cheap family house was hard to come by, and Lewis and Sybil had a long search before they found a tiny house converted from a shop in Wood Street, a scruffy little courtyard just off Smith Square in Westminster. It was infested with bugs, which Sybil loathed and Lewis tackled with expert techniques gained in the trenches. Every morning the family was roused early and armed with knives stuck with bits of soap, to launch the attack. It turned out to be a more successful war than the real one, and when their furniture was moved in, the place began to seem like home. John and Christopher, who thoroughly enjoyed their tiny rooms set opposite each other across an archway, had now started school in Chelsea. Sybil was involved in quite a different job from the Old Vic, where she had been for over three years, playing every conceivable Shakespeare part and loving it. In the Christmas revue of 1917, playing in *Spooks*, a parody of Ibsen, and then in *The School for Scandal*, she had been spotted by Charles B. Cochran, already a well-known producer of revues. He snapped her up for a sketch in a variety bill at the London Pavilion. Now she was playing in a rather maudlin sketch called *The Kiddies in the Ruins* in a show of his at the New Oxford. It was an extraordinary contrast to anything she had done before, not so much the work itself, because melodrama and variety were quite like the nursery drama she and Russell had revelled in during their Rochester childhood, but the company, which was vulgar and earthy enough to break down some of the social inhibitions of her vicarage upbringing and the respectable philanthropy of the Old Vic. (Nevertheless she was still very much in the role of Lady Bountiful when she lined the children up next Christmas to give toys and shillings to their Wood Street neighbours—however sincere the socialist convictions she had learnt from Lewis, she was rarely able to relate to working-class people on any kind of equal footing, and she tended always to equate Socialism with "being kind to the poor".)

By the autumn of 1918 the United States were deeply involved in the war, and Lewis was ordered to confer with his American counterpart in Washington. He was actually in the War Office completing plans when the long-hoped for sirens started to hoot, and the shouting began. He stood still, unable to believe it, until the news was confirmed in the Office: an armistice had been declared and the war was over. Going out into the streets, he found the world had gone mad, not with joy or triumph, but hysterical relief. He left the Ministry and began the dizzy walk home. The first familiar face he saw was Elsie Fogerty's in the middle of Trafalgar Square. They grabbed hold of each other and he told her, "It will be all right now if we are only sensible." Then home to Sybil and the girls, where they hugged each other and shed tears, and he thought suddenly of the boys trying to get home from school on this crazy day. Quickly he set off to meet them and walked them all the way home from Chelsea with big Union Jacks to wave. In the evening, as John remembered, everybody in Wood Street piled what jumble and junk they could find into an enormous bonfire and stood round singing, weeping and drinking as the four-year nightmare ended.

The awakening was like a shadow of the nightmare. Like many others Lewis had a mental war to fight, almost as black as the physical struggle he had survived. Long ago the reforming optimism that saw war as a chance to make a clean sweep of social evils had become a thin thread of determination to get through the war itself. Now, as the period of post-war reconstruction opened out like an endless vista, where was the energy to come from that would fill it with good things, lay the foundations for a firm and healthy society? Lewis was completely drained. He felt the responsibility to put the world to rights as keenly as if it were his own personal task. Yet he was not a politician. He knew that his own work lay in the theatre and that it was creative work. The scraps of theatrical work he had done during the war were positive acts of creation. But they were like feathers in a bucket on a rope, and on the other end of the rope was the earthbound weight of the slaughter he had caused. Slowly, steadily and sensibly, the bucket would have to be filled if he were to restore his conscience to health.

Personally, his responsibilities were enormous. His family was living in conditions hardly better than the worst days of his father's fortunes, and it was perhaps this parallel that made him act as if he were to blame in this. Sybil, unworried by financial problems, operated on a quite simple faith that with hard work and the right attitude, something would always turn up, but Lewis was visited by all the apprehensions and fears for her, and for his children's welfare, that his own mother had experienced. Now, too, he must think of his extended Thorndike/Casson family.

Professionally, the theatre was in a shambles. Looking back later, people would be able to see the valuable groundwork for post-war theatre done by the Old Vic, the N.A.C.B. (Basil Dean's work), and such pioneers as Penelope Wheeler who continued her presentation of Greek plays by working in the camps in France, and Lena Ashwell, who toured Y.M.C.A. huts with musical and dramatic entertainment, helping to create a "people's theatre". But these were like tiny gems obscured by tarnish and bad settings, in contrast to the brilliant gaudy paste-work of most wartime theatre, which had its greatest successes in light entertainment. (The long-running *Chu Chin Chow*, under Lewis's one-time master, Oscar Asche, was still packing in audiences at His Majesty's.) There was no serious theatre of real quality. War casualties included several of the most promising men with whom Lewis had worked—the playwrights Harold Chapin and George Calderon had both been killed, the actor Charles Bibby, and, closest to Lewis, his old friend and leading Gaiety actor, Jules Shaw. Even the two board directors at Glasgow, Jowitt and Morrison, were gone.

As post-war plans began, it also became increasingly clear that serious theatre was to sustain an even more significant loss than these. Granville Barker and Helen Huntington were married in July 1918. Her first husband settled a large fortune upon her, and from that moment on, Barker ceased to regard himself as a professional stage producer. The cause of a national repertory theatre lost its active leader and most brilliant director, not through death, which might have urged on his disciples, but through a conscious decision. In this depressing period of aftermath, Lewis, like many others, felt betrayed, and Barker's retirement shadowed all early post-war attempts to help revitalise English theatre. In later years questions about the real cause of Barker's withdrawal haunted him. Was it that streak of luxury he had detected in his friend at the time of his first marriage, or the innate laziness to which Barker had once confessed? Was it disgust with a society which would not realise the vision of theatre he tried to show it? Was it, quite simply, obedience to the whim of the woman he loved, for Helen Barker had a fastidious dislike of all things theatrical? Was there, as Lewis later came to think, some mystery about Barker's post-war career, and his involvement with the Secret Service, which, if uncovered, might explain his change of direction and his almost complete severance from the theatre? As Barker's brilliant essays and prefaces began to appear, some argued that by turning to writing, he made his contribution to the theatre more lasting and significant, but Lewis would never accept that, and, indeed, you never heard it said by anyone who actually experienced the inspiration of working with Barker in the theatre. To Lewis, the retreat was an abdication, and although he felt no personal bitterness, it added to his own sense of responsibility. He wanted, even more, to help to fulfil Barker's goals for the theatre, but no longer had his shining example.

Politically, Lewis could see how much there was to be done domestically and internationally. Despite the break in his career and his close interest in economics, social organisation and welfare, and diplomacy, he was not tempted to enter the field himself, but watched from the side-lines, reading and discussing policies avidly, sometimes writing to the newspapers, and always conscious of the common man's own responsibility for the society in which he lived. Even in his present state of exhaustion, he could see the probable results of the shake-up the war had given to British society; he rejoiced at the extension of the vote to women and all adult men, heartily approved Labour's new socialist policies and supported the stronger organisation of trade unions.

Through the early months of 1919 Lewis struggled against bouts of morbid depression and got on with day-to-day tasks, greatly helped by Sybil's much more stable and optimistic disposition. Though his black mood was understandable at this time, it could have been that he was suffering the first serious attack of a hereditary depressive illness. No such illness was ever diagnosed in him, but it was detected later in two of his family, and its symptoms were shown often in Lewis's later life, and also perhaps in his Uncle Randal.

The War Office allowed him to take his first professional post-war engagement before he was demobbed. This was as Le Bret in a magnificent production of the swashbuckling romantic drama, Rostand's *Cyrano de Bergerac*, a perfect vehicle for Robert Loraine, already well-known to Lewis and to the public, and now famous as one of the war's most able aviators. He directed and played Cyrano,

123

Nicholas Hannen was in the cast and the play was spectacularly designed by the illustrator and artist E. Dulac, with his eye for bold colour and line. Loraine's training in rhetorical and romantic theatre gave the acting the true panache it required. The right theatrical fare for those emotional times, *Cyrano* had a most successful run at the Garrick, and then at Drury Lane.

Yet while the production harked back to much that was fine on the Edwardian stage, a drama behind the scenes belonged entirely to the post-war theatre: a conflict between the manager, Charles Cochran, with whom Sybil had just finished working, and members of the Actors' Association. Lewis had long ago resigned from its Council and the Association had been almost dormant for several years, but in the social upheaval caused by the war, the idea of trade unionism even in the acting profession had strengthened. The Chairman, Sidney Valentine, was a Conservative, but he gradually came to see that trades unionism was the only way to achieve status and power for actors. In November 1918 he established a new, stronger constitution and early in 1919 a contract was drafted, known as the Valentine Standard Contract, setting minimum salaries and conditions. *Cyrano*, the first production to fall seriously short of these, was rehearsed, then toured in Scotland for three weeks, and held over before its London opening: by that time the company had been employed for twelve weeks but had been paid for only three. At the instigation of Lewis and several other members, an official complaint was lodged with the Actors' Association; and Cochran replied immediately that he would employ no member of the Association in his companies. A long battle took place. The actors did not really want to withdraw their labour, and Cochran did not want a lock-out—at this early point both sides were bluffing. Eventually the Association, standing firm, gained the West End Managers' agreement on the standard contract, and Cochran temporarily retired. A great step on the road towards an actors' union, it was not followed up because of Valentine's sudden death, but it was significant and Lewis, for one, felt the potential strength of solidarity.

At this period Lewis also became involved in the first national organisation for drama, the British Drama League. Several people in the arts believed that professional theatres should co-ordinate their efforts to reach the wider public found by sporadic war-time ventures. Moreover, encouragement was needed for the growth of amateur, community and regional theatre, and for training and study in theatre arts. The idea took firm shape in the mind of Geoffrey Whitworth, a writer and publisher interested in promoting a national theatre. He wrote to Barker about his idea for a League, and a small meeting, with Roger Fry as Chairman, agreed that the object should be "the encouragement of the art of the Theatre, both for its own sake and as a means of intelligent recreation among all classes of the community". A public meeting was held at the Haymarket Theatre in May 1919 and the League's inauguration took place in June. It was clearly a body whose aims Lewis endorsed and he was soon nominated to the sub-committee on Repertory Theatres and spoke at the League's first conference in August. There two important resolutions identified the main area in which the League would work:

1) That this Conference urges the importance of establishing a National Theatre policy adequate to the needs of the people, and a Faculty of the Theatre at the Universities of the country with the necessary Colleges;
2) That this Conference pledges itself to promote and assist collective and individual efforts in the development of the art of Acting, Drama and the Theatre, as forces in the life of the Nation.

Where some might have recuperated from the war by rest and relaxation, Lewis found that by plunging back into his work and taking his militancy and tactical thinking from the battlefield back into the theatre, he was gradually coming to terms with himself and his environment. Financial troubles were eased because Sybil's career was going well. She had taken over a leading role in a new play by Leon M. Lion and Marion Bower, *The Chinese Puzzle*, for which Lion paid her forty pounds a week, the first star salary she had ever received. Then she played the lead in a melodrama at Drury Lane. Russell, doing fine work at the Old Vic, had recently married Rosemary Dowson, one of Rosina Filippi's lively and fascinating twin daughters. Eileen, too, was happily married to Maurice Ewbank, a distant cousin on their mother's side and a naval officer.

The autumn brought an event which served simultaneously as a dramatic requiem for the war, a symbol of international hope, and the beginning of a new artistic era for Lewis and Sybil. It was a production of *The Trojan Women* for the League of Nations Union, performed first at Oxford, without Sybil, who could not be released by her theatre to play Hecuba, then for a few matinées at the Old Vic, and ultimately in a grand gala League of Nations matinée at the Alhambra. Gilbert Murray, as vice-chairman of the League's executive committee, had suggested the production, and Lewis, as

125

director, answered the challenge with tireless alacrity. He had long sessions with Murray, and took advice from his brother-in-law, Arthur Reed, and from Elsie Fogerty. John Foulds composed the music for it—twelve thrilling trumpet chords opened the play—and Lewis found a wonderful man to design the costumes, Bruce Winston, huge, rotund yet graceful. He had been in *Cyrano* and his adventurous use of colour and flowing line would influence Lewis for many years. He worked and worked with Sybil as Hecuba, until they drove each other to despair over her performance, but in fact the war years and her patient work with Elsie Fogerty had given to her much of the sustained passion, the dignity and the powerful, melodious and controlled delivery needed to stir the emotions of her audience and to make them reflect upon their own lives and civilisation. Dozens of eminent people, in whose hands the fate of Europe might lie in the next few years, came to the gala jubilee. But then, and later, Sybil delighted to tell a probably somewhat exaggerated story of a woman selling apples in Wood Street, who greeted her with words to this effect: "Well, dearie, me and my pals went to see you performing at the Old Vic about those Trojan Women. We had a good cry, then a nice walk over the Bridge, and I got them some shrimps for tea. As I see it, that play is just us—haven't we been through the bleeding war? Haven't we lost our bleeding sons and husbands? Yes—I should say we haven't half gone through what them Trojans did—but it done us good to hear 'em all crying and moaning and having to get on with it like us."

For Lewis, listening to Sybil as she lamented over the body of seven-year-old Christopher as Astyanax, and pictured in her dirge for Troy the downfall of a civilisation, all his hopes, fears, joys and griefs must have crystallised in the true catharsis of tragedy:

> Would you be wise, ye cities, fly from war,
> Yet if war comes, there is a crown in death
> For her that striveth well and perisheth
> Unstained.

126

8

Enter a Manager
1920–1924

To impress a nobly-inspired gala audience was one thing; to bring Greek tragedy into London theatregoers' repertoire was quite another. Yet lovers of theatre realised clearly that something momentous was taking place—the birth of a new tragedienne. Lewis felt events moving positively for the first time since the war, and he was determined to seize the time. Much encouraged by his new friend and colleague Bruce Winston, who was full of enthusiasm and a sense of adventure, they put on four matinées of *The Trojan Women* at the Old Vic, and because no West End manager would look at such an uncommercial prospect, that would seem to have been that. But Lewis and Bruce believed that the best way to reach the commercial theatre was by frontal attack. Rather than seek out a high-minded manager who would probably have as little money to put into it as they did themselves, they went boldly to Charles Gulliver who ran the Holborn Empire, "one of the most exuberant of music halls". "Why not," they said, "rent us your theatre very cheaply in the afternoons, when it would otherwise be dark, to put on a series of matinées?" Their direct approach worked. Gulliver was taken with the idea. He let them have the theatre, and before they knew it they had made £200. This was not enough to launch them into full-scale management; while Lewis was pondering his next move, he happened to attend a big dinner at the British Drama League. A few polite speeches were made, but when Lewis rose he launched into a tirade which became one of the most famous in his long line of rhetorical onslaughts.

The beguiling feature of Lewis's wrath on such occasions as these was his selflessness. It was clear that what made him angry was the impossibility of doing in the theatre the things he wanted to do. But where, with many, that sort of frustration might appear to be peevish, with Lewis it became a soul-stirring call of alarm about the whole state of English theatre. He attacked the passiveness and complacency that allowed people who cared about the art of theatre to sit back and watch the purveyors of light entertainment whose only motive was profit. The rift between commercial and artistic interests was so familiar that it could be too easy to accept it as inevitable and unchanging. But Lewis insisted that it was changing— the rift had actually widened. Speculation was growing, far more theatres had fallen into the hands of businessmen who had no knowledge and cared nothing for the business of theatre itself. Unless, he proclaimed, everyone interested in the art—press, public and profession—woke up and took action, there would soon be no English drama of any artistic value.

A grand speech, and it had a more immediate effect than he could have dreamed. Lord Howard de Walden, President of the Drama League, congratulated him on his candour and courage, and Lewis and Bruce, challenging him to match his kind words with deeds, asked him to back a season of matinées at the Holborn Empire. Gulliver had already approved. De Walden put up £1,000; one or two others were persuaded to put up £250; another patron was Sir Hugh Bell, the iron and steel magnate whom they knew from Manchester and Lewis added his own £200. In February 1920 the Casson/Winston management was launched.

They began with *The Trojan Women* and *Candida* (Sybil having long ago fulfilled Shaw's instructions and acquired a husband and children). Then they did *Medea*. In some ways the fiery avenging princess was more suited than Hecuba to Sybil's passion and energy, though she and Lewis doubted at first if she would find her way into such savagery. She was now a vigorous thirty-seven-year-old, yet it was better to have started with the Trojan queen, whose long-sustained grief required enormous discipline and restraint for its effect. Medea made tremendous demands on Sybil's physique, technique and understanding; she had to control the torrents of passion which she found relatively easy to express, even though such selfish vengeance was so far from her own nature. Her performance was another triumph, if not quite reaching her Hecuba.

Having convinced the discerning press and public that Sybil was a tragic actress of real stature, the new management began to lose its way. It put on a play by Sir Hugh Bell's wife, *The Showroom*, which was only a reasonable success, and then a dismal failure called *Tom Trouble*. The season began to falter, and by the end of April, the money had gone and the Cassons were back where they had started.

The next exciting thing was a kind of detour on their road to success: the "Grand Guignol", a scheme dreamed up by the manager José Levy. Grand Guignol was well established in Paris as a varied programme of intimate comedy, tragedy, fantasy and farce, usually ending with its most famous ingredient, the horror play. Before the war Levy had conceived the idea of Grand Guignol in London. In the summer of 1920 the perfect intimate theatre became available, the Little in John Street, Adelphi: "Small, comfortable, in a side street as a Guignol theatre should be—yet within one minute's walk of the Strand," he told the Cassons delightedly. He had approached them because he knew Sybil to be "the best emotional actress now appearing regularly on the English stage", and Lewis, "the most consistently excellent producer I know".

Absurd as it seemed in contrast to the work Lewis had been attempting, he was attracted, drawn by the *structure* of the scheme as the closest thing to genuine repertory to be found in London: a vast range of plays and a permanent company in the most varied roles. Levy wanted a company that could work together as a real ensemble. This, plus Sybil's enthusiasm, persuaded Lewis and he started off happily to select a company and find the scripts.

The most obvious recruit would be Russell, for the blood-and-thunder of Grand Guignol was the culmination of Sybil's and Russell's nursery drama, which had included such ferocious pieces as *The Dentist's Cure*. That, with an unlimited number of grisly murders, had induced their mother to lament that they did not do some "nice" play more suitable for the children in the parish to see: a vicarage sentiment echoed by some of the Grand Guignol critics. Russell accepted the offer with enthusiasm. The other leading player they found was George Bealby, well-known in farce and a most interesting character. Beginning life as an engineer, he was married to Aubrey Beardsley's sister; he was fond of reading Greek drama and poetry, and he turned out to be a great success in the heavy tragic roles of the horror plays as well as in comedy. Other members, carefully chosen, were Dorothy Minto, known to Lewis from the seasons at the Court; Nicholas Hannen, with whom he had worked at Glasgow and in *Cyrano*, and later, the actress who was to become Hannen's wife, Athene Seyler, a fine comedienne and a close friend of the whole Casson family. Later Franklin Dyall arrived, and also, for a while, the young Noël Coward. It proved to be a very happy group with a strong sense of ensemble. Because it was just as important to have a good team of writers, Levy persuaded the French writer André de Lorde, known as *Prince de la Terreur*, to produce one of his own pieces and Lewis recruited two old friends, H. F. Maltby and Reginald Arkell, to write original material.

The first programme, on September 1st, 1920, contained four items. A French curtain-raiser, *How To Be Happy*, was followed by a one-act play from the French of Pierre Rehm, called *G. H. Q. Love*. This, known as the "lavatory" play, caused an uproar, principally because it was set in the cloakroom of a French restaurant and had two doors at the back marked *Hommes* and *Dames*. Next, the *pièce de résistance*, the traditional horror play, *The Hand of Death* by André de Lorde, in which a doctor used his own daughter for an experiment in resuscitation and she regained life just sufficiently to strangle him. The last item was a "revuette" called *Oh, Hell!!!* written by Russell Thorndike and Reginald Arkell.

The public was divided. Some were offended by the ghoulishness; for others it became a fashionable cult to go down to the Little and shudder masochistically. Several critics disapproved. St. John Ervine wrote:

> Too much of the stuff given at the Little is concerned with neurotic prostitutes and lust and drink and general horror. This sort of thing may interest overfed voluptuaries and creepy-crawly people with flabby insides, but I cannot imagine that this fashion will continue to be popular.

The horror plays were high points of the evening. Successors to *The Hand of Death* included *The Kill*, in which a lover is thrown to the wolfhounds by the brutal husband of his beloved, and the most notorious of all, *The Old Women*. Briefly: "The fourth series of London's Grand Guignol . . . offers one item whose horror is more horrific than anything before presented on the London stage. The scene is laid in a French lunatic asylum. The nun in charge neglects the living in order to pray for the dead and leaves Louise, the young girl who has recovered her sanity and is awaiting discharge, to sleep in the same room with deformed and horrible lunatic women. She hears them plotting her destruction, and reinforced by La Borgnesse, they do their grisly will upon her—gouging out her eyes—to the accompaniment of the Requiem Mass, heard offstage." Sybil played the young girl and the old women were played with immense relish by Russell, Athene Seyler and Barbara Gott. A poster, designed as all were, by Aubrey Hammond in a Beardsley style, was banned by the London Underground.

Apart from creating controversy and scandal, which *The Old Women* did especially, because of its implicit religious criticism, the horror plays often troubled the Censor. The Lord Chamberlain, in investigating the license for *The Old Women*, found to his chagrin that the script had been approved for performance in a Parish Hall in aid of a Girl Guides' Jamboree. Lewis had craftily persuaded the vicar of this particular parish to send it in, knowing that a script from such a source would get only a cursory glance from the Lord Chamberlain's

130

readers. Someone, too, asked the R.S.P.C.A. to investigate the treatment of the wolfhounds in *The Kill*. These animals were paraded in the first scene; then their agonising howls were heard offstage. Lewis, receiving the Society's officer with great courtesy, invited him to witness the performances from backstage, where he found that the "howls" were made by the actors blowing through lamp glasses.

Lewis loved these ingenious manoeuvres, his contribution to the whole issue of censorship; he never wearied of the fascinating search for ways of building up an illusion by quite simple theatrical trickery. Convinced of the strength of an audience's imagination, he tried to find the right touch that would set the powers of suggestion going. Here he anticipated Hitchcock. Russell commented later that Lewis produced the plays to create fear and panic, not just sickening horror. "He used suggestion rather than blood-dripping props. We frightened our audiences rather than disgusted them." The critic James Agate, said:

> Mr. Lewis Casson can be trusted to put his money into the brains of his artists and not into the legs of his chairs. He gives us only the kind of scenery which your true lover of acting cares anything at all about; and that is none. His settings are no more than a suggestion of the frame in which the thing portrayed might be supposed to happen. . . . To produce, says Johnson's dictionary, means to generate. Mr. Casson brings forth life; others stifle it with their expensive swaddling clothes.

Of course, part of the reason for the simple sets was the sheer mechanics of presenting four or five scenes on one evening in such a tiny theatre; a feat in itself by Lewis and his indefatigable stage-manager, Cyril Cattley.

Much of Lewis's experience had been in theatres frequented by an intellectual élite. Grand Guignol gave him the chance to bring the same integrity and imagination to popular entertainment. Though his chief enemy in the theatre was commercialism, he was just as frustrated by a protective "ivory tower" reaction to it. Grand Guignol, indeed, was his response to Barker's retreat into scholarship. "If a man believes he can do something," he wrote bluntly in the *Grand Guignol Review*, "his job is to do it, not talk about it. We have so many producers who confine themselves to showing us in expensively bound books and articles in the highbrow monthlies, how badly we do our job and how much better they could do it if they tried."

131

André de Lorde, master of the horror play, insisted that behind the emotions of the "Theatre of Fear" there was always an idea. Agate was the only critic to see what the Grand Guignol plays were doing: "The essence of Grand Guignolism is that, however inexplicable, however ghostly the interference, man shall retain his dignity." The horror plays, with all their melodramatic grotesqueries, were no more or less than a response to a war which had abused human dignity and caused more anguish than could be handled easily in a polite and civilised form. Several plays that Lewis chose dealt directly with the war. There was *Person Unknown*, in which a music-hall actress causes a young man to enlist by kissing him and promising a kiss and a hug on his return. He comes back to claim that kiss, and the sight of his face, blown away by high explosive, makes her die of fright. There was *The Regiment*, which Lewis translated himself. In this a Polish trooper wreaks revenge on his regiment for the bullying he suffered: he puts the germs of hydrophobia into the phials of vaccine with which the soldiers are to be injected. They bark about the barracks and are shot down by machine gunners. Grand Guignol, a clear link between Jarry and Ionesco with its mixture of comedy, tragedy, farce and fantasy, was a significant anticipation of the Theatre of Cruelty and the Theatre of the Absurd. These English seasons were an isolated experiment in the avant-garde modes, having an affinity with German expressionism: an experiment which even some of its participants did not recognise, perhaps because the strength of English theatre was still felt to be in rational situations and realistic structures. Lewis certainly believed that. He was delighted when he managed to persuade St. John Ervine, who had condemned the Guignol, to write for the Little. But Ervine's own *Jane Clegg*, though based on restraint, had contained some of the same ingredients. Now he wrote *Progress*, about a war widow who discovers her scientist-brother elated at his success in inventing a devastating bomb. To prevent him developing his invention she kills him. *Progress* convinced many who had doubted the virtue of Grand Guignol. Sydney Carroll admitted: "The potency of this performance is one of the most moving things I have seen."

Working its way through eight different programmes, the company thoroughly enjoyed the cult they created. After the first year they held an anniversary supper, for which the menu included ghoulish delights like Huitres Royales de Dead Man's Pool, Salade de Rat Mort Cabinet 6, Pêches Melba des Diaboliques and Café de l'Horrible Experience.

Russell, Sybil and Lewis led the acting and while his objective approach as producer occasionally spoilt Lewis's performances—

132

Agate detected sometimes "the corroding influence of a mind too strong"—the Guignol helped to bring Sybil to her full height. In June 1922 her performance as Katharine of Aragon in a charity matinée of *Henry VIII* so impressed Lady Wyndham, the manager and theatre owner, that she offered to back the Cassons in a good play in the West End. Going back into management with her, they began the phase before the zenith of their artistic achievement.

Their domestic life had become, by contrast, more tranquil and stable than for years: no surprise to Sybil who was sure that when she played horrors at the theatre she achieved a release and a cleansing that gave her much more patience and love outside. She always claimed that the children found her more sweet-tempered and angelic after she had played Medea. "All the people I'd wanted to murder, I'd murdered in the play, and all the terrible rages had been raged—and I came out pure like a whitewashed lamb." And perhaps Grand Guignol purged Lewis of the worst of the nightmare of guilt and remorse he suffered after the war.

One important change was their removal from Wood Street, at first to a large and beautiful house on Campden Hill in Kensington, lent to them by a friend, and then to No. 6, Carlyle Square in Chelsea, where they lived for the next eleven years. Aunt Lucy helped them to buy the lease of this comfortable Chelsea house, the home in which they really established the patterns of family life. The household consisted of the six Cassons, John, (in the autumn of 1920) now eleven; Christopher, eight; Mary, six; and Ann, five; and sometimes Sybil's mother. The two maids Alice and Nellie, who had been with Sybil for twelve years, finally left and instead there came Vi Ings, a cheerful and capable girl from Kingsdown. The Reeds were within easy reach in Putney and the Russell Thorndikes, never settled in one place for very long, were often around. Mother Don-Don had her cottage in Dymchurch where they could all spend summer holidays. All the children started school at a Mrs. Spencer's in Battersea; the boys continued to King's School, Wimbledon, and the girls to the Francis Holland School in Westminster. They also began to attend church much more regularly at St. Mary's, Graham Street, which had very high Anglican services like those that had inspired Lewis in his youth. Not that he shared in the Sunday routine, his own faith being now summed up, as he explained to his children, in a generalised belief that "there is a will behind the universe". But he went to church with the family on feast days and festivals.

Presently several important friends joined the family circle. Sybil's mother became for a while the organist to Father Olivier, who had befriended her and Canon Thorndike in their neighbouring parishes in Westminster, and who was now at Letchworth: a friendship that had brought the young Laurence Olivier and his sister and brother into the Cassons' ken. Bruce Winston continued to be a friend and colleague, and Charles Cochran's secretary, Susan Holmes, who had struck up a great friendship with Lewis during *Cyrano de Bergerac*, started to do their secretarial work. Tall and thin, with a quirky smile and a quick sense of humour, Susan was devoted to the theatre, without ever being starry-eyed. Many times over the fifty years and more that she was to work for Sybil and Lewis, her quiet tact would calm a stormy situation. She became a mainstay at home and in the theatre, befriending all the family, young or old, who needed help, comfort or encouragement. She had worked for M15 and Lewis wondered if she was ever asked to spy on her socialist employers. Another friend was Kenneth Ingram, a young publisher who attended St. Mary's, Graham Street, and had first met the Cassons in the annual Christmas pageant, in which he, the Third King, had his train borne by Mary as his page. He was a convinced socialist, and he and Lewis immediately hit it off together, spending long hours hammering out a Utopian future for the world. One of those people who begin by looking middle-aged and then stay like that for the rest of their lives, he became an unofficial Casson, a kind of extra godfather to the children, acquiring the unlikely nickname (for all his dignified appearance) of "Flick".

A steady income from the Grand Guignol seasons, and Aunt Lucy's help with the house, gave Lewis a good solid financial base. He wanted to keep things that way so that his children would have a comfortable but not extravagant home life and a good education. And he wanted to do work that would allow Sybil to develop and display her powers as an actress. Hence his ambition to succeed in the commercial theatre, rather than in some worthy but impoverished theatre in a garret. It does seem that, with the success of *The Trojan Women*, he turned even more than before the war towards Sybil's acting instead of his own. For the next ten years or so, much of his story is completely parallel to hers.

They found the new play for Lady Wyndham's theatre. It was *Scandal*, a social melodrama by Henri Bataille, which their friend Lady Bell translated from the French for them. But then they decided that perhaps an even better choice would be *Jane Clegg*, its reputation already established, as well as Sybil's performance in it. They were right. *Jane Clegg* started the season, presented jointly by "Miss Mary Moore [Lady Wyndham] and Miss Sybil Thorndike" in July 1922. It was well received and they put on four matinées of

Medea as well. Then *Scandal*: the play was undistinguished but the performances by Sybil and Leslie Faber carried it. The cast also included old colleagues and connections—Brember Wills, Rosina Filippi and her daughter Rosemary, Russell's wife. As in his private life, Lewis gathered a congenial group around him. Bruce Winston did the costumes, and the business-manager was Tom Kealy, originally a journalist, who admired Sybil's work and took every opportunity to boost her career in the press. Lewis enjoyed directing the play and added a pretty touch by having the theatre sprayed with attar of roses for the final scene in a rose garden.

Scandal, keeping a steady audience, allowed Sybil and Lewis to launch into an exciting experiment with the first public performance of Shelley's *The Cenci*. Sybil had come across it in her poetry reading some years before, and dreamed of playing the part of Beatrice. It was a hundred years since Shelley's death and the play was now in the public domain. Whether she or Lewis first thought of doing it is now unimportant. They worked so closely that every decision must be regarded as mutual, with Lewis giving the final seal of authority. A little slower with enthusiasm, he probably needed Bruce's excited approval before throwing himself into a scheme wholeheartedly; Bruce, he said, more than anyone, broke down his caution and theatrical Puritanism. Because of those innate qualities, people thought sometimes that he must be a cool and moderating influence but it was not so simple. He sought the exuberance and vitality of such people as Sybil and Bruce so that he could fight his occasional tendency to draw back. He analysed situations deeply, but where they required action, he would shift at a certain point from the analytical stance, and make his final decision impulsively, intuitively, sometimes recklessly.

The Cenci had been banned ever since it was written because of its incestuous theme and its horrific picture of evil and revenge. According to the manuscript Shelley came across, the lustful, murderous and vengeful Count Cenci, among other crimes, raped his own daughter, Beatrice. She arranged for his murder and was tried and tortured for it, maintaining her innocence throughout even though she was technically guilty. In dramatising this, Shelley took the best possible models: there are many parallels with *Macbeth*, *Lear* and other Shakespeare plays: Beatrice's situation and character are like several Jacobean heroines, especially Vittoria Corombona in *The White Devil* who also rouses the audience's sympathy despite her guilt, because of her dignity and courage in the face of cruelty and corruption. It was not until 1886 that the Shelley Society gave a private performance. Even that created a cry of outrage in the press.

But now, after Greek tragedy and Grand Guignol, and in a world more open-eyed to horror, Lewis decided to do it. Applying to the Censor, though this was not technically necessary, he received permission to stage it, and in November 1922 they performed four matinées, so successful that two weeks of evening performances followed.

Where Antonin Artaud would see *The Cenci* as a basis for a Theatre of Cruelty in 1935, the inarticulate response to the extreme pain of human experience, Lewis sought and found its eloquence. In a producer's note, he explained that he saw the play as a symbol of Shelley's own life story. The horror, he felt, was not for horror's sake, but was the only way Shelley could deliver his soul of the revolutionary message that he had to give. Imitating the Jacobean structure, Lewis chose a simple but powerful architectural setting to create "wonderful pictures of kaleidoscopic rotation" so that the action was swift, the tension tight and the cumulative power of the drama enhanced. The 1886 production took four hours, his "would not much exceed two and a half". Bruce Winston designed the costumes with the flow and colour of the fifteenth century, rather than the historically accurate sixteenth century which would be "too severe . . . for my reading of the play". As with Greek tragedy and Grand Guignol, Lewis wanted the moral implication of the horror to emerge; he presented the monstrosities with restraint in order to increase the sense of the "ideal" as Shelley himself suggested.

The success of the production rested on the performances of Cenci and Beatrice. To play this "embodiment of evil" Lewis immediately thought of Robert Farquharson, Herod in the Ricketts production of *Salome*. He was an extraordinary actor, not a professional—he spent most of his time in the land of the Cenci—and indeed he would have lacked the necessary range. His chief gift was for eloquent, powerful evil, combined with great charm. He was tall, dark and statuesque with a commanding physique and a matching vocal range. Lewis knew no one except Barker who had such a command of vocal range and the expression of emotion through rapid changes of vocal pitch. "I should think he could use three octaves, which is very, very rare." Farquharson agreed to do it and was a perfect balance for Sybil's power and majesty. Lewis encouraged the romantic fire which had been so typical of his own early performances, orchestrating the entire production as if it were an opera, sure of every note and tune that he wanted. Robin and Sybil had the capacity and the imagination to work in this method.

The opening matinée attracted not only those who admired Sybil's acting, but also an enormous number of "poets and famous literary people". "The length of the play and the dark passions with which it deals, render it a nerve-tearing experience for actors and audience," wrote the critic J. T. Grein. All agreed that the playing sublimated the horror. "Sybil Thorndike's acting of the unhappy victim of the Cenci's wickedness attains a strength and beauty which transmutes the hardness of Beatrice's character into something majestic." Farquharson's performance "conveys the horror of Count Cenci's personality and seems to exude an aura of wickedness", and the whole ensemble achieved a "rare artistic unity". It was a modern note that lifted Lewis's production of *The Cenci* out of the class of "costume play" familiar to Edwardians into a new kind of historical drama. That new kind was to be shaped in another form by Bernard Shaw, who told his wife after seeing this performance, "I have found my Joan."

The Cenci brought the season at the New to a successful conclusion; besides superb productions and several of Sybil's finest performances, it also did well financially. Lady Wyndham's backing was not called upon; they had finally broken the bastions of West End theatre and created an audience for their own kind of work. In celebration, Sybil and Lewis took a rare holiday, spending some idyllic days in Italy, appropriately enough, at Robert Farquharson's suggestion. He recommended Rapallo first, his own favourite spot, and made all the arrangements, so Lewis could not back out in a typical fit of thrift. It was their first visit to Italy and their first real holiday together. They loved Rapallo, with its tiny hamlets and little churches in the hills, and went for long walks till sundown every day, discussing everything they had done and everything they wanted to do. They found Gordon Craig staying there and took him for a drive. Craig's visionary ideas soon excited Lewis and all three began to spark each other off. Their great scheme was to do *Macbeth*. Craig had twice been disappointed over designing this play, once for Max Reinhardt and then for Tree. Now, hearing Lewis's talk about finding a theatre to present Shakespeare in the West End, he assumed immediately that he had a definite engagement as the designer. Sybil and Lewis moved happily on to Amalfi and finished their holiday just before Christmas. They tried to find a suitable theatre management to mount *Macbeth*, but despite the éclat of *The Cenci*, no one was interested. Lewis dropped the idea for the moment—and was appalled to have Craig on his doorstep with sketches, and bills for fees and expenses incurred. Disappointed again, he did manage to scrounge some money from the soft-hearted Lewis.

Looking at the London theatre in the 1920s, it is hard even now to see its shapes and trends. How much more difficult it must have been to make sense of it all when you were in the middle of it. So many changes were happening, some of which Lewis deplored, some of which he welcomed. The greatest difficulty was to achieve any continuity. The reign of the actor-managers was over. It had kept the theatre stable, or even, according to some, stagnant. Now many theatre buildings were let to speculating businessmen and the "house style" of theatres like Her Majesty's and St. James's disappeared. The landlord, the lessee or sub-lessee, were quite remote from the actor whose work created the income of the theatre. Lewis was fortunate at this point to come into contact with the Wyndham/ Albery family who were the exception to this. Lady Wyndham owned Wyndham's Theatre and the New, which she and Sir Charles had built, and she was the lessee of the Criterion. As Mary Moore she had graced the London theatre with her acting from the 1870s until 1919. Her son Bronson Albery and her stepson Howard Wyndham were both theatre managers. All combined a love of theatre with a fine sense of business, and it was Bronson ("Bronnie") who now took an interest in Sybil and Lewis. Named after the American playwright Bronson Howard, Bronnie was the second son of Mary Moore and the dramatist James Albery. He was married to Una Rolleston (whose father was the Irish poet T. W. H. Rolleston) and had four children. Theatre was in his bones; he was also a trained and practised solicitor. Sybil and Lewis liked him at once. He was courteous, sympathetic and uncannily wise in predicting what audiences would like. They went into a partnership with him which lasted five years and covered their finest productions.

It was uncanny to predict what audiences would like. On one hand Gerald du Maurier, with his impeccable underplaying, epitome of modern comedy, ruled at Wyndham's; on the other, Basil Dean's lavish and exotic production of James Elroy Flecker's *Hassan* opened that same year to much acclaim. *The Cenci* had been a great critical success, but Albery at this point was not to be persuaded to attempt Shakespeare or any other poetic tragedy. Instead he suggested a complete contrast—a light comedy by his old friend Herbert Farjeon, the drama critic, who, with Horace Horsnell, also a critic, had written a romp called *Advertising April; The Girl Who Made the Sunshine Jealous*. Sybil played a film star whose life was a continual promotion of her public image—a novel and up-to-date theme which later would be taken up more seriously. Critics who now considered her to be the queen of tragedy were shocked at the contrast with Beatrice Cenci and Medea, but Sybil enjoyed this light-hearted frivolity and Lewis was always happy to create a balanced repertoire. The play lasted for five months, a very respectable run in those days. They then went on a provincial tour with *Scandal*, *Advertising April*, *Jane Clegg* and *Medea*.

After the comparative leisure of commercial runs, the tour was like old times; they found it refreshing to play to provincial audiences, and Lewis used the tour to rehearse and try out a new Shakespeare production at Birmingham. He decided on *Cymbeline*, because Sybil very much wanted to play Imogen, and Iachimo was exactly right for Robert Farquharson. "We chose it in a spirit of challenge," he told an interviewer. "We want to know whether Shakespeare as we want to do it, will be acceptable to the London public." By this he meant approximating to the conditions of Shakespeare's day and he stated these:

1) Continuity of action: there must be no break in the vocal music by the fall of the curtain and other means.
2) The utmost simplicity of setting consistent with stimulation of the imagination.
3) The utmost richness of costume consistent with the story.
4) The subordination of all characters to the story of the play.

It was a bold play for an experiment, because the Lyceum production, with Ellen Terry's Imogen, was famous. That had been drastically cut to bring out the sweetness of Imogen's disposition and gloss over the play's harshness. With cuts restored, the awkwardness of the play emerged, and several critics found fault with it. The production was as experimental as any of Barker's. Since the story was so unreal, Lewis let Bruce Winston use a Futurist style, with costumes and setting that dazzled the audience with vivid colours and abstract shapes. Ivor Brown, writing in the *Manchester Guardian*, hated to see Shakespeare so "garishly adorned", but his description is evocative:

It was as though an artists' fancy dress ball had spilled its revellers on the stage. There, one saw, was Posthumus, dressed in one of those fashionable bathing costumes they wear at Deauville, there Cloten, to suggest that if you scratch an Ancient Briton, what you find is the Russian ballet. And the closing battle scenes, played in shimmering light behind gauze and round a gigantic scarlet standard, suggested nothing much more dreadful than a ballroom late on in the night's revelry. One could not escape the sensation that here was a tale of the jazz age. The Welsh mountains were too fashionably geometrical to suggest themselves as a suitable spot for the simple life as praised by Belarius.

But Brown enjoyed the language of the play and felt that beneath the dazzle was "the warm radiance of the poet's Indian summer". Sybil and Robert Farquharson both caught "the mellow, lyric beauty of the piece".

Despite a mixed and puzzled reception in Birmingham, Lewis badly wanted to bring his innovative production to London. Albery agreed to try it, and the first night was applauded, but James Agate, often their chief support among critics, hated it. Some recommended it: thus Darlington, in the *Telegraph*, found setting and acting mannered but effective: "The swiftly-changing curtain scenes and light effects give complete continuity of action, and the whole effect is rather to throw the action and poetry of the play into relief than to lose them amid a multiplicity of accessory detail." He hoped that London would flock to the production. The *Morning Post* urged theatre-goers to "repair at once to the New, where they will see *Cymbeline* played probably as well as it has ever been played, and since our actors are rapidly losing the art of speaking blank verse, better than it is ever likely to be played again". J. C. Trewin retrospectively labelled the production as "an odd and lovely collision of the Renaissance with Snow White and Lear's Britain". So this complex experiment did effectively stir or disturb its audiences. But the heady days of Barker at the Savoy were distant now and he, after all, had lost heavily with *The Winter's Tale*, first of his three famous revivals. There was only a limited audience for this "jazz age" production, and at the end of three weeks they took it off. Lewis, accepting temporary defeat, was still quite determined to make Shakespeare succeed in the West End; he would try a different approach next time. It had become a special challenge to him because, for the moment, he had committed himself to West End theatre. He could justify this only with the belief that he and Sybil and his "team" could make good classical theatre popular and available.

The next play, a much better bet commercially, was very popular. They turned to Henry Arthur Jones, famous for his turn-of-the-century domestic dramas, such as *Mrs. Dane's Defence*. He had more or less faded out of the picture because his melodramas did not lend themselves to the lighter style of acting, the "flick and trick performance", as J. C. Trewin called it. But Sybil and Lewis enjoyed the strong emotion of *The Lie* (which had been done in New York ten years before) and they made it into a big success. Misunderstanding, discovery, recrimination, tears and forgiveness, all had full scope, and the most dramatic moment was when Sybil screamed at the sister who had betrayed her: "Judas sister! Judas sister!"

(Though John, on holiday from his training on H. M. S. *Worcester*, asked, "What on earth's a Jute assister?") With the skill of the Grand Guignol and *Medea* put together, Lewis went straight to the emotional heart of the play. Despite the feeling among actors of the day that anything played to the hilt must be "ham", he was sure that audiences still wanted to be moved and to feel suspense, anticipation and climax about real human passions. He was right on this occasion; against all prevailing fashion, the large-scale acting was popular. Some critics were condescending about the play but houses were full and enthusiastic. Jones was delighted, and in dedicating the published play to Sybil he wrote:

> I have had many roaring receptions of applause from English first nighters, but none of them has approached the thundering welcome they gave me when, under the shelter of your wing, myself moved by the inflamed sweep of your acting, I stood beside you to acknowledge the prolonged acclamations that greeted us on the 13th October 1923. How lucky I was, after six years' absence from the London theatre, to return to it in such company as yours.

The year that followed the opening of *The Lie* would be one of the most exciting in Lewis's theatrical life. Long ago he and Sybil had had the idea of doing a play about Joan of Arc, canonised in 1920. While they pondered on this intermittently, Laurence Binyon's name occurred to them. Though he had written few plays, he had adapted the traditional Indian *Sakuntala*, which Lewis had directed four years earlier for the "Union of East and West". With good memories of the piece, Lewis saw possibilities in a co-operative work by the same group; John Foulds had composed music for it and Bruce Winston designed the costumes. Some time in 1922 or 1923, he approached Binyon and asked him if he would like to write a play about Joan of Arc for Sybil.

Meanwhile, and this story is famous, Bernard Shaw had also decided to write a Joan play. As early as 1913 he mentioned it to Mrs. Patrick Campbell; then he was spurred by the canonisation and finally, after he had seen Sybil in *The Cenci*, he settled down to write. Unfortunately he did not think of telling Sybil, and at the same time Lewis was tackling Binyon. One day news of his new play appeared in the papers and threw Sybil and Lewis into a quandary. They longed to do the Shaw, but did not know if he would let them, or how they could avoid offending Binyon, or how Binyon could write his in the circumstances. Lewis decided to tackle the problem

141

directly. He wrote to Shaw explaining the predicament and Shaw replied at once, on a postcard, saying something to the effect that "Sybil plays my Joan". He said that though he had warned off John Masefield and John Drinkwater, he had not thought of Binyon. Delighted, Sybil and Lewis set about explaining the situation as tactfully as possible to Binyon. They need not have worried: he simply withdrew with the comment that Shaw would write it much better than he could.

So Shaw finished *Saint Joan*, telling Sybil that because he had used so much authentic material, it was "the easiest play I've ever written". One autumn day he read it to a select group invited to lunch at Ayot St. Lawrence: Sybil and Lewis, Bronson Albery, Mrs. Shaw and a friend of Shaw's. From all accounts, Shaw read beautifully. Sybil and Lewis were over the moon about the play, from the ridiculous opening lines, "No eggs! No eggs! Thousand thunders, man, what do you mean by no eggs?" right through to Joan's final prayer, "O God that madest this beautiful earth, when will it be ready to receive Thy saints? How long, O Lord, how long?" Bronson Albery was far less impressed and so was his wife when she read it. It seemed to them an odd mixture of Shavian humour, unfashionable costume drama and poetry, but the Cassons' enthusiasm was overwhelming and the Alberys recognised a time to throw caution to the winds. *The Lie*, though, was doing well, so Shaw allowed the Theatre Guild in New York to present the première of *Saint Joan* in December 1923. But in February he asked if a closing date for *The Lie* could be set and rehearsals for *Saint Joan* begin. And so, despite the success of Jones's play, Bronnie agreed to take it off in March.

As designer, Shaw and Lewis thought at once of Charles Ricketts, who had continued over the years to take an active interest in the theatre. John Foulds composed the score. For the next few weeks comings and goings at Carlyle Square included frequent conferences in which Lewis's rumbling voice alternated with the shrill, almost querulous piping voice of Ricketts as he brought sketch after sketch to discuss, drawing on his decorative skills which rivalled Leon Bakst's, and basing his designs on exquisite French illuminated manuscripts. Strains of French peasant music, or warlike marches, would sound in the sitting-room as John Foulds tried out his ideas.

It was important to find actors able to handle the vocal interpretation in an almost operatic way. People who could speak "bigly—in the Shakespearian manner", as Sybil put it. Lewis and Shaw, meticulous about the casting of every role, knew between them a large number of actors. The Archbishop was Robert

142

Cunningham, both actor and singer. The Dauphin was Ernest Thesiger, experienced in classical and modern drama, with a beautifully quirkish comic style. With his long thin face and limbs he was perfectly shaped for the perpendicular lines of Ricketts's fifteenth-century costumes, and he used his fastidious manners and movements so well that after the first rehearsal Shaw told him not to change anything. In complete contrast, Bruce Winston was La Trémouille, his rich robe displaying all his rotundity, and Robert Horton played Dunois. A heavy burden fell upon the three actors in the Tent scene: the Earl of Warwick was Lyall Swete, a Bensonian who had been with Lewis in Oscar Asche's company at the Adelphi, and with the Barrymores in New York. He could convey "the real aristocrat and the real cynic without any romance or any true religion". Lewis originally cast himself in the role of Cauchon, Bishop of Beauvais, but Albery persuaded him not to combine so large a role with producing. Instead the Irish actor Eugene Leahy was Cauchon and Lewis played the Chaplain de Stogumber, the fiery persecutor of heretics, quite unable to imagine the consequences of his condemnation of Joan, and utterly broken by seeing her at the stake. The other crucial part, the Inquisitor, was given to O. B. Clarence, a distinguished actor already playing in *The Lie* with Sybil. His performance captured definitively the power and strength of the Church, so absolute and uncompromising that it could afford to dress itself in mildness, kindness and reasonableness. Other names in the first cast were Raymond Massey as Captain La Hire and Canon d'Estivet, and the boy actor Jack Hawkins, as Dunois's page in the scene where the wind changed direction on the Loire. Several other players had worked with Lewis before: Victor Lewisohn, Lawrence Anderson, Matthew Forsyth, Zillah Carter.

Shaw and Lewis produced, a combination made possible by their mutual understanding and their methods, which were both similar and complementary. Shaw, who conducted the morning rehearsals, would act out all the parts. Accounts of his "acting" vary. Sybil thought him really better than anybody in all the parts. Ernest Thesiger was unimpressed, but found it easy to take direction from Shaw's performance; Jack Hawkins, whose part Shaw read "in a ridiculous falsetto", thought he was quite mad, but set about faithfully mimicking him. Lewis considered his acting to be very broad, and did not believe he could have sustained a characterisation through a whole evening. "But," he said, "in giving a vivid half-minute sketch of a character as a demonstration, I know few better."

At the first rehearsal Shaw's reading to the cast helped them unconsciously to absorb the shape of the play and to gain a general idea of the characters and much of the actual detail of music and phrasing in the dialogue. Then he plunged straight into rehearsal, "blocking" included, without any lectures or discussion, teaching the actors what he wanted but also listening to their points of view. Sybil found him gentle and "courtly", with the suggestion of a volcano underneath. "If anyone set himself against him it would be to discover the force in him, but nobody ever does." Shaw, in his turn, told Mrs. Patrick Campbell, "Sybil never let me doubt that she regarded me as far superior to the Holy Trinity as producer." For Lewis these morning rehearsals were a marvellous opportunity to detach himself from the scene and observe what was happening. He retained a vivid memory of Shaw's method. "At this period of rehearsals G. B. S. would be on the stage with the company, when he could talk freely to the actors and interrupt and interpret. He was always patient, but quite persistent in getting eventually exactly what he wanted, so far as the actor was capable of it. I never remember his teaching any actor an intonation parrot-like, but he had the power, the skill and the vitality to make his version seem the obvious and only one, and one can certainly say that by the time rehearsals were over, every phrase and pause had been considered and deliberately passed, either as his intention or as near as the actor could get to it. He was always open to argument, and would do his utmost to get round a difficulty rather than make an intelligent actor do something his instinct told him was false."

When the whole framework had been set, Shaw retired to the circle and let the scenes run through without interruption, while he took notes which often meant further work on the stage. Lewis spent much time following up and implementing the notes Shaw had taken in the morning. (Or, as Shaw pretended to think, undoing his work.) Sometimes he had to "translate" Shaw's intonations for the English actors. Shaw's Irish melodies were often too long and elaborate for an English actor to retain or reproduce, but without them much of the significance and emotional appeal of the lines could be lost. One of the faults Lewis saw in Shaw's directing was its slowness. "He wanted every word to be slow enough to get every idea over . . . he wouldn't let the audience miss a single point if he could help it." So Lewis spent a great deal of time quickening up the performance—after the first night he cut twenty-five minutes off the running time, "without cutting a word, or, I think, losing any ideas". Shaw was quite agreeable so long as the actors kept the run and phrasing and the actual interpretation of each word.

Another weakness that, as usual, dogged Shaw's work, was his tendency to overdo the comic side. Perhaps when we get to Heaven we shall find that Shaw was right and that his often tiresome humour is a true manifestation of the Divine. Lewis saw it as the "eternal schoolboy" in him. He had a great love of slapstick and "dressing up" as opposed to costume, and the same instinct led him in his productions to underline the comic, which Lewis then tried to restrain. Lewis was also in complete command of the technical aspects and final co-ordination, which Shaw, at this stage of his career, could not be bothered with. Having approved of Ricketts's appointment, Shaw intervened little in the matter of sets and costumes, except to insist that Sybil had real clanking armour. In fact, at the dress rehearsal he suffered the feeling of dismay common among writers when the visual side of the play suddenly becomes predominant. "Scenery and costumes have ruined my play," Sybil remembered him saying. "Why can't you play it in plain clothes, as at rehearsals? Sybil is much more like Joan in her ordinary jumper and skirt than when dressed up like this with her face all painted."

But Ricketts's sets and costumes, with their simple, luminous, medieval colours, and their aspiring, perpendicular lines, were a beautiful setting for the eight scenes. Far from overloading the production, they provided tableaux on which the eye could rest. The production's prompt-book has every technical detail closely recorded, down to the correct grouping for the "supers" in their individually-designed costumes; and it indicates a production bold and uncluttered in its effect.

Because of Shaw's renown, Sybil's reputation and the interest in a play about Joan of Arc, the first night of *Saint Joan*, March 26th, 1924, was a real gala night in the theatre, reminiscent of some of Irving's at the Lyceum, or Tree's at Her Majesty's. The audience was thick with such celebrities as Sir Johnston Forbes-Robertson, Ellen Terry and Mrs. Patrick Campbell. Reserved seats were strictly allotted. When Jacob Epstein sent word that he would be unable to attend, his ticket went immediately to the director and writer J. B. Fagan. At five a.m. the first person arrived to queue for gallery seats. The management provided 150 teas for the queue and opened the doors for them an hour early. The theatre was packed despite a strike, and the whole atmosphere was electric.

As the lights dimmed, John Foulds stepped into the orchestra pit to conduct the overture, many of its tunes based on authentic French music. Then the curtain rose upon Ricketts's light but sturdy representation of the castle at Vaucouleurs, and the comic scene between de Baudricourt and the steward. Sybil, in the wings, felt for once in her life no stage-fright at all, as she listened to the now-familiar words. Few moves are marked in the prompt-book; and those few are used to clarify an idea. For example, on de Baudricourt's line, "The milk was short yesterday," is the direction "A fresh thought which is emphasised with an out-stretched arm." About three minutes into the play and then Sybil's voice was heard from off-stage, "Bright, strong and rough," as Shaw wanted it. "Is it me, sir? . . . Be you captain?" Many disliked the northern accent Shaw imposed on the Maid, but Sybil found it a key to Joan's simple straightforward approach to her tasks. She based her speech on Lancashire, which she knew well, and the rough, warm Cornish of a maid of hers, producing, as she said, "What Nigel Playfair calls Lumpshire". The direction continued to be restrained. For a three-page section after her second entrance there were no moves, so that when she did move, on the line "Ten like me can stop them with God on our side," the impact could be felt.

The second scene, the ante-chamber at Chinon, was more elegant in design, with a beautiful curtain, a medieval tapestry design of a hunting scene, and some exquisite angels mounted above the Dauphin's throne. Costumes exploited the elaboration of fifteenth-century dress with exaggerated silhouettes and a range of jewel-colours like a stained-glass window. In this scene, after the fun and games of Joan's recognition of the Dauphin, came her earnest discussion with him alone. Many critics condemned her informal language to the Dauphin, especially when she addressed him as "Charlie". But the scene depended on their relationship, shown by more frequent moves, which indicated the points where Joan exerted most influence, and where she forced strength into him.

The third scene, the short one on the banks of the Loire when the wind changed, was played in front of a drop-curtain, with the river scene painted on it. By then, according to the revised running time, the play had lasted fifty-eight minutes (longer on the first night). It was the point which Shaw marked, when first reading the play to the Cassons, with the comment "Well, that's all flapdoodle. Now the real play begins."

There followed the twenty-three minute scene between Warwick, Cauchon and de Stogumber, in which they thrashed out the issues of heresy and nationalism. The arguments are as close as those in *Don Juan in Hell*, and this first production showed what was probably the only way in which the scene could work; actors and director putting their trust in the vitality of the argument. So the only movement in the entire scene, entrances and exits apart, was de Stogumber's rise to make his rash and angry accusation of Cauchon, "You are a traitor!"

The next scene, Rouen Cathedral, was lofty and impressive and cold, emphasising Joan's insignificance; the few gestures marked in the prompt-book indicated her growing isolation. The one interval occurred after this. The audience had been able to follow, unbroken, the dramatic shape and development of Joan's career.

After the interval, the Trial. The reactions of the court were carefully structured to bring out the tension and meaning of the scene, almost word for word a transcription of the actual trial until Joan's passionate outburst and denial of her recantation. "Sheer poetry and pure Shaw," said Sybil. "His two great speeches—the loneliness of God, at the end of the Cathedral Scene, and the great cry against imprisonment in the Trial scene, those are the ones, and when people say Shaw wasn't a poet they should just read those speeches and consider whether they could have been written by anyone except a poet." Immediately afterwards came Lewis's reversal as de Stogumber. His agony after watching Joan burn was so real as to be almost unbearable. No one else could bring an audience so close to raw emotion without being ridiculous. And in making this scene so powerful, Lewis took the audience from complete identification with Joan and prepared the way for the Epilogue.

Very few people were impressed with this at first, except Lewis and Sybil. Many critics condemned it for irrelevance and silliness. Part of the reason was Shaw's broad direction. "There is," Lewis allowed, "an intensely comic idea in the canonisation of a Saint by the Church that had burned her, but at the first production, he so over-emphasised this with overplaying and funny business, that although Ernest Thesiger and I induced him to modify this considerably at rehearsal, it still shocked the audience far more than was necessary and marred the essential beauty of the play's design."

The Epilogue's unpopularity may have lessened the sense of triumph at the end of the opening night, but the occasion was still glorious; Lewis and Sybil felt that they had in some sense fulfilled themselves, whether or not the play was a "success". The next morning they woke to mixed notices. The impact of Shaw's un-romantic and modern approach to history was too strong for the play to be properly assessed at once. Productions and acting were praised, but the real significance, even of Sybil's Joan, was not caught until later. Agate soberly catalogued her qualities without being roused to flights of eloquence:

Joan was excellent—boyish, brusque, inspired, exalted, manner-less, tactless, and obviously, once she had served her turn, a

147

nuisance to everybody. The part is one which no actress who is leading lady only, and not artist, would look at. But Miss Thorndike is a noble artist and did nobly.

Desmond MacCarthy found Sybil's Joan obscured the angelic side, but he found it difficult to tell whether the lack of sentiment was Shaw's or hers:

> Mr. Shaw so dreads the sentimental . . . is so desirous that our response to beauty of character should be as ascetic as possible that I am inclined to lay the blame on him in the first place, but there is no doubt that Miss Thorndike stresses this aversion to anything which might move us first by its loveliness, only afterwards by its significance.

(Yet when Ludmila Pitoëff played Joan in 1930, MacCarthy found her too pathetic. It was, after all, this very quality of putting significance before loveliness that made the play and Sybil's performance endure.)

Lewis announced level-headedly over breakfast, "Well, we are good for six weeks on Shaw's name," and hoped Albery would not regret taking off *The Lie* to make room for the Cassons' wayward saint. But when they reached the theatre that day they could not get near the box-office. Throughout the seven-month run that followed, houses were packed and the queues continued as playgoers showed their instinctive knowledge that here was something not to be missed. On October 25th (as Lewis and Sybil celebrated their forty-ninth and forty-second birthdays respectively) the weekly takings, £2,533 14s 6d, and attendance, 9,268, broke the New Theatre's record. *Saint Joan* was withdrawn finally to make room for Matheson Lang who had booked the theatre earlier, and they went off on a provincial tour of *The Lie*. Then they came back to London, took the Regent Theatre, still with Albery, and ran *Saint Joan* again; the play had become part of their lives.

For many years afterwards, the whole family lived and breathed *Saint Joan*. The first family holiday away from Dymchurch was motoring through the château country in France, visiting all the "Joan" spots. All the children soon knew every word, every inflection, and every note of music by heart. For vast numbers of people Sybil became identified with Joan; the production gave them a quite transcendent experience that broke the limitations of time and space. Christopher Fry said once that Sybil conferred on him "one grain of eternal youth", because seeing her in later years always transported him at once to the New Theatre in 1924, where for him, a fifteen–year–old boy in the gallery, her performance "pierced the great distance between the stage and the theatre roof with such precision that it recreates itself for me still". And for Elsie Fogerty, friend and beloved teacher of Sybil and Lewis, *Saint Joan* became the greatest of her memories of both of them: ". . . it achieved at the New Theatre in 1924, that rare triumph of a perfect cast, a perfect production and that curious fitness to the public mood of the day which together showed it to stand apart from all other plays of Shaw". Gradually the performance took on the perpetuating quality of myth. J. C. Trewin wrote thirty years later: "But Joan's single–minded glory shone, the strength of a peasant girl divinely possessed, a 'dear child of God', a warrior saint in a world not yet ready to receive her. Joan, as Sybil Thorndike played her, grew to a pillar of faith and fire. She had a timeless quality."

Though the effect was timeless, it was impeccable timing by whatever god oversees the theatre to bring together Shaw, Sybil and Lewis, Charles Ricketts and Bronson Albery at a moment when all their powers were at a peak. Lewis's role was pivotal and complex. His own thinking had been shaped and influenced by Shaw's writing, especially the idea of the evolutionary Life Force, most cogently expressed in *Man and Superman*. (Objectively, indeed, he might have ranked it above *Saint Joan*.) In fact he would have seen that first production of *Man and Superman* as a manifestation of the Life Force operating in his own life, since it caused a great leap forward in his mind and in his career. Another manifestation of the Force was Sybil herself; possessing some of Joan's qualities of "the genius and the saint", she had helped him to "dare and dare". So he was the perfect interpreter of *Saint Joan*, understanding its message intellectually and intuitively, including the final statement that the world is still not ready for its saints and supermen. At the same time, he had the desire and ability to work on all the practical tasks and problems that would put the ideas effectively on the stage—the desire that seemed to have withered away in Barker. Through his earlier work with Ricketts and his later alliance with Bruce Winston, he had nurtured his visual understanding of theatre, so that he could confidently leave the design in their hands. On the business side, the Casson/Albery alliance made a strong management team because Bronson's more worldly wisdom stabilised Lewis's rather volatile approach to money matters, while his own zeal and enthusiasm operated like the Life Force for Bronson, overriding any initial reluctance. Business relations for the production were so cordial that Shaw and Albery never even arranged a written contract. And

149

Lewis's belief in the nature of theatre, in particular his faith in the power of the voice to create emotion and understanding in an audience, showed him the path to be followed in rehearsing all the actors—including Sybil, who must be disciplined so that her sweeping passion and uplifting energy had definition; and himself, who must bring the audience to a piercing awareness of what the burning of Joan really meant.

9

A Leading Part
1925–1930

With his half-century Lewis was at the height of his career. One is so used to measuring his work by Sybil's, seeing how she achieved stardom and an unassailable position as Queen of the English stage (shared with Edith Evans) and how Lewis was virtually the Svengali who made this possible for her, that it is easy to forget how important his own work was in its own right. He was now among the top ten in his profession. A comparable figure was Basil Dean, his old friend from Manchester, who was also in West End management and would be responsible for such successes as *The Constant Nymph* and *Young Woodley*, as well as the earlier *Hassan*. There was J. B. Fagan, who had opened the Oxford Playhouse in 1923 and also produced several important plays in London, including O'Casey's *Juno and the Paycock*; Barry Jackson, director of the Birmingham Repertory Theatre, was now leasing various theatres in London, doing such plays as Shaw's *Back to Methuselah*, Ibsen's *Rosmersholm*, with Edith Evans, Pirandello's *Six Characters in Search of an Author* and three modern dress Shakespeares. Out in Hammersmith Nigel Playfair, at the Lyric, was mounting such famous productions as *The Beggar's Opera* and *The Way of the World*, in which Edith Evans played Millamant. In Shakespearian theatre there were W. Bridges-Adams at Stratford, Robert Atkins and Andrew Leigh at the Old Vic. Two other important figures were Nugent Monck, who converted the Maddermarket Theatre, Norwich, into an Elizabethan playhouse, and Terence Gray, who in 1926 was to found the Festival Theatre at Cambridge. These were the men who carried the torches lit by the Edwardians Frank Benson, Forbes-Robertson, Barker, Boucicault and Asche. From Russia had come Theodore Komisarjevsky, bringing the influence of Stanislavsky and other Moscow artists to London. Younger men were just beginning to emerge—John Gielgud playing his first Romeo for Barry Jackson, Noël Coward, whose controversial success *The Vortex* was in the same year as *Saint Joan*. These were years of great activity and creativity in the London theatre. Aldwych farces,

Edgar Wallace detective plays and musical comedies jostled for audiences with Shakespeare and new classics such as Ibsen, Strindberg, Chekhov and Shaw and new plays from America and Europe as well as Britain. Cinema had not yet captured a large entertainment market, so success in the theatre could still mean big rewards in fame and fortune as well as in artistic fulfilment.

For Lewis, as for several of these men, (there were very few women directors at this time) the game was to juggle artistic, commercial and popular theatrical balls in the air and not let any drop. The post-war boom was over and theatrical ventures were risky financial investments, especially as social unrest continued to make popularity hard to predict. It seemed clear that there was only a limited audience for most serious, experimental or classical theatre, though you could strike lucky with a *Saint Joan* which captured the popular imagination. Some of Lewis's colleagues got round the problem by going out of central London where expenses were high, to such little theatres as the Everyman at Hampstead or Komisarjevsky's theatre at Barnes; and serious theatre-goers would faithfully make a suburban pilgrimage to see interesting new plays and designs and watch the development of such budding talents as Peggy Ashcroft's. Experimental theatre on a shoestring budget might even exist in the middle of London: Peter Godfrey's Gate Theatre, for example, which opened in a Floral Street warehouse during 1925. This was the fringe theatre of the 1920s. Others were committed to one theatre or to one kind of drama, like Bridges-Adams at the Shakespeare Memorial Theatre.

The other way to keep faith with your art was to intersperse your work for the run-based commercial theatre with occasional productions for the numerous theatre societies of the 1920s. These were modelled on the still active Stage Society and mounted for two or three performances on expenses only. There was the odd occasion, as with *Journey's End*, when a Society's play became a hit.

Lewis's own ideal was still repertory, with a balance between popular and minority interests and a variety of types of play, so he did not want to commit himself to one kind of theatre or drama. Nor would he have wanted now, at this point in Sybil's career, to seek the comparative anonymity of the suburbs or the anxious struggles of provincial theatre, such as Barry Jackson underwent at Birmingham. So he, like Basil Dean, centred his work in London's West End, a huge and glorious market of varied wares spread out around Shaftesbury Avenue and Charing Cross Road, for a large public to wander through, trying on this, picking over that, and always moving on to see what else was offered. And on the side he gave his occasional services to societies and groups that asked him, like the Jewish Drama Group, maybe, or the Royal Academy of Dramatic Art where he did a Masefield play in 1926. There were sometimes Sunday night productions or gala matinées, such as a grand *Hamlet* production at the Lyceum in December 1926, Lady Bell's *Angela* which Queen Mary chose for a charity matinée in 1927, or some special revival, such as a series of *Everyman* performances given at the Rudolf Steiner Hall in 1928, with Sybil, Russell, Eileen and Lewis. At the drop of a hat they would fit in somewhere a couple of flying matinées of *Medea*—to them this was refreshment rather than an added chore. Emlyn Williams described their god-like descent for such a matinée when he walked on in an open-air performance of *Medea* as an undergraduate at Oxford: "I admired the professional bustle with which the Cassons packed before the dash for the London train: as they streaked across to the Canterbury Gate, the youngest middle-aged couple I had ever seen—'Lewis darling, the thermos!'—and into a waiting taxi."

In this way, just as time and space were transcended by the very act of theatre itself, so in his varied activities, a one-night production might be more significant in the total pattern of his life than a more humdrum production that ran for months. During the first run of *Saint Joan*, for instance, he directed the first British production of Toller's *Man and the Masses* for the Stage Society. It had been performed in Berlin, but nowhere else in Germany; in Moscow at the Theatre of Revolution; and in New York by the Theatre Guild. Now London was to have the chance to experience the grim social poetry of German Expressionism. It was the year of the first Labour government under Ramsay MacDonald, but no playwright of the masses had yet emerged, nor was there any tradition of that kind in Britain. Lewis called upon Aubrey Hammond to design it, remembering those sparse macabre sets and posters for the Grand Guignol. The play was performed on the same stage as *Saint Joan*, so Hammond used part of the set as a basis for a strange, stark, red scaffolding structure. Penelope Spencer choreographed modern dance movements for it, and John Foulds composed the music. Sybil played The Woman; George Hayes The Nameless One; Milton Rosmer The Husband; and Lewis The Guide in a translation by Louis Untermeyer. Lewis found it rather like producing Gilbert Murray's Euripides, and he used for the choruses the same idea of composing expressive tableaux and emotional speech to bring out the plight of the workers. The critic E. A. Baughan praised the effect highly: "The cry of the workers to be delivered from the factories—'Down with the factories, down with the machines!'—was poignant in its thrilling passion." J. T. Grein found the masses "wonderfully attuned in rhythm and movements", the whole creation like a litany (though he meant that pejoratively). He liked Sybil's performances as the idealist, conceiving her part in the spirit of Saint Joan, and found the production said more than the words themselves. The production, for a serious minority of theatre-goers, showed how the German drama was reflecting the deepest concerns of its people through a near-abstract form of theatre.

Abstract in another sense was *The Verge*, a spiritual allegory by Susan Glaspell, in which Lewis and Sybil acted with the Pioneer Players, for Edith Craig. Sybil found it one of the most exciting plays she had ever been in. Both these plays might have fitted into true repertory, where minority plays could be subsidised by more popular ones, or perhaps into an experimental studio attached to a main theatre, a Russian idea not yet thought about in England. As it was, these important experiments were being informally subsidised by the commercial theatre which earned the participants their daily bread.

Another kind of experimental drama was in the new medium of wireless. Lewis, who had followed its scientific progress with enormous interest, was just as excited by its artistic potential. When the British Broadcasting Company began in 1923 he was very soon involved in its work, directing some of the first dramatic productions. He did seven plays in 1924, including Russell's *The Tragedy of Mr. Punch* from the Grand Guignol, Maeterlinck's *The Death of Tintagiles*, Rostand's *The Fantasticks* and a Gilbert and Sullivan. He also gave a talk on the History of Dramatic Representation in the very early days and did an abridged version of *Medea* and the death of Queen Katharine from *Henry VIII* with Sybil. His belief in the power of the spoken word made wireless very attractive. In a later talk about the broadcasting of Shakespeare he spoke of "a magic dance of words, a symphony of sound" which could be created out of any well-written play, in prose or verse, a creation built out of the component parts of tone, rhythm, and melody. Much though would be lost. "The 'feel' and mutual stimulation of a live audience, the sweep and majesty of full-voiced rhetoric in the great outbursts and the answering thrill of an audience roused to enthusiasm. Moreover strong emotion which would deeply move a highly-charged audience, may be merely embarrassing to the fireside listener; and the microphone abhors any sound approaching violence."

Listening to, or creating, drama for the wireless was still on the fringes of art and culture. The centre of Lewis's and Sybil's activity was the commercial theatre. Pursuing their now quite lucrative careers, they continued in management with Bronson Albery. Their next play, *The Round Table*, by the Irish writer Lennox Robinson, did not give Sybil any great scope; though she loved it, it failed and was withdrawn in three weeks to be replaced with *The Lie*. They went off on a provincial tour of *Saint Joan* and planned another major production which was to be Shakespeare's *Henry VIII*.

Now Lewis did find a way of making Shakespeare popular. He chose the play so that Sybil could act Katharine of Aragon, a beautiful part for her, and also because he could see how a lavish production could enhance the masque-influenced qualities of the play, yet remain simple. This he had learnt from *Saint Joan*. He and Albery took the Empire Theatre—a very large stage and auditorium—and began to muster their forces. By now Lewis had something very like a permanent company: Charles Ricketts designed, John Foulds did the music and Penelope Spencer the dances. Bruce Winston made the costumes, the business-manager was still Tom Kealy and the treasurer Susan Holmes. Actors included Lyall Swete, Lawrence Anderson, O. B. Clarence and Eugene Leahy from the *Saint Joan* cast, with Norman V. Norman as Henry VIII, a stalwart and experienced man of the theatre whom Lewis knew well. Lewis liked to keep up old connections and so he cast Ada King, an old colleague from Manchester, and Beatrice Smith from Glasgow. This company was remarkable for the number of young actors who would become famous. Anne Bullen was a beautiful vivacious young actress, Angela Baddeley, whom Sybil had first met in child parts at the Old Vic during the war. Jack Hawkins was again in the cast, and the pages were played by Carol Reed and Laurence Olivier, in his second engagement, at £3 a week. "We had better talk to Canon Thorndike's daughter," his father had said when it was decided that he should go on the stage, and she and Lewis, having been greatly impressed by his nine-year-old Brutus at the All Saints Choir School, were delighted to give him the start he needed.

The production, unlike any other Shakespeare Lewis had done, did not follow the Poel tradition so closely. He had contemplated the creation of a Jacobean stage, but found that it would be much too expensive to build an apron on the huge stage of the Empire (and would reduce the audience drastically). He did not want the extreme ideas of design that had alienated critics and public in *Cymbeline*, but he had a clear grasp of what Ricketts could achieve in combining authentic artistic sources with modern principles of scene design. These would avoid the old-fashioned error of placing a solid figure against perspective scenery. All scenery with which

155

the actors had close contact was either in three dimensions or as tapestries. And, in keeping with what he called the "operatic" style, he used pools of light to concentrate attention on the main characters.

Again, Ricketts proved his skill in creating elegant, decorative, unfussy effects by careful selection of scenic features and props. The costumes were based on Holbein, Wolsey's palace was modelled faithfully on Hampton Court, but he went out to King's College, Cambridge, to find inspiration for a marvellous stained-glass window of Esther and Ahasuerus for the Trial scene. There were several superb tapestries, the most impressive depicting the four horsemen of the Apocalypse, as an ironic background to the fall of Buckingham, and later of Wolsey. Two more were Gothic and one was of David and Bathsheba in what Ricketts called "the most rolypoly Romano-van-Orley style", whatever that means. Doing some research in heraldry, he incorporated the arms of Katharine, Henry and Anne. He worked very quickly, dashing off up to forty designs in one day, then moving them about the floor with his foot, grouping the characters, judging the effect and accent of the colours. Then the execution of costumes was delegated to Bruce Winston, who shut himself in the wardrobe for weeks on end. (Jack Hawkins found him there one day surrounded by a mass of velvet, silk and damask in bales, looking exactly like a medieval cloth merchant.) Ricketts enjoyed working with Winston though he admitted that in their enthusiasm "we both have a hopeless influence on each other". He was less happy with the scene painters, accusing one of doing "abominations in colour and painting which lighting had not quite cured". He worked indefatigably himself and would often be found right through the night painting, stencilling, making properties and jewellery. The Apocalypse tapestry and the window were entirely his work, and on the day of the opening performance, he noted in his journal: "December 23, 1 a.m. My contribution since yesterday's rehearsal (all day) has been a pomander, a rosary, two jewels, a mask, and two hours before the performance I was adding the arms of England to a half of the Spanish shield." This attention to detail gave to each visual feature a perfection like the bloom on a piece of fruit.

Ricketts's methods were paralleled by Lewis's. Just as Ricketts chose his focal objects, Lewis chose his moments. The prompt-book for the production is fascinating, with great emphasis on pageants and processions in all the public scenes; visual effects that must have pointed the contrast between the pomp and circumstance of public life and the passions of private life. The production exploited every chance for ceremony and formality. Wolsey's banquet must have rivalled the Field of the Cloth of Gold—numerous fanfares, a masquers' dance, a pavane, a jigge, a lavish feast, and dozens of supers in brilliant costumes, individualised to be part of the whole composition. Here is the entrance of the food, according to the prompt-book:

> Food procession starts here in following order: 1st servant enters R. with oysters and places them in front of Vaux for inspection. 2nd servt enters L. 3rd servt enters R. and they meet C. holding Brown cake and Peacock in front of Wolsey. Then exit L. and R. respectively. 4th and 5th servt enter R. with iced cakes to tops of both tables. Bow and exit L. and R.

In dramatic contrast was the sombrely elaborate procession as Buckingham was led to execution, foreshadowing Wolsey's own fall. The trial of Queen Katharine, with its huge stained-glass windows in the background, might have dwarfed the human drama, but Sybil's proud stubbornness was tremendously moving in such an awe-inspiring scene. Between this and the sumptuous coronation came the more intimate third act, beginning in the tranquillity of the Queen's apartments, with the song of "Orpheus with his lute". Next, the conflict between Wolsey and Katharine, without their public masks for once, and then the moving scene of Wolsey's fall. The gaudy coronation became an expression of hollowness and ephemeral splendour, with its brilliant heraldic flags, its intricate procession (forty-three actors involved), and its battery of drums, trumpets and bells. After the hymn "All Nations Bow", the prompt-book has a gloriously comprehensive sound cue to mark Queen Anne's entrance: "All spare Thunder sheets, Cannons, Tanks, Stage-hands and other impedimenta to be used as noises off on this cue." There followed the death of Katharine, Sybil's other important scene and the last real human interest in the story, certainly in this production: a scene aided by Lewis's quiet dignity as Griffith. At the end of the play he cut most of Cranmer's part—the man entered too late to be a really interesting dramatic figure—and again, for the final baptism, he emphasised pageantry.

The first night was again a gala. The audience included Ellen Terry, a former Katharine, and Forbes-Robertson whose Buckingham was famous. The performance was long—thirteen scenes and three intervals—but unlike *Cymbeline* nothing outlandish jarred a warm appreciation of the production's splendour, and its acting was praised, especially Norman V. Norman's, and Sybil's magnificent portrayal of pride, dignity, anger, pain and patience.

Agate wrote that, in suffering "she moves you to the shattering depths of spiritual pity".

Henry VIII ran for over three months. At last Lewis had achieved a West End success with Shakespeare, the first since Barker's. Some people even preferred it to *Saint Joan*. After *Henry* there followed a short revival of *The Cenci*, and then *Saint Joan*. A London theatre-goer in 1926 was able to see a full display of Lewis's and Sybil's best work. They were at the zenith of their careers.

The state of the nation was less happy. The revival of *Saint Joan* was cut short by the General Strike, which brought Lewis into active politics for a few days before the capitulation. His work for the Labour party had continued through the years. When the strike began he was fervent in his support of the T.U.C. and lent his car to its leaders for their meetings with the government. At first he felt that his own duty was to keep his own work going as far as possible. So, though most theatres closed immediately, the revival of *Saint Joan* opened at the Lyceum, and there were ingenious manoeuvres to get a complete cast together. Young Jack Hawkins set out at six in the morning to walk the eight miles from his home in Wood Green to the theatre. He arrived five minutes late for rehearsal, and such was his sense of discipline under Lewis's authority that he apologised but did not explain why he was late. Somebody told Lewis, and he was immediately invited to stay at Carlyle Square where he soon felt like one of the family. For John and Christopher it became a great game to walk on as monks in the trial scene and get their friends to join in. A handful of people would turn up to see the performance, and Lewis or the stage-manager would go out and ask them to come down to the front row. "We shall feel more cosy." But the lack of transport and the street disturbances made it impossible to continue, and they had to close. Almost with relief Lewis threw himself into the strike wholeheartedly and set off to the North to be a courier, sharing for a few days in a kind of communal life in Carlisle, and eating, sleeping and talking with the strikers. It seemed as if a socialist society was really in formation and he found it inspiring. He told Sybil: "This strike will go on and on until the government comes to its senses. The spirit of the people is marvellous." When J. H. Thomas capitulated to the government he shared the strikers' bitter sense of betrayal and disappointment.

Back in London he started work on a new play which ranked with *Jane Clegg* among his favourite productions. It was *Granite* by Clemence Dane, whose *Bill of Divorcement* had been a great success for Basil Dean in 1922. Lewis and Sybil, going down to Devon to meet the author, struck up a great friendship. Winifred Ashton was

158

her real name, a most exciting person, beautiful, large, and generous, and always in long flowery dresses. Her black hair was coiled at the back of her head and her whole appearance was regal even when washing up or weeding the garden. A woman of enormous and contagious enthusiasm, she had been an actress and was also a painter and sculptor. Her greatest success was as a novelist and writer. When she was looking for a nom-de-plume she told a friend: "I want a name that will be memorable and roll off the tongue, like 'Westminster Abbey' or 'St. Clement Dane's'—ah, that's it. I shall become Clemence Dane!" And she did, though Lewis nicknamed her "Clemmie-the-Dane" which she rather liked. A real Renaissance woman, she knew a great deal about literature, art and history, she had a particular passion for Nelson, and based Sybil's character in *Granite* on Emma Hamilton. Lewis and Sybil began a friendship which lasted till their deaths, though sometimes stormily, for Winifred could be stubborn and self-opinionated.

Granite is a sort of morality play set on Lundy Island, the tiny, bleak, wave-lashed island off the Devon coast. Sybil played Judith, living a harsh and loveless life with her stern husband Jordan, played by Edmund Willard. A Nameless Man appears, saying that he has been wrecked and has climbed the cliff to their lighthouse. They take him in, and he promises to serve Judith. He serves her by killing Jordan so that she can marry his gentler brother Prosper, played by "Beau" Hannen, but later Prosper, too, becomes a cruel master and she regrets the influence of the Nameless Man. His power grows and he ends by killing Prosper and, at the end, by dominating Judith. It is a study of temptation and possession, reminiscent of Middleton's *The Changeling*; Judith has sold her soul to the Nameless Man, and as the little maid says: "The Devil always gives you your wish, and then when you're sorry he laughs." Lewis played the Nameless Man, a terrifying performance from his first strange and wild appearance at the window to his ghastly, unforgettable laugh of triumph. (It must have been about then and under its influence that Ann wrote a spine-chilling detective play, *Louis the Strangler* which the four children put on in the drawing-room.) The title *Granite* conveys the impression the play makes, the hard, cold quality of Judith's life, isolated and comfortless, and the relentlessness of the Devil, carrying out her most evil thoughts but bringing her no joy. There is just enough hint of warmth and light to throw the "granite" into relief.

Lewis harked back to the simple, stark realism and selective detail of the Grand Guignol, against which the symbolism could take effect. The storm at the beginning set the mood for the large-scale

159

acting he coaxed from the actors. Some critics still found the mixture of realism and symbolism unsatisfactory and embarrassing. Clemence Dane had not managed to fuse the two modes as Ibsen would have done. Charles Morgan pointed out: "If this stranger is the devil, then Judith's soul is his prize and Miss Dane, taking wings of faith and poetry, must plunge without swerving into spiritual flight. But if he is a man, then his prize is Judith's body and Judith's farm. He becomes not a dark angel but a blackmailer." But St. John Ervine wrote, and this must have caused Winifred some chagrin, that Lewis's performance almost made good the defect:

> Mr. Lewis Casson's acting as the Nameless Man was powerful in its sinister quiet. There was something unearthly and inhuman about this figure, as if Mr. Casson had made up his mind to be more devilish than Miss Dane was prepared to be, with the result that he almost recovered for the play what she had lost through her efforts to square the intellect.

Granite was perhaps too grim to attract a big audience. It ran for six weeks, but many of those who did admire it, such as Mrs. Patrick Campbell, were haunted and went back several times. "How easily one forgets most of the plays one sees," concluded St. John Ervine. "How difficult it is to forget this one!"

Lewis now turned to the most haunting play of all, *Macbeth*. Having nursed their ambition for several years now, he felt emboldened by the success of *Henry VIII*. So he and Albery took the Princes Theatre and again he asked Ricketts to do the designs. Granville Bantock composed the score. His work was very modern, often influenced by oriental sounds. For Macbeth, Lewis asked Henry Ainley, whom he had first seen at the Court, a gloriously handsome actor with a golden voice. Though he lacked intellect, Lewis felt that he could make him see what Macbeth was, and then he would add "a mysterious magic of his own" and act everybody else off the stage. Shaw was so interested that he agreed to help in the direction. So, that autumn of 1926, the now-familiar machinery for a lavish Casson production began to roll.

Princes Theatre was not ideal. The stage was too small and shallow for some of Ricketts's best ideas and it could not take a trap-door. He had wanted to have the battle scenes on several levels, with actors appearing from below and disappearing, and to have Lady Macbeth rise from the ground in the sleep-walking scene and sink back into it at the end "as if she had approached the place up a flight of steps". But he was confident that after all the years of discussing the play with Lewis, something would emerge, "as it is too packed with thought for nothing to happen". Perhaps it was *too* packed, because when Lewis brought him the model stage to work from, he commented, "The work will be superhuman, like placing the Atlantic inside a duck-pond, or Durham Cathedral inside a bathing-machine."

Lewis soon assembled a strong cast, headed by Ainley, Sybil, and himself as Banquo, with Basil Gill playing Macduff. Jack Hawkins played Fleance and served the function of "assistant assistant stage-manager". Another young member of the company was Peggy (Margaret) Webster, daughter of Ben Webster and May Whitty, who would later become a Shakespearian director herself.

As usual Lewis was stern, brusque and demanding at rehearsal. Young actors were terrified, though he did not have quite Basil Dean's reputation for reducing everybody to tears. This was partly because Sybil was there to offset his bullying. "Lewis!" she was heard to cry at one point when he was rushing round like an avenging fury. "Will you listen to me for a moment?" "We haven't time for talk now!" he bit back. "Just get on with it." "Oh, he's impossible!" she said in a whispered aside to Ainley that boomed through the theatre, "I can't think why I married him." Her robust response to his shouting and cajoling and rare bits of praise made everyone else feel better. And then he could go on to be just as unrelenting as before. Once he told an actor he was pleased with his work. "I'm glad you're satisfied, sir," the gratified man replied. "I said I was *pleased*," Lewis retorted with a growl, "I am never satisfied."

His aim was to get the ideas from the actors and "mould" them into what he was trying to do. With speech, his prime concern, he would, if he could, take the actor's own way of saying the thing, grasp his intention, and then make it much more vivid by increasing pitch and range and fitting the speech into the "orchestration" of the whole play. If he thought 'it necessary, he would impose his vocal ideas more firmly: he had developed from Poel an extraordinary technique for illustrating what he wanted. This is how Peggy Webster described it: "He would give you an idea both of the tonal quality and the emotional content that he wanted, by pouring forth a stream of total gibberish, precisely scaled and cadenced and rhythmically exact. Some actors found it extremely disconcerting—a cart-before-the horse process. So it was, until you learned to translate back from what your ears heard to the truth of the thought behind it. You then got the hang of it and realised that, far from wanting you to make a noise without any thought, Lewis would

161

pounce like a hawk on any noise that was not truthfully thought-filled."

Lewis became interested in some of the textual problems and made some interesting changes based on the idea that the text contained errors of mishearing. He had Macbeth say "My thoughts whose *matter* yet is but fantastical", instead of "murder", and he gave one of Macbeth's lines to Lady Macbeth, altering one word: "Who dares *no* more is none." Shaw came to rehearsal and would sit up in the circle taking numerous pencilled notes, usually aimed at clarifying the action. Lewis was so immersed in the complexities, as well as preparing for his own performance as Banquo, that he felt the need of Shaw's more detached viewpoint and incorporated many of his ideas. The company sometimes felt it was rather interfering of Shaw when it was neither his play nor his production. Jack Hawkins remembered one day when the final lines of the play were being spoken:

So thanks to all at once, and to each one,
Whom we invite to see us crowned at Scone.

Shaw bounced up at this and insisted, "No! No! It should be pronounced SKOON!"

At which point the young John Laurie, playing Lennox, took matters into his own hands. ". . . he strode to the footlights and in his splendid rolling voice said: 'Mr. Shaw, you are talking rubbish. I am Scots born and bred. The place is called SKON. It always has been SKON and no Irishman is going to change it.' "

But the main struggle Lewis had was with Ainley, who was suffering from a mental collapse and drinking heavily. By prayer and determination they got him through the first performances. ("There *is* something about this play," Lewis told Sybil near the opening night. And they took hands in the dressing-room and spoke a psalm to overcome the play's black magic.)

As dress rehearsals began, Sybil felt trammelled by the lavishness of the production, even the gorgeous wasp-like dress and huge cloak that Ricketts gave to her. Taking her cue from Lewis, she told an interviewer that she would have preferred to do it in the Elizabethan style without scenery, and added ruefully, ". . . but we know by experience that we cannot earn our living this way." The sets were magnificent, sombre, but with a proliferation of colour in the banquet and the final scene of victory for Malcolm, but it was an unwieldy production. The dress rehearsal was a nightmare, lasting from seven thirty p.m. to two a.m. John and the other children went to it: "Nothing went right. Scenery got stuck in the changes, backdrops came down in the wrong places, people put the wrong clothes on and everyone got fratchier and fratchier. At one point, Lewis, only half-dressed in Banquo's battle dress and a Nordic helmet all awry on his head, leaned through the house curtain and had a furious and technical musical discussion with the conductor. As he dodged back with a biting last word, his helmet fell off and rolled into the footlights from where he had ignominiously to retrieve it." When there was some trouble over a scene change Lewis—as Banquo—was to be seen frantically pulling on a fly-rope. After this fracas the atmosphere at Carlyle Square was black indeed, though Lewis was not too morose to accept the notes he had asked his son to make.

The first night ran for three and a half hours. Not the over-whelming triumph *Henry VIII* had been, it was still a powerful piece of theatre. Agate wondered, as indeed Lewis did, "Does unabridged Shakespeare really suit the picture stage?" but he found the production handsome "if a trifle Christmassy". J. T. Grein saw clearly what the production was aiming at with "its barbarism, its sense of chaos and blood overtaking Duncan's old paternal aristocratic rule, its heavy, ominous atmosphere". The music contributed greatly to this doom-ridden feeling. Bantock used woodwind, heavy brass and wailing bagpipes to create an uncanny and discordant accompaniment to the disintegration of Scotland and Macbeth, as evil and disorder overtook them. Charles Morgan regretted the lack of swiftness and the cumulative force. "The play's progress is like that of some vast decorative chariot, to which eagles are uncomfortably harnessed." The eagles were Sybil and Harry Ainley. But as the week went by they began to soar more freely, especially as the audiences were so enthusiastic. Then, once more the *Macbeth* curse descended.

Ainsley's health began to crack. He would wander off into dark corners of the stage, mumbling his lines and missing his entrance cues. Lewis appointed Jack Hawkins to be his "shepherd", a happy choice, for Jack worshipped him and treasured his charge devotedly. "I would go up to his dressing-room for five minutes before he was due on stage, and he would greet me with 'My dear boy!' and I would reply 'Ready, sir?' 'I think so. Let us go down.' Going along the corridor there would inevitably be the regal enquiry, 'Well, what have we been doing today?' 'Sir, I had ballet class this morning and fencing class this afternoon.' 'Splendid! Splendid! Keep working, keep doing everything.'" Finally one night near the beginning of the run, Jack, watching from the wings, heard his idol's voice get rougher and hoarser, until by the end of the performance his voice had gone completely. He was shattered to see and hear Ainley's agony. It was to be three years before Ainley, then forty-seven, could act again, and sadly ironic that one day, Jack himself would have to undergo the same pain.

The understudy, Hubert Carter, now took over the part; a big tough character actor who, rumour had it, drank raw bull's blood to keep him strong. He regularly risked killing Sybil as he clutched at her in the Throne scene, and he abandoned the whole fight routine when it came to the final battle with Macduff. Lewis finally placed an assistant stage-manager behind each piece of scenery, so that when Hubert came near, they could whisper, "Macbeth has to *lose* the fight, Hubert! You've got to *lose!*" But he only roared the louder and plunged more fiercely into the attack. "That really is pretty awful, isn't it?" John remarked to Lewis, watching his performance one night from the wings. To which Lewis replied, "Ye -es, but I'd much rather have it than a lot of namby-pamby acting that we see so much of. It has got guts and power, if nothing else. He's too big for his acting ability, that's all. It's better than being too small for it." That was always the worse of the two evils for Lewis. But the truth was that Hubert Carter could not begin to touch Harry Ainley's tarnished brilliance, and the production was only a limited success.

A pattern was beginning to emerge— *The Cenci*, followed by *Advertising April*; *Saint Joan* followed by *The Round Table*. Now *Macbeth* was followed, in February 1927, by *The Greater Love*, a romantic Russian melodrama by J. B. Fagan, which allowed Sybil scenes of noble self-sacrifice and passion, though Agate said she was not "scrumptious" enough for the part. Basil Gill was a deliciously stern hero. Fagan and Lewis directed together. They disagreed about one actor, the young Charles Laughton, a scruffy, inaudible man who used to rehearse in a dirty old mackintosh. Fagan wanted to fire him, but Lewis said, "Let him be. There's something potentially right about his acting," and he turned out to be funnier than anyone thought possible as a Russian general, and walked away with all the notices. The play was not a great success, but lots of people did enjoy wallowing in its delightful intrigues and excesses.

In the summer, great excitement—they were invited to represent English theatre at an international theatre festival in Paris, run by Firmin Gémier, founder of the Société Universelle du Théâtre. Believing firmly in the diplomatic power of drama, Gémier wanted to invite a German company to Paris as early as 1919, but had to abandon the plan. Now seven nations were to contribute to the first festival of its kind—from Spain and Russia came dancers; Holland, Denmark and Japan sent drama; and Italy sent opera. Germany was not represented, though there had been great hopes that Reinhardt would bring a company from Austria. The British Drama League, affiliated to the Société Universelle, invited Sybil to represent England. She and Lewis wanted very much to go, and wondered how they could get financed. Most of the other countries subsidised their actors and had organised companies to send, but in England this was unthinkable. Sybil said publicly: "In both of these matters this country is, of course, behindhand; we never have dared to think of asking for a subsidy." Instead, she and Lewis approached all the original company of *Saint Joan*, the obvious play to take, and asked them to join the venture on a co-operative basis. They would also perform *Medea*. The idea was so appealing that almost everybody agreed, though Ernest Thesiger was unable to accept. All took little more than expenses for what turned out to be an applauded, if unlucrative, week; Russell went to play Warwick, and Mary was his page, her first speaking part.

They sent the complete Ricketts set, which looked superb in the elegant Champs-Elysées theatre, and Tom Kealy had the bright idea of sending the whole company to Paris by air. Lewis and Sybil had never flown before and thought it a splendid idea, so they set off from Croydon in a Handley-Page, rather green with excitement and sickness. Lewis was unaffected by the motion; but not Sybil who, as the star, had to greet a huge crowd of French people waving flowers and hats at them on their arrival, and make a grateful and complimentary speech. After a quick visit to the Ladies, where she brought up all her breakfast, she obliged with great aplomb and then they were borne off by an old wartime friend of Lewis's.

The performance went beautifully. The French thoroughly enjoyed seeing an English tragedienne who had been compared to Bernhardt and Duse, though she modestly disclaimed such comparisons. And they found her Joan interesting to compare with Ludmila Pitoëff's recent performance in a simpler production at the Théâtre des Arts. Sybil's was nobler, more inspiring, more vigorous, Pitoëff's frail and more moving. Expenses were huge and the festival attracted enthusiastic but rather small audiences, so everyone was out of pocket, none more so than Sybil and Lewis; but as they had thoroughly enjoyed the whole adventure and made great friends with Firmin Gémier, they felt no regrets and whisked the whole family off to Wales for a carefree stay in Portmadoc. It was the children's first visit to what, one day, would be Lewis's house, and though a little awed by Aunt Lucy's grand ways, they loved seeing the Welsh hills and the other landmarks of Lewis's childhood, and meeting their various cousins at Tallsarnau.

In the autumn Lewis and Sybil accepted an engagement for the Old Vic, almost a holiday in itself, especially for Lewis. He was able to drop the burden of management and production and get down to acting which, he still felt, was his real craft. The Old Vic theatre was being renovated, and Nigel Playfair had lent his Lyric, Hammersmith, for a season. For a few months Lewis devoted his energies to being Sybil's leading man in four Shakespeare plays. And what energy it was! He started by playing Petruchio to Sybil's Katharina in a production of enormous gusto and spirit. "His was the triumph of virility over femininity in tantrums," wrote J. T. Grein, but there was an underlying gallantry that softened the attack. With freedom and abandon, Lewis threw himself zestfully into the part, with little regard for subtlety, and reminded audiences that he was no shadow to Sybil but a true sparring partner.

Then he played a controversial Shylock. Ever since Macklin, in the eighteenth century, had foregone the red wig of comedy and made of the Jew a realistic figure, the part had become progressively attractive to actors. Lewis felt they had lost touch with the character Shakespeare created. "*The Merchant of Venice*," he said, "has suffered particularly from Shylock being played by actor-managers, and attempts have been made to get sympathy for Shylock by making him an heroic representative of a noble race." He decided to discard these traditions of Shylock and to play him as he felt Shakespeare had written him, "a mean little miser with glimmerings of good in him". With much more realism than his recent predecessors, he spoke in the accents of the Jews in the modern East London ghetto, creating an unforgettable portrait which some thought the best Shylock since Irving. St. John Ervine, impressed but not convinced, found the performance by far the best in the production, but thought it lacked "the magnificence of baffled rage, and the courageous abandon of a man whose life is filled with despair". Quite a correspondence followed, Lewis insisting that the text indicated Shylock as a mean, miserly, malicious, cunning, cruel coward, with no evidence to suggest anything of what St. John Ervine wanted— "dignity, nobility, generosity, sympathy, real love of his child or moral greatness of any kind". It was a well-tempered disagreement between two friends, which Lewis thoroughly enjoyed, especially as it brought more attention to his performance.

Next came Henry V, described as "sensible, not a showy king, who delivers his harangues, fine sentiments and royal heroics with as much regard for their content as for their music". He wooed

Sybil, as his Katherine, with great wit and feeling. The season ended with *Much Ado About Nothing*, a joyful treat for both of them. Perfectly balanced, they danced through the play, Sybil glowing with mischief, wit and charm as Beatrice, Lewis relishing every moment of comedy as a soldierly, resolute Benedick. They played at a great pace, but lost none of the subtlety. The season was a delight and they must have wished they could go on playing those lovely parts together and not worry about making money or conquering the world.

But the world was beckoning, and with an alluring invitation. Shaw decided that he could not hold over the rights of *Saint Joan* in South Africa any longer. Lewis and Sybil had spoken vaguely of doing their own production there, and now Shaw told them that if they really wished to go, they had better go at once. Their positions in the English theatre were so high at this point, in esteem if not always in financial reward, that a year away could not harm their careers. They loved touring, and they longed to see Africa, so they set about planning a whole repertoire.

Just before their departure, they did one more production, which turned out to be a complete error of judgment. This was *Judith of Israel* by E. de Marnay Baruch. Judith was a character Sybil had much wanted to play and this version was originally written for Sarah Bernhardt. The production, with music by Granville Bantock, was as spectacular as any of their earlier ones. Lewis engaged dozens of down-and-out, out-of-work actors to play the crowd of starving people he needed, and at the dress rehearsal they all turned up in juvenile make-up. He raged at them, "I didn't engage you to look beautiful, but because you looked starving!" The cast was good and expectations were high that *Judith* would be comparable to *Medea* but more easily popular. Baruch, though, was no Euripides and everybody agreed that the play was totally inadequate. Agate's opinion was typical: "Dr. Baruch has turned a great story into a novelette and degraded the punch of great drama to a sentimental fillip." Sybil and Lewis lost £8,000 on this fiasco, but, undaunted, they completed their preparations for the tour.

They would take *The Lie*, *Jane Clegg*, *Saint Joan*, *Medea*, *Henry V*, *Much Ado About Nothing* and a new production, *The Silver Cord*, Sidney Howard's study of a possessive mother, which Lilian Braithwaite had played in London. Great was the pandemonium as they packed up to leave. Mary and Ann were to go too, "to play pages and things". Vi would be left in charge of the house. Lewis had the mammoth task of overseeing the packing-up of scenery and costumes—just like the Canadian trip from Manchester.

Just before they left, the British Drama League and the Société Universelle du Théâtre gave a special dinner for them and made a presentation to help make up for the losses on the Paris trip. But the occasion, perhaps, was more significant because it expressed the affectionate feelings of so many theatre people. They set sail in April, 1928, on the *Windsor Castle* from Southampton; a huge send-off by countless friends and relations, a party that captured the excitement and energy and enthusiasm they both felt as they set off to discover the third world.

South Africa was a dazzling patchwork of experience. They went straight from Cape Town to Johannesburg and played an eight-week season. To satisfy an immediate demand for some Shakespeare, which they had not prepared, Lewis cabled at once for the *Macbeth* costumes and had the sets built on the spot. He added to the enjoyment by playing Macbeth himself. Their other main dates were at Durban, Bulawayo, Livingstone and Cape Town. Everywhere the size and beauty of the country exhilarated them, the broad sweep of the veldt and its changing patterns of light, the splendour and force of the Victoria Falls by daylight and by moonlight, the deep coolness of the Rain Forest. They went everywhere, did everything, met everyone, or so it seemed, admiring the vigour of Bantu and Zulu dances, intrigued by a lion-tamer who used yoga, inspired by a visit to General Smuts. They were treated like royal guests—Sybil boasted indeed that she had received a letter addressed to "Miss Sybil Thorndike, Africa". And without our modern familiarity with foreign countries through films and colour supplements, each experience had the shock and clarity of the unexpected. Though they had prepared for the journey by reading and talking to people, they were still surprised at what they encountered, especially by their experiences of apartheid. They sought introductions to the natives in their churches and kraals, and their politeness as guests of the country did break down when they found their audiences in Johannesburg were to be all white. By furious argument they persuaded the management to close the dress circle to whites in Johannesburg and let the blacks come in. Playing *Medea* to this audience suddenly became quite different as Sybil found each line of oppression and suffering ringing through the theatre to the black Africans. Medea became black, Jason white, and their terrible meeting acquired a new pressure.

Early in the New Year, 1929, the Cassons set sail for England again, full of new thoughts, feelings and memories, with a wider circle of friends than ever, but quite ready to face a London winter. After nearly a year away, the South African tour had made a break in the Albery–Casson association. They did not seek immediately to renew it; without ill will on either side, the split became permanent, for Albery turned to other concerns and soon established a firm partnership with John Gielgud, and Lewis and Sybil pursued their own way. The loss, if any, must have been theirs. Without a permanent company, the only hope for steady growth in the theatre lay with such a wise and caring manager as Albery. He could lead the way skilfully through the commercial tanglewood without being lured by the sirens of philistinism or trapped by unrealistic idealists.

Still, their first season in 1929 was with just such another manager, Leon M. Lion, who had directed one play with Sybil and now wanted to do *Major Barbara*. Nothing could have delighted them more. There had been talk, a few years earlier, of reviving *Candida*, but this was much more of a challenge to Sybil, who found Barbara a marvellous successor to Joan. "Major Barbara," Lewis wrote in an article ostensibly by Sybil, "is starting off today with Joan's enthusiasm to reform the world. Her great fight is still before her and it may well be that she will have to make Joan's sacrifice before she wins victory." He played Adolphus Cusins, and loved the part for its association with Gilbert Murray, and he co-directed with Charles Macdona, responsible for many Shaw revivals in the 1920s. Chiming well with the concerns of the day, the play was quite popular: it had a fine cast, Baliol Holloway as Undershaft, Eric Portman as his son, Margaret Scudamore as Lady Britomart. The partnership with Lion seemed auspicious, so Lewis made plans to continue it and they did *Mariners*, another play Clemence Dane had written for them. It was a rather grim piece which Lion directed with Lewis as a pathetic and saintly clergyman married to the wreck of a once seductive barmaid (Sybil) whom he protected from the disapproval of the neighbourhood. In a sense, a reversal of the *Granite* relationship. It was not popular and soon came off. As if determined to pursue a "harrowing" line of plays, they put on next a double bill of *Jane Clegg* and *Medea*, a combination with which Lewis had experimented in South Africa. He liked contrasting the two studies of an unhappy wife, one a drab and realistic picture of Edwardian marriage, the other a royal witch in the surging measures of Euripides. But Lion's real enthusiasm was for Galsworthy, and Lewis appeared in his new play, *Exiled*, a rather sad piece which the author called "an evolutionary comedy", looking at those sacrificed in the process of social evolution. Lewis played a gentle English squire, his coal-mining property taken over by a modern industrialist who will probably close it down. Satisfying to act, it was not sensational enough to be among Galsworthy's more popular works.

If sensation was lacking on the stage itself, backstage events that autumn amply compensated. In September the collapse of a production called, ironically enough, *Open Your Eyes*, left a whole company of actors stranded without pay. This encouraged the two actors' bodies to consider forgetting their differences and to work for improved professional conditions. Over the years the Actors' Association had lost influence. It had made progress after the *Cyrano* upset in 1919, and under Sidney Valentine contracts had been drafted, but all this had faded after Valentine's death; Lewis was no longer a member because he was a manager, and—by his own reforming zeal—ineligible. In 1924 a rival organisation, the Stage Guild, appealed to those who were against trades-unionism and the principle of a closed shop. Not at all Lewis's cup of tea, it represented all the different sections of theatre—actors, managers and writers—but Lewis was completely out of sympathy with it (although its Joint Secretary was called Louis Casson, just to make everything confusing). At the time of the General Strike fear and uneasiness about trades-unionism increased; many actors deserted to the Guild. The Association was dissolved except for a skeleton committee. Lewis continued to hope for a trades-union movement, and now at last the time was imminent for the founding of an actors' union.

In October, then, the almost defunct Actors' Association called a meeting to try to unite with the Stage Guild. They passed a resolution urging actors and actresses to form and unite in one effective organisation and abandon everything that might prejudice this result. A momentous meeting followed at the Duke of York's Theatre in December, with A. M. Wall, Secretary of the London Trades Council, in the chair. Hundreds of people in the profession came together at last and passed unanimously a motion proposed by Ben Webster to form a British Equity Association (the name taken from the American body, already seventeen years old). It was a tempestuous three-and-a-half hour meeting. Members of the Actors' Association and the Stage Guild argued fiercely; their bitter recrimination wasted much valuable time and energy. Then there was a crucial argument between those who wanted the new body to be an affiliated trades union and those wary of political implications. Here Lewis, a moderating influence throughout, made his strongest contribution. No-one could have been more strenuously in favour of affiliation but, aware of the destructive acrimony he had heard, he argued against affiliation because of the importance of keeping the loyalty of what he called "indispensable folk". He remembered so clearly the disaster of his own reform movement which by its extremism had almost destroyed itself. If he had learnt anything from his years of Socialism and long council meetings of the British Drama League, it was to proceed cautiously on matters so important and controversial. His influence was beneficial. The meeting ended with a sense of triumph that the theatre was at last on the threshold of organising itself for the modern world.

10
Various Parts of the Forest
1930–1940

The dawning of a new decade found Sybil and Lewis frolicking in *Madame Plays Nap*, one of their frothiest and least substantial comedies ("A Dash of History, a spot of Fiction and you have a Legend"). As usual when they made one of their now customary switches from tragedy and high drama, critics and audiences were in several minds how to treat this Napoleonic intrigue. Some revelled in what Agate now defined as Sybil's desire to "disen-duchess herself", others heartily disapproved of her descent from the heights of *Saint Joan* and *Medea* to play a silly coquettish little Parisienne, especially as the play lacked any real sparkle or wit. Lewis spent hours doing an elaborate make-up as Napoleon, and made an energetic stab at what W. A. Darlington called "a poor pasteboard figure of a Napoleon, so lacking in sense, brains and gumption that not even Mr. Casson can do anything much with him". Agate was prophetic when he said in their defence that "Saint Joans do not come into the market every day, and Hecuba and Christmas audiences have comparatively little to say to one another". This indeed was to be the problem for Sybil and Lewis now and for many years to come. *Saint Joan* had been so perfect as a play, as a part for Sybil and as a production that it was hard to match it, and hard also to find any other measure of achievement. Stuck with the Saint Joan image, Sybil was trapped in it, not just by some of her audiences but by her own love of the part, and also by the dearth of large dramatic roles in new plays. Sheer economics made a classical repertoire out of the question. The two of them were a living argument for state subsidy and a national theatre.

A few months before, they had presided at a luncheon at the House of Commons, with an M.P., John Beckett, and another manager, Maurice Browne, to try to encourage the idea of such a theatre, and Lewis had emphasised the importance of continuity and security for actors and actresses: "They cannot work in the team spirit, or with the calmness necessary to artistic expression if they feel they may be out of a job in a few weeks' time." And he added that, on average, only one out of five plays succeeded. Soon afterwards, Geoffrey Whitworth took over as Honorary Secretary of the Shakespeare Memorial National Theatre Committee (S.M.N.T.), after the death of Sir Israel Gollancz, and, finding it a rather undynamic group, enlisted some new recruits, Lewis included. Lewis was already working hard towards the establishment of Equity. He and Sybil, both on the first committee, had long discussions with the Websters, Raymond Massey, Godfrey Tearle and Felix Aylmer, hammering out a constitution. The fact that they had neither been actively involved with the Actors' Association recently, nor ever joined the Stage Guild, made their presences all the more valuable. In May, 1930, at a general meeting in the New Theatre, Equity was really founded, with a twelve-point list of objects, of which the most important was to establish an enforceable contract. Besides this work Lewis sat on the Council of the British Drama League, during the 1930s a "flying buttress" of the National Theatre movement. Agendas, minutes, proposals, resolutions, plans, arguments, strategies, buzzed around his head and his diary was stuffed full of meetings, formal and informal. Out of words, words and more words, he believed the dreams would finally be spun into reality.

Meanwhile, in their own careers, Sybil's and Lewis's policy was just to *work*, to keep practising their craft in front of an audience, to devote themselves to "theatre" as such, and not to turn their backs because it could not fulfil their highest aspirations. For Lewis there was the urgent need to earn good money, not to be lured into building unsellable organs at the expense of his family's prosperity. Two spectres, Barker and his father, confronted him if he were tempted too far towards a higher vision—away from the more practically satisfying sight and sound of a well-packed house night after night. So, over the next few years, Lewis's career became a dizzying sequence of activity, sometimes brilliant, sometimes banal, diverse, diffuse, confusing, often separated from Sybil by thousands of miles, its continuity provided more in his committee work than in his acting and directing.

Madame Plays Nap was followed by two of the high spots. First, a play by Benn Levy at the Arts Theatre Club, which Bronson Albery had opened a few years earlier for non-commercial work. This, *The Devil*, was a fascinating modern morality about a Mephistophelean curate who tempted all the characters but failed to win them because they valued their own consciences more than his offerings. It was acted superbly by Sybil, with Dennis Neilson-Terry, Diana Wynyard, Jean Cadell and Ernest Thesiger. Then, for the Stage Society, Lewis played Socrates in Clifford Bax's play, a

173

beautiful part for him; though it had only the usual weekend, it must rank amongst his most important performances. The first half was almost straight Platonic dialogue to which he brought his Shavian experience; indeed, too, his personal method because in private argument his way was sometimes to lead opponents craftily up the garden path until they had trapped themselves in some patent absurdity or contradiction. The second half, Socrates's trial and condemnation, was more straightforward, moving theatre; Lewis was able to convey all the Socratic values and, at the same time, to portray the man and his heroic stand, all with a humour forbidding sentimentality or pomposity. Agate wrote: "Nobody need be ashamed of having wept at the demise of one who, as well as looking absurdly like Socrates, reminded us, in his snub-nosed, venerable ugliness, of both Tolstoy and Verlaine, and contrived, such is the whimsy of this actor, to encompass the fun of all three."

In August, Lewis and Sybil set off on a provincial tour under the Daniel Mayer management, with *Ghosts* as the most interesting addition to their repertoire. In Mrs. Alving Sybil found a part worthy of her. She had played it already at the Everyman, Hampstead, and now Lewis acted opposite her as the hypocritical Pastor. It became a mainstay of their work, and it seems the more surprising that Lewis never did any further Ibsen. He would have provided them both with good significant parts, the blend of realism and symbolism, of social and spiritual meaning, that excited them in many plays they loved. Perhaps the heaviness of the Archer translations, still in general use, put them off.

The tour took them into the New Year. Then they went into His Majesty's with another revival of *Saint Joan*, still with Daniel Mayer. They had qualms about this, Sybil suggesting to Shaw that perhaps now she should leave it to the younger generation. But the temptation to get back to it was overwhelming and it excited them to see what sort of impression it made seven years later. They felt there was a clear parallel between Joan's France and contemporary India, striving for recognition and identity. There were two additions to the cast—Dunois was Robert Donat, a promising young actor who had started his career at Liverpool; and Bernard Miles, in a humbler capacity, shared with another man, turn and turn about, the great honour of fastening Joan's manacles. He thoroughly imbibed the philosophy which he felt the Cassons put before him. "You set my sights and aims once and for all at the very highest," he told them later, "taught me without ever saying it in so many words, that the theatre is a great and noble profession, worthy of the most strenuous effort and exercise of the imagination." Again the production was an inspiration, and, with appropriate timing, Sybil became a Dame of the British Empire in the Birthday Honours. At forty-eight she was the youngest actress-Dame and felt particularly proud because it was under a Labour Prime Minister. The news, a struggle to keep secret, was announced on the first night of *Marriage By Purchase* in which Lewis directed her at the Embassy with Donald Wolfit. Together they went to Buckingham Palace; together they enjoyed the floods of congratulation. But for the rest of the year they worked apart, Lewis appearing in a newspaper drama called *Late Night Final* and then directing and acting opposite Gladys Cooper in Somerset Maugham's *The Painted Veil*. "Mr. Casson," wrote Charles Morgan in *The Times* "contrives to portray dullness without being in the least dull." Sybil was kept busy with filming and a production of *The Knight of the Burning Pestle* at the Old Vic with Ralph Richardson.

She was so busy indeed that she missed Lewis's extraordinary and moving experience, late that year, when Gandhi came to London and lived for a few weeks at Kingsley Hall. Meeting him through Muriel Lester, who also ran Bow settlement, watching his simple manner, listening to his quiet speaking and following his patient and diligent attempts to work with the British government at the Round Table Conference, made a deep impression which remained in Lewis's mind through the increasingly turbulent political years ahead.

In 1932, another grand tour, prompted again by Shaw, who wanted to release the rights for *Saint Joan* in Australia. This was the sort of excitement they wanted. But how could a Commonwealth tour be financed? Lewis had never sufficient funds to underwrite a major undertaking like this, though he could usually lay his hands on a few hundreds or a thousand if that was the only way. Now the Cherniavsky Bureau entered the scene, three Russian musician brothers who had turned impresarios. Lewis and Sybil had already met them, and they arranged to co-operate with the Australian management, J. C. Williamson and Tait. A new idea flowered. Why not precede the Antipodean tour with a visit to Egypt and Palestine, with some help from the British Council and the Egyptian government? Gradually the tour took shape on a big scale. Lewis planned an enormous repertoire. As well as *Saint Joan* they took *Macbeth*, *Granite* and *Captain Brassbound's Conversion*, Sybil playing Lady Cicely Waynflete for the first time; and on the lighter side, *Madame Plays Nap*, *Milestones*, an Arnold Bennett-Edward Knoblock comedy which they had done at Manchester, *Advertising*

April and *The Painted Veil*. It was a vast campaign to plan, prepare and rehearse.

One result of the less satisfying artistic work of these years was a certain blinkered effect on Lewis. He and Sybil took it for granted that "theatre" was a Good Thing. Any play was better than no play. Working in the theatre was a satisfying and fulfilling occupation. The two girls, Mary and Ann, who had been taken out of school at thirteen and twelve to go to South Africa, never returned to the Francis Holland School, but took their places as young actresses. Ann was happy to do so, but gradually the complete lack of alternative plans and questions about her future began to trouble Mary. Lewis assumed without consultation that she would be included on the Australian tour. There seemed no similiar problem for John and Christopher because they were both in the Navy, but Christopher had become unhappy there and finally left. He, too, turned immediately to the theatre, but it was a positive choice. Mary made her stand and was left out of the touring company, so only Christopher accompanied Lewis and Sybil on this tour, and Ann as far as Egypt.

To increase the pressure of activity the lease of the Carlyle Square house ran out; as it was getting too cramped for the whole family, they moved to a much larger house at 74, Oakley Street, where Sybil's mother was already established. Here, with much more room for their own activities, the four children could expand, and Mrs. Thorndike's comfort and safety were assured. But the uprooting did not help Lewis much. He became so strained and tense, whirling in a frenzy of rehearsals and administrative chores that seemed unceasing, that he brought himself to the verge of a nervous breakdown. Happily, John and the rest of the family forced him to take a break from rehearsals and go off into the country with Ann for a week or so. By the time they set off in March 1932 he was his old brisk, energetic self.

Alexandria, Port Said, Perth, Adelaide, Melbourne, Sidney, Brisbane, Wellington, Auckland. Impressions of this tour filtered back to England by the usual route—Sybil's enthusiastic scribbles which told of a variety of places, beautiful and wretched; fascinating people; glorious outings, packed houses and grateful audiences, sea-board rehearsals, company friction or joyous cameraderie and tiny oases of calm retreat. Sometimes her phrases were pure poetry as when she described the New Zealand hills as "lion green", and when challenged, "I mean the sort of colour a lion would be if it was green." But usually everything merged into one great whoop of delight and for those at home the various ports of call became just dates to be checked off. She and Lewis were the mother and father of the company, with the unique closeness that only a tour, even more a foreign tour, could establish. They were also its leading players and Lewis its artistic and administrative director. Further, their international standing had grown, so ambassadorial roles and duties were considerable. Sometimes their left-wing politics got them into trouble at public functions, but usually a genuine, gracious appreciation of all they saw and heard won their audiences' hearts. Contact with home was close. At Christmas there was even a trans-world phone call between Lewis, Sybil and Christopher in New Zealand, and John, Mary, Ann and Mrs. Thorndike in Oakley Street.

At last, early in 1933, they set off from New Zealand back to England, passing through the Panama Canal, where Lewis's grand-father, Captain Holland-Thomas, had once walked, carrying his boat. In the West Indies they received news that Mrs. Thorndike had died, and then, just before their arrival at Southampton, a telegram from Lewis's brother Randal with news of Aunt Lucy's death. Sadness made this homecoming, with its grand reunions, most poignant, but soon they were settled back in their new home and immersed once more in the London theatre.

While they had been away there had been great progress in Equity. It was clear that in so overcrowded a profession there could be no progress on conditions and contracts if a pool of actors was still available outside Equity. There must be a "closed shop". The positive moves for this came from the top of the profession. Dame Marie Tempest got a group of leading actors, including Lewis and Sybil, to pledge themselves not to work with non-members. With this encouragement the council of Equity sent out a memorandum to all members, making the "closed shop" effective from January 1933. The first test came in February over a production in which the comedian George Robey was to appear. To get round the problem of non-membership he offered to make a "donation" to Equity in lieu of subscription, but the General Meeting rejected this. It looked as if a strike was the only option left, but the crisis was averted when someone pointed out that Robey had a financial interest in the production, and was thus an employer outside Equity shop. Every-one sighed with relief because George Robey was a popular member of the profession. Later he and his producer allowed Equity to use the Savoy Theatre for a meeting. Lewis and Sybil missed this drama, and also missed the withdrawal of an entire cast from a production at the Duke of York's because the management had broken the Equity contract. Their return was warmly welcomed— there were still hard battles ahead, most importantly to get the "closed shop" principle included in all contracts; and at the next A.G.M., when Lewis was elected vice-president in place of J. Fisher White, and Sybil was elected to the executive commitee, they both became members of the council.

United in aims and aspiration, Lewis's and Sybil's careers now diverged more than ever before. During the next five years Lewis acted in fifteen London plays of which he directed four. Only once did he appear in the same theatre a second time, and Sybil's career was equally scattered. Concentrating more on acting, he moved into the "middle-age" range of parts and created several memorable portraits. Directing Lewis was something of a challenge because he always felt he knew exactly how it should be done and had little or no reticence in telling everybody. But, in the long run, he usually managed to keep on good terms.

Immediately after his return from Australasia he was in Gerald du Maurier's revival of *Diplomacy*, then in *Ballerina*, Rodney Ackland's adaptation of a best-selling novel, romantic and lavish, its sets by Aubrey Hammond, dresses for the star, Frances Doble, by Rex Whistler, ballets by Anton Dolin. All this left the director, Sinclair Hill, rather out of his depth and he was grateful to Lewis for helping to pull the thing together. Still, it was not much of a success and in a few weeks Lewis was busy directing again, this time Shaw's *On the Rocks*, with Nicholas Hannen, a political extravaganza set in 10, Downing Street. Not the impressive study of politicians *The Apple Cart* had been, it showed Shaw at his most facetious. Lewis played Sir Jafna Pandranath, an Indian which suited him because, as Sybil said, "he has a lovely speech in which he's frightfully rude to all the English high-ups; so like him". The most lasting effect was that Lewis went off to the Battersea Dogs' Home about this time and bought a "Dutch Barge" dog, whom he called Jafna, and placed in residence at Bron-y-garth, his inheritance from Aunt Lucy.

Lewis began 1934 down at Kew, playing for the People's Theatre run by Nancy Price. She and Sybil had once been rivals when they both played Lady Macbeth at Stratford in 1916. Since then Nancy Price had moved largely towards directing, with such notable premières as *Lady Precious Stream* in which Mary appeared. Playing the English chaplain in *Nurse Cavell*, Lewis found himself in the company of Robert Speaight, one of Poel's actors in the younger generation, and a promising newcomer, William Devlin, who had been a great success in the O.U.D.S. . Then he was in an American play, *Men in White*, directed by Gilbert Miller. Winner of the Pulitzer prize in New York during the previous year it dealt with the novel theme of the medical profession, the conflict between dedicated work and private life. The "men in white" were actually at work in a crucial scene when the young surgeon-hero had to operate for septicaemia on a girl who had tried to get an abortion after an affair with him, his fiancée standing by all the while. (One critic commented that he could actually smell the iodoform.) Lewis played a selfless specialist who represented the work ideal. Such is the theatre's influence that one member of the audience trained as a surgeon as a direct result of Lewis's performance.

Next, Lewis did a production for a fairly new management, H. M. Tennent, directed by Hugh ("Binkie") Beaumont. He seemed a very go-ahead young man and Lewis was keen to work with him, so when Beaumont invited him to direct a play with Douglas Fairbanks Jr. and Gertrude Lawrence, he accepted. But when he read the play he found it so weak and shapeless, that he thought it was sure to flop, despite such popular stars. Beaumont was reluctant to believe this, so Lewis tried to make the best of a bad job. Finally the impossibility of the script became clear and he turned in desperation to Clemence Dane and asked her to write him something quickly. She obliged with *Here Lies Truth*, later called *Moonlight Is Silver*, which opened at the Queen's Theatre in September 1934. A fairly light-weight examination of suspected marital infidelity, it was only a moderate success, hardly surprising in the circumstances, but Lewis felt that Beaumont blamed him, even though he had voiced his uneasiness from the start. At any rate, as Tennents' grew in influence and prestige, they never offered Lewis another production.

His next part was his one and only foray into detective plays, a police superintendent in *Line Engaged*; "one of his best essays in rubicund persuasion", said Charles Morgan. It was directed by Auriol Lee. Though he and Sybil were not working together, their careers crossed or ran parallel from time to time. Auriol Lee had directed Sybil in *The Distaff Side* by John Van Druten, one of the most successful modern dramatists, who had made his name with *Young Woodley*. Now Auriol Lee asked Lewis to be in Van Druten's latest work which she was to direct, an anti-war play called *Flowers of the Forest*. He liked it at once. The first and last acts were set in the present (1934), the middle act in 1914 and 1916. Lewis played a parson of great patriotism and little imagination; and the plot examined the lives and attitudes of his two daughters (Marda Vanne and Gwen Ffrangcon-Davies) as they moved through various stages of patriotic idealism, disillusionment, bitterness, acceptance. The focal character was the lover of one of them, played by Stephen Haggard, a soldier and poet killed in the war; he reappeared through a young pacifist, his medium, who in a trance spoke his now tranquil thoughts from beyond the grave. It was both moving and disturbing.

Though Sybil read the play she had no chance to see it because she herself went off to New York in *The Distaff Side* and was away about seven months, the first time she and Lewis had been separated since the war. They hated it, but wrote to each other every day and Lewis went over to see her for Christmas.

He kept himself extra busy, doing lots of radio work, and then set off for a few days on an exciting foreign trip of his own to Russia, as part of a delegation to a drama festival in Moscow and Leningrad. They were not allowed to see very much of the country; Lewis, aware of this, never felt that he had gained much impression of the country, only exhilaration on his visit to the Hermitage in Leningrad and irritation at the repressiveness of the regime insofar as it affected him. They saw some interesting productions—a Yiddish version of *King Lear*, Nemirovich-Danchenko's production of Shostakovitch's *Katerina Ismailova*, and some beautiful children's theatre. He was struck by the absence of good original plays—they were either trivial or irritating in their facile pro-Soviet message. This, more than anything, told him of the restrictions on freedom. They did see one of Okhlopkov's productions "in the round", but silence about Meyerhold was noticeable. Lewis refused to kow-tow to rigid bureaucracy. On one occasion they were delayed for hours in a shed without food, waiting to board a boat that was already in the dock. At midnight he stood up, and with great panache led his group to the dock, singing the imperial national anthem at the top of his voice. No arrests followed; they boarded the ship and sailed. Peggy Webster, who told this story, also remembered doing scenes from *Macbeth* with Lewis on the Soviet ship going home, to the great delight of the Russians. Lewis broadcast about his trip but did not relate any anti-Soviet stories: he felt he should praise rather than condemn and so his talk was mainly a eulogy which he hoped might help to ease Anglo-Russian tension.

There was great drama in Equity just now over the move to include Clause "M" in the contracts: "The artist shall be required to work only with members of the British Actors' Equity Association." The Council decided that these contracts were to begin in January 1935. At once two disputes arose, the first over Ivor Novello's *Glamorous Nights*, to open at Drury Lane, the second over Daniel Mayer's production of *The Beggar's Opera*. Again the status of the whole profession was in question and its solidarity tested. Meetings of the council and the executive committee were fraught. The principle that "the show must go on" was imbedded, and suspicion still lingered that union solidarity must be unpatriotic and unseemly, but everyone in Equity recognised the progress already made towards fair treatment. The fight for strength and unity must go on. At one meeting the atmosphere was suddenly lightened when Lewis decided that Sybil's opinion and vote were so necessary they were worth a transatlantic call. Everyone sat solemnly waiting while he put a call through to her New York hotel. But they had not quite reckoned with Sybil's huge delight at hearing his voice, delight which crackled and squeaked all through the room.

"Sybil, it's me—Lewis. Listen, I'm at Equity—"

"*Daarling* Lewis! How lovely! How are you? Are you all right? Oh, I'm missing you all—"

"Yes, yes, listen it's about Clause 'M'—"

"Where are you? Are you at Equity? Oh, give my love to everybody. Is Godfrey there? Darling Godfrey! And May and Ben? Angels! Just think of you all there and me here!"

"Yes, they're all here. Now listen, we need to have your vote—"

"And you Lewis? Are you all right? Are you eating enough? And clean clothes and everything?"

By this time the whole room was convulsed and it probably did them all a power of good.

Later a general meeting at the Criterion Restaurant loyally supported the council's insistence on Clause "M". But what action should be taken? Would there have to be a strike to enforce it? And would a strike succeed? Lewis, recognising the sense of determination, made a heroic speech in the true Gandhi spirit, advocating non-aggressive action: "If we called a strike tomorrow we could close every theatre in London tomorrow night," he said, his confident tones ringing through the room. "We are not going to do it. There will be no strike. We are going to win this fight by a steadfast refusal of every single member of Equity to sign any contract which is not the Equity contract containing the closed-shop principle."

His rhetoric won the day. No strike was called. Instead consultations took place between Equity, the Ministry of Labour and the Society of West End Managers, and out of this grew the London Theatre Council, an arbitrating body of ten managers and ten Equity representatives, with a chairman approved by the ministry. The first chairman was Lord Esher, whose theatrical interests were well known, and Lewis became a member of the Equity panel. The first test of its authority was in a dispute with the old enemy, Charles Cochran, who did not want Equity to approve his contracts. Equity members refused to sign them. Cochran said he would not proceed with productions, but after negotiating with the London

Theatre Council agreement was reached and Cochran was given a certificate of registration for approved managements. The negotiating machinery worked. During the next few years Equity business was to be a matter of extension and consolidation.

While all this went on, Lewis had the thrill of welcoming back John who had been out in the Far East where he had met and become engaged to Patricia Chester-Master. Neither Lewis nor the rest of the family had met her yet. He rushed John up to Bron-y-garth to show him the changes that had been made there. One of the extra activities of the last year or so had been his journeys up to Wales to stay and work on Aunt Lucy's house which he had now inherited. He loved going there and employed his architect nephew Hugh, son of his brother Randal, to convert it. The most striking change Hugh made was to open up the ground floor so that you could look right across to the window overlooking the Traeth as soon as you entered. Aunt Lucy's old maid Sarah was still in residence as housekeeper; Lewis was full of plans and expectations about a real family home that linked him completely with his own childhood and was such a pleasurable prospect for his children, his brother and sisters, in-laws, nieces and nephews and perhaps, soon, grandchildren. On this trip, the first for several weeks, they found a good resting-place for Jacob Epstein's marvellous eager-looking head of Sybil, and rushed back to London again, where Lewis was actually playing a Welshman, Owen Glendower, in *Henry IV* Part One.

Robert Atkins, for some years artistic director of the Old Vic, had asked Lewis to play Glendower at His Majesty's. One of the sporadic attempts to do Shakespeare in the West End (Sybil had played Emilia in *Othello* at the Savoy a few years earlier, with Paul Robeson and Peggy Ashcroft) the "excuse" for this production was that George Robey, disputes with Equity now forgotten, played Falstaff. It was a large-scale production under Sydney Carroll's management, and Lewis acted expansively, relishing the music of the language and spinning Welsh magic with his words and phrases. In contrast, George Robey had some difficulty with the language. "I can assure you," he told the audience in his first-night speech, "I have had great difficulty with the words. But, as you have heard, I have mastered a few of 'em. I have understood most of them . . . and I feel that when you come to see us again I shall have a little more to say to you." He was quite ashamed that all he could do was "talk to the audience", exactly what Lewis thought was right: "That's it! That's the real Shakespeare Falstaff," he said. "Warm, vulgar, huge and outrageous, talking to the audience as his friends and fellow-conspirators. He doesn't have to try to be an actor. He *is* an actor." Lewis enjoyed working with Atkins, perhaps the most experienced Shakespearian director in the country and agreed to play Quince for him that summer at Regent's Park Open Air Theatre.

Before Sybil's return, John's fiancée Patricia arrived from China to be engulfed by the rest of the Casson household. "Pat a darling. Just what we expected," Lewis cabled to New York. Within a few weeks Sybil was back and the family was complete again. Patricia just had time to begin to know them all before the grand Knightsbridge wedding took place and they departed to Egypt. The family she got to know was more eccentric than it realised. To the Cassons' complete unselfconsciousness, promoting individuality to the point of oddity, had been added the flamboyance and theatricalism of the Thorndikes. The six of them formed a very close group, each having a different combination of the family traits, so that they all understood and complemented each other. The relationship between Sybil and Lewis had shown the children that "love" could tolerate any amount of argument and independent activity so long as it was part of a search for what was truthful, good and fulfilling. This search all six carried out with fierce intensity. A Casson was rarely idle. If you stepped into 74, Oakley Street and happened to find them in (which was not that likely anyway, because they lived at so fast a pace), the impression might be of a sort of artistic monastery, each member pursuing his or her discipline in solitude, with ardent dedication: Lewis working on his elaborate line-learning system which involved filling up whole notebooks with a nearly illegible scrawl; Sybil keeping up her music by running through a few Bach fugues; John mysteriously manipulating billiard balls to improve his conjuring skills; Christopher practising ballet steps; Mary singing; Ann working on poetry. At meal times all converged on the basement dining-room where loud, quite unmonastic, discussions took place. It was taken for granted that everyone had an opinion about everything; that they thought deeply and felt passionately about their opinion, that they could and should articulate it, and that the opinion could actually have an impact on the outside world. Music, theatre, religion, ethics and politics were the chief topics, the last three burning most brightly. It was nothing to find yourself covering the nature of patriotism over the soup, the responsibility of democracy during the roast beef, the limits of pacifism while you attacked your jam tart, and the existence of God as you sank back with your coffee. All was conducted fortissimo, with beautiful delivery and a gamut of expression from screams of laughter to shouts of anger. The extraordinary thing was that after it all, there were no feelings of discord, resentment or animosity, even though for each of the children the resolution of some of these questions would mean a significant personal crisis. The whole mode of conduct was a steady natural growth from the exciting but cosy family life at Carlyle Square, to the expansion in this larger and more rambling house at Oakley Street. But to a newcomer it was almost overwhelming.

The branching-out from the family centre continued. Now it was Lewis's turn to set off for America, without Sybil. He was to be Lord Palmerston in Laurence Housman's *Victoria Regina*, a play which had only a club performance in England because it was too near the bone in its treatment of recent members of the royal family for the Lord Chamberlain to license it. But Gilbert Miller, the impresario who put on *Men in White*, saw the production at the Gate and thought it a good vehicle for Helen Hayes. He engaged Lewis and a good supporting cast, and the production was so successful that it earned Housman more than all his other writings put together. Like Sybil, Lewis felt lost to be separated, though he did, we understand, find some feminine consolation—identity never divulged. He gave a fine performance, enjoyed acting opposite the beautiful and accomplished Miss Hayes, and had a full social time seeing all their New York friends and theatre people. The biggest events he missed at home were the death of King George V in January 1936, the second family wedding, when Mary married William Devlin, and the birth of his first grandchild, Anthony, in March.

When Lewis returned, he and Sybil started to plan some work together. They had begun to feel that if they did not do this themselves, they might find themselves on divergent careers for another ten years. The only thing was to get a tour together and this they did, under the experienced management of Barry O'Brien. While some actors dreaded long weeks of theatrical digs, unfamiliar theatres and dreary train journeys, Sybil and Lewis rather enjoyed themselves. It was a chance to revisit old haunts, catch up with old friends and detach themselves for a while from the skirmish of the London theatre. Christopher and Ann went with them, and a small company. They took a varied repertoire of simple productions. There was the wit and gentle sentiment of Noël Coward's one-acts, *Hands Across the Sea* and *Fumed Oak*, performed with Shaw's *Village Wooing*, "a Comedietta for two voices in three conversations", which Sybil had already performed in London. Some performances of a new production of *Hippolytus* were more exacting, and something put it into Lewis's head to take a look at D. H. Lawrence's plays. He got hold of a script of *My Son's My Son*, written in 1912 but not published or performed then. Like his other early plays, this was a beautiful slow-moving naturalistic study of a collier's family, just the sort of play Lewis would have been delighted to find on his desk at the Gaiety, Manchester, if its youthful author had thought of sending it there. Instead it had remained as a draft for more than twenty-odd years. Now Lewis presented Walter Greenwood's completed script with Sybil as the garrulous old mother and Christopher as her impudent young miner son.

Naturally he lavished most love and attention on *Hippolytus*, Christopher in the name part and Ann as his tragic stepmother Phaedra. Sybil played Aphrodite and the Nurse, as well as her old part of Artemis, and Lewis played the Henchman, with the long speech on Hippolytus's death which he had heard Barker do many years before. For economy's sake he had the characters themselves as the Chorus, sitting on each side of the stage and slanting towards screens at the back behind which they disappeared before entering to play their scenes. The device meshed everything together in a most satisfying way as they watched and reacted to Phaedra's predicament. Gilbert Murray, who came to see the production, thought it was more truly Greek than anything Lewis had done before. Lewis himself felt that he had got a little nearer, though not all the way, towards solving the problem of a Greek chorus in the modern theatre.

The whole tour was like doing a good provincial repertory season, but mobile. They were out of London to the end of the year and playing in Blackpool, Sybil remembered, when the King abdicated. Like almost everyone in the country, they sat by the wireless and wept as they listened to his simple explanation, knowing that they both found each other's support quite indispensable in their work.

Their next enterprise was also a provincial tour, but very different. Miles Malleson, actor, writer and socialist, collaborated on a play about the Tolpuddle martyrs, *Six Men of Dorset*, based on the diary of George Loveless, leader of a group transported for conspiracy because they fought the landed gentry through their Friendly Society, forerunner of the trade union. Malleson showed his play to members of the T.U.C. who became interested, particularly Ernest Bevin and Walter Citrine, key figures in the Congress and on the National Council of Labour. With their enthusiasm the T.U.C. sponsored the production, and Malleson asked Lewis to play George Loveless and help him to direct. So, just as he had used his political experience and conviction to further his own profession in Equity, now he could use his professional work directly in support of his political beliefs. Since the National Government had taken office in 1931 and Ramsay MacDonald had been ejected from the Labour Party its motive force had come more and more from Transport House and the T.U.C. This production was truly about grass-roots Socialism.

They toured *Six Men of Dorset* all over England, visiting mainly the industrial towns and several places where unemployment was still very heavy. Because of the T.U.C. sponsorship, houses were packed with trades-unionists; Lewis and Sybil got the chance to see and talk to working-class people about their social and economic situation. The play itself was only adequate as a vehicle for the idea of a labour movement. It had the great merit that it never proselytised, but it was episodic, with a number of characters—William Cobb, Robert Owen and Thomas Wakely being lightly drawn— and only Lewis, as George Loveless, was able to give it continuity. This he did, making a moving and compassionate portrait, with Sybil as his wife, almost for the first time giving him a supporting performance. The company worked with great energy and conviction but the play did not reach London, where it might have created more of a national stir.

Despite the limited impact of *Six Men of Dorset* it did seem as if some of the causes Lewis was fighting for were going to be won. The groundwork for Equity was laid. Lewis, still vice-president, endorsed the seventh annual report, while grumbling about its complacent tone. At the time that this report appeared, meetings of the National Theatre Committee had reached a degree of excitement not felt since the early days of Barker and Archer's scheme. Funds now stood at £150,000. The search for a suitable site had begun, and there was great hope that the L.C.C. would provide a site, possibly on the South Bank, for which redevelopment plans were being projected. Though Shaw was against it because of the sleazy neighbourhood, Lewis did not think this mattered; what went on inside the building would be much more important. He also thought there might be some potential in a link with the Old Vic. But now, in 1937, the Committee heard that the French Institute had given up a plot of land in South Kensington and the Office of Works was putting it up for auction. Everyone got very excited, but Lewis was horrified when he saw it. The whole area, a kind of oblong with a wedge stuck on, was little over 200 feet long and 130 feet wide. Some committee members were worried if it could hold the two stages they wanted. Lewis was convinced it could not hold even one, and he was most concerned at the lack of storage space for true repertory. (He remembered those frantic trips across the river for

Frohman's season at the Duke of York's in 1910.) However, the prospect of owning a site was so encouraging that the committee went ahead, acquired it for £75,000, and appointed Edwin Lutyens to design the theatre.

Lutyens, the most famous architect in Britain, was aided by Cecil Masey, who had helped to build the Phoenix Theatre, and by a building committee consisting of Ashley Dukes, Bridges-Adams from Stratford, Nicholas Hannen, Geoffrey Whitworth (chairman of the committee), Sidney Bernstein, managing director of a chain of cinemas and of the Phoenix, and Lewis. The committee was excited about its task and even Lewis was resolved to make it work. They met frequently in a Pall Mall office to work on the technical specifications, pooling the wisdom they had gleaned from practical experience. Then, as Geoffrey Whitworth remembered, they would adjourn "to Rosa's Edwardian restaurant in Jermyn Street, to resume more light-heartedly the discussions of the morning over plates of succulent beef and glasses of undiluted ale". It was a happy time and Lutyens's final design was "a marvel of concentrated amenity" which never, in the event, went beyond the drawing board.

Pursuing his own career, Lewis again went his way separately from Sybil. He took over a part in Elmer Rice's *Judgment Day*, presented by Ronald Adams and Stephen Mitchell at the Phoenix, and set in a totalitarian state. Lewis played one of the judges at the trial of two men and a woman, wrongfully charged with attempted assassination of the dictator. It was a grim play, well received by the limited public prepared for such stern matters; the figures of Mussolini, Hitler and Stalin hovered in their minds. It was a time when Churchill was regaining his influence, rearmament had begun in earnest. Young British Socialists and Communists were fighting in Spain and pacifism was on the wane. Lewis's family divided on this issue, Sybil, Christopher and Ann maintaining their pacifism throughout, Lewis, John and Mary accepting, in varying degrees, the idea of war.

Turning from political plays, Lewis worked for the first time with J. B. Priestley in *I Have Been Here Before*, probably the best new play he directed or acted in during the 1930s. Based on Ouspensky's theories, it fascinated Lewis who believed that many apparently supernatural phenomena were to do with time-warps. Ouspensky worked on the idea of "eternal recurrence"—everything that happens has happened before, but there is a possibility of changing the pattern by an act of will. Lewis played the professor who expounded the theory, one that did not overwhelm the human

187

interest, for Priestley had a rich talent for portraying realistic characters whose lives you cared about. Rather, the idea provided a moral framework in which to examine motivation and responsibility. Wilfrid Lawson, hitherto almost unknown, gave a performance that touched greatness as the man whose positive act was to break the pattern. Laurence Irving, grandson of Henry Irving, designed the production and Lewis directed, being careful to keep the balance and tension between the philosophy and the situations. Agate thought it was his finest performance since Socrates and lavished praise on the whole production, "so interesting in thematic material . . . so novel in treatment, so loyally produced, and so flamboyantly and dimly acted according to the integrity of the part and moment, so gloriously independent of playwriting stuff". Lewis and Jack Priestley got on very well together and began a friendship which would flourish over the next few years as they shared a good many social and political views.

Just before Christmas Gilbert Murray asked Lewis to do a matinée of *The Trojan Women* for the League of Nations Union. As chairman of its Executive Committee, he was anxious to give it some boost at a time when the League's power and influence were ebbing frighteningly away. The international scene looked much less auspicious than during the performances in 1919 but the production was full of the splendour of Lewis's early work. Bruce Winston dressed it again and helped with the direction; John Fould's trumpet music was used; Penelope Spencer choreographed the chorus; Sybil of course was Hecuba, Ann played Cassandra and William Devlin, now Lewis's son-in-law, was Menelaus. After making a great success as King Lear a couple of years before, he was now at the Old Vic. Margaret Rawlings was Helen, and Lewis played Poseidon and Talthybius, reminding his audience just how moving and impressive his astounding vocal delivery could be. In a single breath, climbing in a very slow steady rhythm, he would speak the lines:

> Up from Aegean caverns pool by pool
> Of blue, salt sea where feet most beautiful
> Of Nereid maidens weave beneath the foam
> Their sea-dances, I their lord am come,
> Poseidon of the Sea.

The production contributed to the whole mood of appeasement which would look like weakness only in retrospect.

Sybil had now been asked to go to New York with Priestley's *Time and the Conways*, and, though she was not particularly keen,

Lewis persuaded her that it would be fun, and she would earn good money, always a major consideration. It looked as if he, too, would get out there, in *I Have Been Here Before*, but the plan did not work out, so Christmas Eve found Sybil and the rest of the company sailing miserably across the Atlantic, desperately homesick and depressed. Lewis felt guilty at having let them miss their wedding anniversary together. However, during the run, Christopher was taken ill in Boston, where he was playing in *Murder in the Cathedral*, and she was glad to be on hand. It did make them determined to consider their personal lives more carefully when making professional decisions. Half of Sybil's company seemed to be having matrimonial difficulties and often the crises were precipitated by their professional commitments.

Sybil returned in the spring of 1938 to one of the happiest engagements she and Lewis had had for years. This was Lewis's magnificent production of *Coriolanus* at the Old Vic, with Sybil as Volumnia and Laurence Olivier as Coriolanus. It was Lewis's first production for the Vic. Because of Sybil's early association with it, the idea has sometimes got round that Lewis was always an "Old Vic man". He had, as we have seen, played a few odd roles quite unofficially during the war, but otherwise his only engagement for Lilian Baylis was the Lyric Hammersmith season in 1928. Low budgets at the Vic led to an emphasis on the acting of which he heartily approved. "What you want at the Old Vic is generous acting," he told Harcourt Williams, who was in charge of productions at the beginning of the 1930s. The last few years had seen the emergence of several major actors who were apprenticed to the classics at the Vic, and whose shining talents contributed to a gradual rise in the prestige and quality of the theatre's work: Peggy Ashcroft, John Gielgud, Michael Redgrave, Ralph Richardson, Charles Laughton, Alec Guinness, William Devlin, the director Tyrone Guthrie and many others. But Lewis had never been able to afford a long-term commitment to such a poverty-stricken organisation. Nor was he much tempted by the idea of working for Miss Baylis. Though he warmly admired her work from a distance, they would never have been able to establish a working partnership. Working with Miss Horniman had been difficult enough, with her eccentric and amateur approach, but Miss Baylis was much more idiosyncratic, untutored in the values of theatre and acting, and downright stingy into the bargain. She in her turn would have found Lewis domineering, demanding too much control to fit her idea of an artistic director. So they always kept a respectful distance from each other. In November 1937 she died, affectionately

189

mourned. Tyrone Guthrie was put in charge of the Vic, an exciting, innovative, flamboyant young director with whom Sybil had worked a couple of years before. His enthusiasm was contagious, his whole approach warm and generous. He believed that the best way to achieve success, financial and artistic, was to *risk*; to invest all the heart and soul and money you could muster. Then you would get a return that was worth the struggle. His sense of adventure sometimes coincided with Lewis's ideas, as when his production of *Hamlet* in a ballroom at Elsinore—having been rained out of the castle—led him towards the development of the open stage, work that would finally bring some of Poel's ideas to the mainstream of Shakespearian production. Sometimes he was accused of gimmickry and waywardness. But his creativity was unquestioned; Lewis quickly agreed when Guthrie offered him the challenge of directing Sybil and Larry Olivier in a tragedy rarely revived.

Another reason why Lewis could accept this offer was the dwindling of his financial responsibilities. Two children were now married; the other two both self-supporting. He and Sybil decided to give up Oakley Street and move into a flat. They had watched the building of Swan Court, a large block at the top of Chelsea Manor Street, and Sybil found it most attractive in a monastic sort of way. Number 98 was vacant, a two-bedroomed compact flat on the sixth floor with a grand view westwards, so they packed up Oakley Street, let Russell and his family move in there, sent a lot of stuff to Bron-y-garth, and generally took up a simpler style of living. They would have no staff. Vi and her sister Nan, who had been at Oakley Street, moved back to Kent. Sybil undertook breakfasts and the odd supper or snack, and they took their other meals in the restaurant in the block. It was very satisfactory. Lewis even found a corner of the sitting-room where he could mend china, a hobby he had taken up in order to have a manual craft.

Coriolanus was a great success. Olivier's fire and spirit, and his air of heavy brooding, were exactly suited to the proud young Roman general. He caught the perplexity and uncertainty that made the play tragic. Sybil's Volumnia was full of passion and dignity, supplication and tenderness. They made a wonderful match for each other, and she and Lewis were delighted to think that Father Olivier's son had fulfilled his early promise so excitingly. William Devlin was a forthright, fiery Aufidius. Lewis got Bruce Winston to do the costumes, enjoying the revival of their old alliance. In rehearsal he gave most of his attention to vocal delivery. Olivier had a superb voice and a breath control as remarkable as Lewis's, but up to that time he had not fully developed his vocal potential. He and

Lewis started to have breath competitions. Lewis said one day: "You've got to do this speech all in one breath." "I bet you couldn't," said Larry, but Lewis did. Still, Larry usually won their competitions; Sybil used to boast that he had a longer breath than anybody she knew: "He could do the Matins exhortation 'Dearly Beloved Brethren' twice through in one breath. Lewis could do it one and a half times, and my father once."

Most of the critics praised the production. Charles Morgan wrote: "There is only one thing to do: keep up the pace and beat the drums, and this Mr. Casson's production does vigorously." The set was not the majestic pictorial Rome of Alma-Tadema, who had designed Tree's production, but a grim stronghold which put you in mind of Stonehenge; the costumes, never gaudy, showed a darker aspect of the grandeur that was Rome. The red cloak of Coriolanus glowed "like sullen fire" said Agate, and so did Olivier's performance. Agate also noticed his vocal development: "Vocally Mr. Olivier's performance is magnificent: his voice is gaining depth and resonance and his range of tone is now extraordinary." It was one of those productions that grew in the memory so that disagreements on interpretation seemed trivial in retrospect. J. C. Trewin recalled the première as "lightning streaked". "Olivier . . . rose like flame on marble. In the supplication Dame Sybil stood for eternal Rome . . . She spoke for the centuries."

Just after *Coriolanus* opened came the exciting moment when deeds for the National Theatre site at South Kensington were handed over. Someone unearthed an ancient ritual called the Ceremony of the Twig and Sod which Lewis and the rest of the committee organised for the eve of Shakespeare's birthday. A scarlet marquee was erected, the Kensington M.P. handed over a twig torn from a Kensington tree, lying on a sod of Kensington earth. Shaw received this quaint presentation and spoke on behalf of the committee, pointing the way in which a small and dedicated group can sometimes move towards a national institution: "People sometimes ask me, 'Do the English people want a national theatre?' Of course they do not. They have got a British Museum, a National Gallery, a Westminster Abbey, and they never wanted any of them. But once these things stand, as mysterious phenomena that have come to them, they are quite proud of them and feel that the place would be incomplete without them." The Fleet Street Choir sang some madrigals, and the whole event gave the idea of a National Theatre much more national significance than it had ever had. Coinciding with Lewis's work at the Vic, it also turned his mind positively towards the idea of amalgamating the National Theatre committee with the Old Vic. Over the next few years his own involvement with both bodies would be crucial.

After *Coriolanus*, Lewis took over a part in Karel Capek's *Power and Glory*, like *Judgment Day* a political drama about totalitarianism and the individual. Presently he undertook a most enjoyable Shakespearian production. Ivor Novello, actor, writer and composer of such romantic musicals as *Glamorous Nights*, wanted to do some Shakespeare, so he took the Theatre Royal, Drury Lane, and asked Lewis to direct him in *Henry V*. It was quite clear that this should be no cranky experimental production but a big, exciting affair, like *Henry VIII*, appealing both to Shakespearians and to Ivor Novello's fans. Lewis had a wonderful time. Contradictions in his character sometimes made it hard for him to commit himself to one approach or another. The Puritan in him fought with the Anglo-Catholic's love of pageantry and the conflict was carried into his artistic work. But when events pushed him in one direction or the other, he would jump wholeheartedly that way, and the sense of relief at having the choice forced on him increased his energy and enthusiasm. This time the theatre and the actor's reputation "justified" a spectacular production which the Puritanical side of him might have gainsaid. Accepting that, he seemed to glory in its lavishness. This production, he decided, was to be a bridge. "It has a great deal that belongs to the present way of producing Shakespeare," by which he meant the simple directness of the Old Vic and Stratford, "but it is also perhaps the last in the Tree tradition." It was also to be a bridge between popular and "high-brow" entertainment.

The play was designed by Edward Carrick, son of Gordon Craig; Ivor Novello composed most of the music himself, and one of the actors contributed heraldic and historical details. There was a huge cast. The note was magnificence, which had been lacking in much of Lewis's work in recent years. It was, W. A. Darlington said, "a piece of pageantry whose sober magnificence made a fine frame for the poetry". Indeed all the critics were enthusiastic. Ivor Brown wrote in the *Observer* of its "tapestried splendour" and forgave the slower pace it needed—"the glorious torrent of words is bound to be a little dammed with the pikes and battlements and heraldry. But Mr. Casson's job has been most ably done."

Ivor Novello, Welshman and musician, understood Lewis's approach to the poetry, and he was a most dashing and romantic young king, the epitome of chivalry. The trumpets sounded glorious, the whole play moved with great style and its battle scenes were worthy of Cecil B. de Mille. There must have been the usual rows and crises but none worth relating. Alas, theatre audiences were unimpressed. The production opened on September 16th, when Neville Chamberlain was beginning negotiations with Hitler in Berchtesgaden on the question of Czechoslovakia. As Ivor Novello led his troops eagerly into one European war, Britain's leader tried desperately to prevent another. On September 30th the piece of paper was signed that would bring "peace in our time" and the British public rejoiced and turned their minds thankfully away from the subject of war. The play closed. Novello, disappointed, comforted himself with the knowledge that "though *Henry V* was a financial disaster people really did love it, and particularly people whose opinion I value".

Lewis was also disappointed but he, too, knew he had done some fine work on it. Rewarding work seemed to be offering itself more consistently than for some years. Sybil had just opened as the schoolmistress in Emlyn Williams's *The Corn Is Green*, the most successful part and play she had found recently. Now Guthrie offered Lewis another Old Vic production, none other than his all-time favourite, *Man and Superman*. Of course, he accepted eagerly. The play, now over thirty years old, presented something of a problem in design. Should he put it back in the 1900s, or treat it as modern? He decided on modernity: "As soon as you get actors in what is frankly 'costume' as 1905 dresses would appear, you get a slight sense of artificiality, of their not treating themselves quite as 'real people'. The play 'dates' only in the smallest and least essential matters." It was probably the last time it could be done like this without any sense of "gimmickry". Even so, there were criticisms because, in a modern realistic production, Lewis did not modify the Shavian musical approach he understood so well. On the whole the revival was much appreciated, and Anthony Quayle's Tanner was lively and attractive. A critic in the *Observer* remarked with sly amusement on Lewis's progress since the first production: "It is strange to think that the redoubtable Mr. Casson . . . the autocrat and Napoleon of many a stricken field of rehearsal since then, can ever have played the mild Tavy, whom Ann treats as a boa-constrictor treats a rabbit. But thirty-three years is a long time."

Lewis also acted in *The Rivals*, directed by Esmé Church, and then she and he were asked to head an Old Vic tour to the Mediterranean. Apart from the production of *Hamlet* at Elsinore in 1937, this was the first time the Old Vic had performed abroad, a bold venture artistically and politically. The British Council sponsored the tour to improve various cultural relations. They were to visit Portugal, Italy, Egypt and Greece, and there was quite a stir in the press at the idea of the Old Vic going to a fascist country. At no point did Lewis accept the boycott as an effective weapon, and he hoped very much that positive good could be achieved by visiting Italy. He said, "I feel that at a time like this, when the world is in a state of strain and tension, it's particularly important not to let what, after all, are political differences interfere with the ordinary human relations between nations." He and several others in the company took their responsibilities as cultural ambassadors very seriously. Indeed, his political knowledge made him an excellent choice to make many of the official speeches. His experience abroad was also invaluable because it was all quite new to the Old Vic. They took eight productions: Guthrie's modern-dress production of *Hamlet*, with Alec Guinness, which was very popular (Lewis as Polonius); *The Rivals* (Lewis as Sir Anthony Absolute); his own *Man and Superman* and *I Have Been Here Before* (he liked this even better than his original production); *Trelawny of the "Wells"*, *Henry V*, *Viceroy Sarah*—the only play he was not in—and *Libel*, a courtroom drama requested by the Egyptian Government because it was an examination text for their law students. As usual, the logistics needed to get everybody and everything in the right place at the right moment were vastly complex, and Lewis was often irritated by the somewhat happy-go-lucky attitude to stage-management compared with his own more rigorous standards.

There were forty-two in the company, including six technical staff and a business-manager, and nearly twelve tons of scenery. The acting company included Alec Guinness, Anthony Quayle and his wife Hermione Hannen, Cathleen Nesbitt and her husband Cecil Ramage, Andrew Cruickshank and Curigwen Lewis. Lewis's nephew Owen Reed came as well and, as he had always been very close to Lewis's family, it was like having a son with him. Esmé Church promised Sybil that she would look after Lewis too.

The only thing that marred the trip for him personally was that when they set off he was not only leaving Sybil behind, but leaving her in a weak and barely convalescent state. Just after Christmas, which they had spent at Bron-y-garth, she was taken ill at the theatre during *The Corn Is Green* and rushed off to hospital with an appendix about to burst. She protested "I can't go to hospital. I must finish the week." "Then you'll die," said the doctor. Ann, who had sent for the doctor in the first place, managed to reach Lewis on the telephone and he tore down to the theatre and took matters out of Sybil's hands. He and Ann went with her to the hospital, and the surgeon pulled her through a very dicey operation.

It was all so sudden and unexpected that the whole family, as well as Sybil herself, felt the shock of it. She and Lewis had always had excellent health and, like many healthy people, had come to rely on it and to feel that illness was almost a sign of moral weakness, especially if it meant committing the unpardonable sin of "missing a show". Sybil spent some of her convalescence with Ben Webster and May Whitty, who were ardent Christian Scientists and she became interested in their attitude to pain which was so similiar to hers. Before this she went up to Bron-y-garth with a full-time nurse, who became, in typical Casson fashion, a close family friend. It was there that Lewis addressed the first dozen or so of his daily letters to her. These are the first batch he wrote which still survive and they reflect beautifully the rush and bustle of foreign touring, and his ever-developing thoughts about the state of Europe.

The tour started in Lisbon where a large amount of Old Vic scenery fell into the harbour: an inauspicious start. As usual, the beginning of a big tour put Lewis into a depression which reminded him now of his arrival in Montreal in 1912 and the disastrous personal consequences. But he felt quite safe this time: "I can't see myself falling on Esmé's bosom." The Spanish War was in its final stages and almost everyone he met in Portugal seemed to be pro-Franco, and heartily relieved that the "red menace" had been crushed. The company set off on their second boat trip, to Marseilles, and took the train to Milan. Lewis was struck by the contrast between the cities. Where Marseilles was dirty, scruffy, smelly and lethargic, Milan was orderly, clean, prosperous, energetic and efficient. Never blinded by his left-wing outlook, Lewis looked at Mussolini's Italy without prejudice and had to see that some of it was good: "Whichever way England and France go, they'll have to tidy things up and make life more livable than it is now." However, talking to the Italian actors revealed their great discontent about the plays they were allowed to do. As he had seen in Russia, the writers were ceasing to write plays at all: "I'll break out about this before I leave, I'm sure."

There was no doubt that the tour did oil some wheels and promote Anglo-Italian relations on some levels. He was intrigued by the way in which Italian stage-hands and Old Vic technical staff managed to communicate with each other, forming a language of their own, like English and French soldiers during the war. The plays went very well in Milan, Florence, Rome and Naples, especially *Hamlet*, and he was pleased that so many of the company were young and gave so lively an image of England. He said on the radio afterwards: "They [the Italians] could see that we have a new generation of young and vigorous youngsters who are going to carry on the theatre's tradition."

Whatever happened politically, Italy was as beautiful as ever. While they were in Naples, Lewis went off on a reminiscing jaunt to Amalfi, taking Andrew Cruickshank and Curigwen Lewis with him down the same winding roads as he had been with Sybil, and through the same steep-roofed villages. He revisited the hotel, still run by the same family, and was delighted to find in the sitting-room a portrait of Sybil, hanging beside one of Ibsen, who had also stayed there, and a picture of the whole family at Dymchurch. On one bedroom door was an imposing sign announcing that Mussolini had occupied it in 1921, and on another, a similiar sign read: "In this room in 1926 stayed Miss Sybil Thorndike." Their holiday was so vivid to him that it seemed time had stood still. He found this was literally true because that day he dropped his watch and it broke; so, a couple of days later, sailing from Syracuse, he threw it impulsively into the sea "as a sacrifice to Poseidon", in gratitude for his time in Amalfi with Sybil.

On they went to Cairo, where he saw many of the people he and Sybil had met in 1932, and even bumped into the Alberys and had a pleasant relaxing time with them. Usually, as everywhere on the tour, days and nights were filled with rehearsals, performances, functions and social events, and any gap he filled himself with sightseeing and walking. Typically he was "tempted by the look of the hills behind Cairo—I never can resist hills". He was quite envious of Sybil in Wales. But as she was still quite weak, he often needed to write reassuringly to her, raising her low morale. Unusually, his chronic worrying about money had infected her; she felt guilty at having to pay expensive doctors' bills, and at losing so much in earnings which she could have spent on much better things. His response was comfortingly down to earth. On the lowest possible level, he wrote, she was simply an earning machine that had broken down and had to be repaired to make money again. And he teased her about the wonderful use she would have made of her earnings: "I think it is rather conceited of you to think you would necessarily have done more valuable things with the £800 odd salary that has not been drawn." And he added that Athene Seyler, who was replacing her, could make just as good use of it. Surprisingly, he seemed for much of the time to be more optimistic about the international situation than she was. He wrote that if war did come, he thought it was still more likely to be against the Russians than against Hitler. Again, he said he did not think the world so much worse than it had always been.

196

One of the most interesting people he met was Sir Osman Pasha, Egyptian Secretary of Finance, who had been educated at Balliol and married an English barmaid. Lady Osman, entirely unself-conscious about her origins, was very popular in Egypt; Lewis found her warm and jolly. In Alexandria they saw the Greek National Theatre Company in *Electra*. Lewis was not overly impressed, even with Katina Paxinou, whom he found too old and "fish-wifey", although he enjoyed her "fine heavy voice" and some of the cries and moans she made were "beautiful". (She received them very graciously in a rather "grande dame" manner.) He felt that the problems of presenting a chorus had not been solved any better than in his own productions, and the whole thing, though large-scale with impressive moments, lacked the "brooding religious tone" he would have liked. He also saw a very famous Egyptian comic actor whom he much enjoyed and in Rome, an Italian *Macbeth* played by Ruggeri. Surprisingly, Ruggeri had *under-played* and was solemn and serious, making Macbeth "a sort of troubled saint".

Next, to Athens, sailing past Rhodes and Naxos and other islands whose names rang through Lewis's head as lines from the Greek plays. The day were full in Athens and he could not get to Delphi; he had to content himself with trips to Elevsis and Corinth, and a thorough exploration of the Acropolis. He did manage to visit the Theatre of Dionysus alone and spoke the whole of the Henchman speech. After disappointment at the unromantic first view of Piraeus and Athens, it all lived up to his expectations and he longed to have Sybil there and to explore it all properly with her.

Finally they sailed to Malta. Lewis had been there with Sybil when John was stationed on the island and he found many people to greet. Social life here was intense and Lewis, who (with Esmé Church) had borne the brunt of it throughout the tour, began to get irritated with some of the company's lax attitude: "I do dislike actors. Much groaning because they haven't been asked [to all the parties] and when they are asked they get something they want to do more, and then get out of the official ones." The vast amount of naval activity was apparent. The ships were all "so horribly ready" for war; one night the theatre emptied halfway through as all the men were ordered aboard. While the Albanian crisis came and went, thoughts about war changed every day. Once Lewis wondered how they would ever get home because their route was overland through Italy. Yet, at another time, he was still insisting that matters were no worse than before; "Hitler and Mussolini doing what they have been doing for years." He was amused at a view he heard that "the world will never be peaceful till the day Franco's widow tells Stalin on his death-bed that Hitler has been assassinated at Mussolini's funeral".

Anyway, the situation remained stable enough for them to get home. At the end of April he was safely reunited with Sybil, glad to find her almost completely restored to health and relieved that the tour was over. It had been stimulating, exciting, and exhausting. He had seen and heard so much of past and present and discussed the uneasy future with so many different people. Now all that could be done was to watch, hope and pray.

Through the summer news grew blacker and war become inevitable. He had one last engagement, playing Colonel Pickering in a revival of *Pygmalion* with Margaret Rawlings. Then war was declared and immediately he joined the Air Raids Precaution Service in Chelsea. Despite all the bitterness and disillusionment he had felt by 1918, and despite Sybil's pacifism, he accepted this war completely and he would have joined up if he had been young. As it was, John was in the Navy and thrown into active service at once; Christopher, a staunch pacifist, had settled in Dublin and was out of the fray. Lewis's son-in-law, William, volunteered for the Wiltshire Yeomanry and was called up in November.

As the war machines began to grind down towards the younger generation, Lewis felt desperately disappointed that his own generation had failed. Predictably though, he was soon stamping with impatience at inactivity during the "phoney" war. Theatres were closed for several weeks and then gradually re-opened. What Lewis could not have foreseen was this war's different attitude to the arts. Long months of uneasiness meant that people were more mentally prepared for the event; several, remembering the frivolities of the London theatre from 1914, were determined that now the theatre should be put to good use. Basil Dean, who had run camp theatres in the First World War, founded E.N.S.A. (the Entertainments National Service Association) which through the war would bring entertainment to the troops.

Despite opportunities provided by this new "management", many actors were thrown out of work, but Equity found that no agreed terms of employment were violated. Indeed, in some instances, terms had even been improved. Nevertheless, the council felt that with the new tasks ahead, Equity would need a more national voice; it decided at last to apply for affiliation to the Trades Union Congress because of that body's increasing authority in national affairs. The decision created a personal crisis for the President, Sir Godfrey Tearle, who had always opposed affiliation.

Having held openly and steadfastly to this belief he did not feel that he could legitimately remain in office. With some sorrow, and even, Lewis remembered, some bitterness, he felt compelled to resign. Lewis was elected to the presidency, and held the position throughout the war. Before he knew it, he was also vice-chairman of the London Theatre Council and the newly-formed Provincial Theatre Council. Suddenly and rather unexpectedly, the outbreak of war had made him the chosen leader of his profession.

11

Battle Scenes
1940–1945

A second body would enlist Lewis's help, one totally new which proved to be the war's most important development in the care of the arts. Lewis came into it soon after it began.

The driving force was a remarkable Welshman, Dr. Thomas Jones. Though unknown to Lewis, he shared some of his background. A graduate of Aberystwyth (founded by Sir Isambard Owen, husband of Lewis's friend and half-aunt, Ethel Holland-Thomas), he lectured there before moving to Glasgow University. A friend of Lloyd George, he virtually formed the first Cabinet secretariat in 1915; and among other activities he had convened a meeting to discuss the wartime encouragement of the arts. In 1939 he was just as eager to prevent a cultural black-out; as secretary to the Pilgrim Trust, a charity founded with two million pounds from Stephen Harkness, he saw a possible way and got together with Lord de la Warr (President of the Board of Education) and Lord Macmillan (Chairman of the Trust). On de la Warr's initiative, a Committee (later Council) for the Encouragement of Music and the Arts was formed to administer £25,000 from the Trust to promote amateur and professional arts through the country. Soon the founders, led by Tom Jones, gathered a team of eager and sensible people who never lost themselves in a turmoil of bureaucratic procedure, conflicting ideals, and worthy verbosity. Lewis, attracted to the scheme by Tom Jones's unpretentious enthusiasm, became director of professional theatre activities.

C.E.M.A., the inevitable abbreviation, sponsored several companies, including E. Martin Browne's Pilgrim Players and Donald Wolfit's Shakespeare company. The usual arrangement, designed by Lord Keynes of the Treasury—later to have a much greater part—was that C.E.M.A. gave a guarantee against loss, rather than a straight grant, to selected non-profit-making companies, exempt from Entertainment Tax. Lewis started to work at once on his own pet scheme to associate C.E.M.A. with the Old Vic.

Already he was dreaming of a state-subsidised National Theatre.

After years of ambling in the byways of site-committee meetings, it seemed that a grand highway was opening towards the Barker-inspired destination. Why should not all the C.E.M.A. drama activities, starting now from scratch, be co-ordinated with the Old Vic? And the Vic grew into a National Theatre organisation over the whole country? Lewis's mind flashed back to pre-war ideals. As long ago as 1911, he had said about the place of theatre in the community: "Remember that if it is to live, it must be built of blood and iron, not gold, and the gold that builds the mere shell, the outward symbol of the idea, will flow in easily enough", sentiments appropriately Churchillian in flavour.

Just when C.E.M.A. began to operate, and while these possibilities ran through Lewis's head, John Gielgud approached him. Gielgud had achieved the minor miracle others had attempted for the last twenty years—to persuade Barker back into the theatre. At that time Barker was living in France. Though he took no active part in theatre, his deep interest remained. As soon as war broke out, he had written to Gielgud: "If this war is to go on for long, something should be done to save the theatre from falling into the pitiable state (from the point of view of the drama itself) into which it fell during the last. And I think you are a chief among those who can do this." He proposed a scheme whereby plays should be performed on a non-profit-making basis. Gielgud, a fervent admirer, seized the chance to suggest that Barker himself should direct such a company. Predictably, he refused. Pressing again, Gielgud asked him to direct *King Lear* which Guthrie had just proposed at the Old Vic. They had already asked Lewis to play Kent; and hearing this, Barker suggested an unorthodox plan: he would work on the production if his name were not mentioned and Lewis—to be announced as director—would direct with him. Anxious to bring Barker back to the theatre, Lewis agreed to what he called "this humbug", and he and Gielgud immersed themselves in Barker's Preface to *Lear* and began to correspond with him. (Lewis's letters from Barker were lost in the blitz, but Gielgud's survived.)

The action, they insisted, would be unimpeded, with emphasis on this and the poetry. Roger Furse designed a very simple set. Costumes, Italianate seventeenth century rather than ancient British, allowed for a fully Jacobean development of each character. The cast, a fine one, included, besides Gielgud and Lewis, Nicholas Hannen (Gloucester), Jack Hawkins (Edmund), Robert Harris (Edgar), Cathleen Nesbitt (Goneril), Fay Compton (Regan), Jessica Tandy (Cordelia), Stephen Haggard (Fool), and Harcourt Williams, another persuaded Barker disciple (Albany).

201

Lewis set the main lines of the production according to Barker's ideas. After the brief exposition the opening scene must frame Lear with formality, ritual and dignity, so that he is seen as "king" with only a few glimpses of the "man" beneath. At his entrance to Goneril's castle he "springs away" (in Barker's phrase) and his action and direction provide the "master-movement" right through the storm scenes to Lear's exhausted sleep when captured. After the single interval (the end of Act Three), great attention had to be paid to the "to-ings and fro-ings" of Albany, Goneril, Regan and Edgar, following Barker's instruction that "an exact and unblurred value must be given to each significant thing". Then the "marvellous moments" between Lear and Cordelia would take care of themselves.

Meanwhile, Gielgud, absorbing himself in the dramatic poetry, full of freedom and power, yet always with its "anchorage in simplicity", built his performance on Barker's belief that the two sides of Lear's character could be combined: "The old man pathetic by contrast with the elements, yet terribly great in our immediate sense of his identity with them." In his preface Barker's chief instruction to the actor was to "comprehend the character, identify himself with it and then—forget himself in it", in the same way that Lear abandons himself to the storm. In correspondence he then helped Gielgud to realise this, fully mindful of Gielgud's own reality as an actor: "Lear is an oak. You are an ash. We must see how this will serve you." The strength of Barker's interpretation derived from his implicit understanding of Shakespeare's craftsmanship. Far from finding *King Lear* "unactable", as Charles Lamb did, he saw that the meaning of the play would emerge only by faithfully following the *theatrical* movement. "This contrast and reconciliation of grandeur and simplicity, this setting of vision in terms of actuality, this inarticulate passion which breaks now and again into memorable phrases—does not even the seeming failure of expression give us a sense of the helplessness of humanity pitted against higher powers? All the magnificent art of this is directed to one end, the play's acting in a theatre."

At the beginning of April, two weeks before the production opened, Barker appeared and quietly took up the reins. No longer auburn-haired, he was the same slim figure whose voice and movements carried a contained vitality that was charismatic. Expectation was high, both among older members of the company who knew him and wondered if their memories had grown rosy or if he might have lost his touch, and among younger actors who had been fed on stories of a god-like man. Few were disappointed. Gielgud described the illuminating experience: "In the very few

days in which I had the privilege of working with him, I could see
no trace of effort in the use of his superlative gifts—no lack of
sureness in his authority, no hint of tentativeness or uncertainty in
his approach. From the moment he stepped through the stage-door
of the Old Vic, he inspired and dominated everyone like a master-
craftsman, and everyone in the theatre recognised this. He had only
ten days to work with us on *King Lear*, but they were the fullest in
experience that I have ever had in all my years upon the stage."
Guthrie saw things differently. Dropping into rehearsal from time
to time, he found Lewis, a master-craftsman in his own right,
playing the raw apprentice, hanging on Barker's every word. He
was unimpressed.

Barker's strength was in his complete integration of inner and
outer necessity. He worked meticulously on details of movement,
pace, intonation and characterisation, but always by explaining the
thought and feeling to be expressed, rather than by imposing a
pattern of sound or gesture. For actors who had absorbed some of
Stanislavsky's ideas of inner motivation, or who had experienced
the simplicity and clarity of Michel St. Denis, Barker's work was
not a reversion but a natural extension. Lewis, as impressed as he
had been as a young man, noticed how deftly Barker shifted,
adjusted, extended, modified, so that each detail fell into place in the
total pattern. How magically Barker could fill a pause: "He was a
master of silence," Lewis said once. When Lear entered with
Cordelia in his arms there was one such silence. "There should be a
long still pause, while Lear passes slowly in with his burden,"
Barker wrote, "while they all stand respectful as of old to his -
majesty." He knew why the silence was needed, and he sensed
when it was right: "Dumb and dead, she that was never apt of
speech—what fitter finish for her could there be?"

He worked his cast hard, never letting them relax into a belief that
the performance was fixed. Harcourt Williams wondered if this was
right, if the "scaffolding" would still be too visible at the first
performance. But if it was, Barker was not there to see. After the
dress rehearsal he left. It was his last production and Lewis never
saw him again.

A whisper had gone round the theatre world that Barker had been
there, despite his insistence on official secrecy. (Lewis believed that
Barker's mysteriousness was indeed a matter of Official Secrets
though his evidence for this remains mysterious too.★) Even

★He delivered a letter to the Society for Theatre Research for safe keeping. It related to Barker
and has now disappeared. I believe it to be some information about the nature of Barker's
work in Intelligence, which Lewis believed had continued after the First World War.

without this excitement, *Lear* was felt to be the first real theatrical occasion of the war. Though Gielgud was indeed an "ash", he felt confident that, with Barker's guidance, he had achieved "some of the range and gradual ebb and flow of the character". Charles Morgan liked the way the whole production was based on a trust in the play's stagecraft and in "a company whose accomplishment collectively and individually is equal to every demand made upon it". If only Barker had remained for the performances he would have been able to see that there *was* a change from 1914: the response from the audience showed that the theatre was unlikely to fall again into that "pitiable state". Gielgud was pleasantly surprised by the enthusiastic and sensitive response. He wrote to a friend: "It is wonderful that people are so ready to come and seem to be so still and moved, even with all this trouble in the world. I think the superb poetry is a sort of comfort and release." Russell and Sybil had played in *Lear* on that very stage during the air raids of 1916 as part of a wild scheme by an eccentric do-gooder. Now, in 1940, as an invasion of Britain appeared imminent, the new *Lear* was recognised as important in far more circles than anyone had dreamed.

Encouraged by the success, Gielgud remained at the Old Vic to play Prospero in *The Tempest*; and Lewis played Gonzalo. The directors, George Devine and Marius Goring, had both worked with Michel St. Denis, and the cast included Jessica Tandy (Miranda), Alec Guinness (Ferdinand), Marius Goring (Ariel), and Jack Hawkins (Caliban).

During this production Lewis had a personal grief. Just after Dunkirk, John, in his first command in the Fleet Air Arm and in charge of a bomber squadron on the *Ark Royal*, was shot down over Norway. The Admiralty telephoned Sybil when it received the news, and since someone had seen John's 'plane dive down, pursued by a Messerschmitt, he was posted "Missing, believed killed". Sybil went straight to the theatre to catch Lewis before the matinée. Taking in the news at once, he stood in his dressing-room, tears flowing all over his make-up, and as with Will's death twenty-five years before, thought first of the family. Sybil must go straight down to Patricia and her children, near Winchester and tell her to move at once to Bron-y-garth. Then he went on stage, and played unfalteringly, until the last scene, though every line about the drowned Ferdinand seemed to refer to his own loss. But when Ferdinand and Miranda are discovered playing chess in the grotto and the father and son are reunited he just broke down and wept on stage. John was so very full of energy and action. Patricia never believed that he was dead, but Lewis and Sybil dared not hope.

As in the First World War, Lewis tried to sublimate his grief and turned to his own patriotic efforts. The Old Vic and C.E.M.A. gave the opportunity. As if newly roused by his youthful ideals, Lewis found that he wanted to be in on the new cultural crusade as much as he had wanted to be in on the military battles of the first war. Obviously C.E.M.A. would receive a great boost if he, as its drama director, and Sybil, with her enormous prestige, lent their talents to it, but in truth childlike enthusiasm for a new adventure had urged him to set up an Old Vic–C.E.M.A. tour for Sybil and himself. They would take a production of *Macbeth* to the mining valleys of South Wales, sponsored by local education authorities and the Miners' Welfare Commission. Relinquishing his C.E.M.A. administrative duties to Ivor Brown, he took up the new task energetically.

The lavish, romantic spectacle of his Drury Lane *Henry V* he threw out with something like a sigh of relief. He devised a very simple, compact production, introducing it by a brief prologue which suggested the relevance of the play to Britain in 1940; it was about a time of savagery, murder and spying in which a ruthless dictator grows in tyranny and evil as he strives to keep himself in power. They used screens for the sets and dressed the play in comfortable, workmanlike costumes reminiscent of the period of the 1745 rebellion, with kilts and tam o'shanters; a chorus linked the scenes and explained the action. While educational in its method— and in that sense helping the development of theatre-in-education, this *Macbeth* in no way diluted the emotional and poetic content of the play, but rather intensified it. Lewis believed, correctly, that the Welsh audience would relish its tragic passions.

While rehearsing, with a lively, close knit cast which included Ann and her friend Freda Gaye, and several others who became as close as family, glorious, unlooked-for news arrived that John was safe and in a prison camp in Germany. Patricia heard the news through one of Lord Haw-Haw's broadcasts; at first Lewis was panic-stricken that it might not be true, but the Admiralty confirmed the news, and tears flowed again as the family was able to rejoice fully.

Bombing raids had now begun in earnest, and Lewis and Sybil returned from rehearsal one night to find that Swan Court had been hit and their flat was uninhabitable. In another raid, the warehouse where all their theatre stock was stored—costumes, scenery, scripts and many papers—was also hit, a sad historical loss which has made this record of Lewis's life and work not only more difficult but more necessary. Guthrie, deciding that rehearsals should be finished in Wales, announced cheerfully: "Leaving Paddington at noon—if

Paddington is still there." So, at the age of sixty-five, bereft of house and chattels, Lewis set out with Sybil, like a strolling player, to tour thirty-seven towns and villages in ten weeks. They loved it.

The tour started in Newport before a full and appreciative audience. That night's events showed how terribly appropriate the play was. In a big raid, the manager's house, where Lewis and Sybil were to have stayed, was completely destroyed. His two children, like Macduff's, were killed, though his wife was saved; Sybil was touched to hear that she had visited the captured German airman in hospital.

Again and again, raids interrupted their journeys and performances as the 'planes sped over towards Liverpool. The winter was cold; often, after a long, wearing drive, they would find themselves shivering in an unheated hall, in an empty, hostile-looking village, trying to sort out the dozens of stage-management problems fresh in each new place. After one bleak look, Lewis would take a breath, throw aside his hat, coat and stick, and start heaving the furniture round himself, testing the often rudimentary electrical system, and generally making himself at home in what was to be their night's theatre. Younger members of the company would set to as well, more efficiently sometimes, but never more vigorously. And as curtain-time approached, doors of the little slate-roofed cottages would start to open, and through the dark streets the serious-faced miners and their wives and families would march, often from valleys miles away, as intent as if they were bound for chapel and just as devout and concentrated as they filed into the hall or school. Lewis played with all the emotional rhetoric of a Welsh preacher and these audiences were sensitive to it and responded with rapt corporate attention. At the end, at the company's request, they would sing hymns as their own contribution to the evening, and then everyone together sang "Land of my fathers" in Welsh, reaffirming their communal warmth and hope.

Afterwards, the hospitality, to be received with as much grace as a tired actor could muster. Lewis and Sybil, believing their roles as guests to be as important as their parts in the theatre, would meet the varieties of food, accommodation and landladies with gratitude and humour. Freda Gaye recollects how the terrible question of allotting the accommodation had to be settled. "I will not share my bed with another man!" one actor announced; and Lewis declared: "I will not take another company on tour unless they are all married couples!" Showing an interest in the households they joined was tiring as well. "I am not a servant of the public, I am a servant of the theatre," said Sybil forcefully, as she battled with political discussions where she found herself a "a Conservative when we were with Communists and a Communist when we were with Conservatives". Her own memories were vivid. In the Rhondda Valley she thought of *The Corn Is Green*, Emlyn Williams's play in which she had played a dedicated teacher who encourages a young boy to look beyond the mines to the dreaming spires of Oxford. On admiring the beautiful valleys, which she thought must compensate for the hard work in the mines, she was politely reprimanded and told that the country air was of little comfort to a man with silicosis. She loved to recall the Welsh boys brought in at each place to play Young Macduff in mime, while she spoke the words off-stage. One child sat silently in the dressing-room while political discussion raged around him and then announced in his strong Welsh accent and with a dignity that ended the argument, "We made a *great* mistake after the first war." One young bystander watched the company unload and asked, "Which is the Dame?", receiving a scornful reply from his friend, "They're *all* dames." The tour's favourite story was when she spoke at a big gathering of educationalists, and the local dignitary introduced her as "a famous member of the oldest profession in the world".

Freda Gaye tells a revealing story of Lewis's attitude to theatre and costumes. On one occasion the van with the scenery was delayed and the actors' faces grew more and more apprehensive as they contemplated the bare hall, wondering how they could perform to a full audience in their own shabby clothes. At last the van arrived. Cries of relief from everyone except Lewis, who looked a little crestfallen. "You're disappointed, aren't you, Lewis?" said Sybil. "Yes," he replied. "I thought the actors would have to *act* for once." On another occasion he scolded a young man for complaining of an unresponsive audience—it was the actor's job to get the response. The seriousness with which he took this responsibility was sometimes too much even for Sybil. "Oh, Lewis," she said one evening, "let's not teach them anything tonight—let's just do the play!" Still, he loved the simplicity of the staging and the clear sense (without which he was never quite comfortable) that they were serving a social and cultural need.

The South Wales tour was such a success and they were so warmly welcomed wherever they went that the account at the end of ten weeks was firmly black. They had no need to call upon the guarantee against loss which C.E.M.A. had provided and Lewis, the C.E.M.A. director, delightedly took off his hat to Lewis, the actor/producer, and arranged to extend the tour to North Wales.

In January 1941, a year after the formation of C.E.M.A., what amounted to an Old Vic/Sadler's Wells festival took place at Burnley in Lancashire, where the company had based its headquarters after being bombed out of its London theatre. Guthrie had toured the main company in Lancashire, also with a C.E.M.A. guarantee against loss, and a third company was touring opera and ballet. For eight weeks Burnley became the centre of some of the best available English theatre. One can detect Lewis's hand in a programme note that expressed the happy meaning of this provincial season. "One of the most important and encouraging symptoms of the turmoil we are now enduring is the dispersal of the treasures of art and culture throughout a wider area of the land and a wider range of the people." Though the C.E.M.A. enterprise was still small and its coffers were only occasionally refilled with a little more from the Pilgrim Trust, matched by the Treasury, the avowed policy of providing "The best for the most"—a slogan coined by Ivor Brown—was being steadily fulfilled by practical action, not buried beneath a load of planning. Members refused at any time in those early years to let red tape tie up personal initiative.

So in March 1941 Lewis came home—to the land of his fathers, to the culture which had nurtured him, and to his house and family. His daughter Mary was living at Bron-y-garth with his daughter-in-law Patricia and her three children, and a large number of friends and relatives who, at various times and in various states of need, were offered warm, but sometimes eccentric, hospitality. Sybil's sister Eileen was there, recovering from a nervous breakdown, and her two younger children, Elizabeth and Sybil (known as "Donnie" after Mrs. Thorndike). Eileen had been in Cambridge touring with students from the drama school she ran when she collapsed, and as Lewis could not get there himself, he sent Patricia, fast becoming the person to turn to when things had to be organised, rescued or generally coped with. Winding up Eileen's company herself, she reported to Lewis that only one of its members was worthy of attention. This was Paul Scofield, then a young ex-student of Eileen's with little experience. Lewis promptly offered him a job, but as soon as he arrived in Wales he went down with mumps and infected half the company. That aside he stayed in Lewis's mind, and the fact that Patricia had "discovered" him was firmly established.

So the Bron-y-garth household grew, a refuge for homeless friends and family. Russell's two youngest children, Georgia and Rhona, were there for a time, and Esther's daughter-in-law and baby. It was an eccentric household, not because of Mary or Patricia, who laboured to keep the household running smoothly and sanely, but because of the Celtic mystery that seemed always to affect the place, manifested in those years in the increasing strangeness of Sarah, the housekeeper, (a character not unlike Strindberg's Vampire cook in *The Ghost Sonata*), who drank and brooded and sent unpalatable, meagre dishes to the table. Lewis worked hard to be happy there, and was (we must presume) delighted when, in April, 1941 Mary gave birth to his fourth grandchild, myself.

Macbeth went just as well in North Wales; quieter audiences but no less enthusiastic. There followed an Old Vic production of *King John*, co-directed by Lewis and Guthrie. By this time a few companies were venturing into London, following a brave effort by Wolfit, and the Old Vic went to the New Theatre for two weeks. A programme note bears witness to serene determination: "If an air raid warning is received during the performance the audience will be informed from the stage. Those desiring to leave the theatre may do so, but the performance will continue."

Four fine Shakespeare productions had taken Lewis into wartime theatre. Now, with his firm faith in the power of theatre and the receptivity of the audiences, he wondered if the time was ripe to offer Greek tragedy to the Welsh people; he proposed a new Old Vic-C.E.M.A. tour, this time of *Medea*. Some of the council, surprised by the choice, wondered if Lewis were taking his evangelism a little far. He offered to do *Candida* as well, and he could crow over the doubters when the audiences, as he had predicted, took the strong passion and rhetoric to their hearts and were less attracted to the cleverness of Shaw. "This is the play for us," one miner said, "it kindles a fire"; and another, with his own eloquence said, "There's no light pastry about this—it's good solid meat." Again the domestic and practical difficulties of touring were considerable, but there was no doubt that the hunger Lewis hoped to satisfy really did exist, and it was encouraging to be working not in isolation but as part of a national operation as carefully planned as military strategy. How Lewis must have revelled in the contrast between his work in the two wars! Though, acting as he was in such investigations of evil as *Macbeth* and *Medea*, we can hardly say that he was not involved in the blackest aspects of humanity.

During this tour Guthrie sent a young man to see if Lewis could find a job for him. Douglas Campbell, who would become Lewis's son-in-law, hitch-hiked all the way from Glasgow to Tenby, and in his first encounter with Lewis and Sybil became tangled in a political debate. He was a pacifist, though his violence in argument, matching the fire of his bright red hair seemed sometimes to belie his convictions. His father had known Keir Hardie, and he had been brought up in an atmosphere of poverty and generosity. Socialist idealism was his creed, not Christianity. Largely self-educated, he had met Guthrie while lorry-driving and expressed his ambition to be an actor. Guthrie remembered him and recommended him to Lewis. After that first meeting, Lewis said: "That's an opinionated young man. But I like him and I'm glad he's with us." Plunging into the tour with immense energy, Douglas soon began to develop his skills as a fine actor and to accept Lewis's theatrical ideals. His friendship with Ann was established, but as they both kept falling in love with other people, they had not then the remotest idea of marrying each other.

Lewis, looking for another play to add to the repertory, was glad to hear from Laurence Housman who had completed some plays on the Old Testament, and wanted to offer one. Lewis chose *Jacob's Ladder*, the first new play presented by the Old Vic during its association with C.E.M.A. Soon after the tour opened Lewis had a career choice that caused some searching of conscience. Ivor Brown was appointed editor of *The Observer* and Lewis was asked to take over from him again as Drama Director. Because C.E.M.A. activities had expanded so much this was now a more-or-less full-time position in London; in accepting it, Lewis would not continue touring. This saddened him. He felt himself to be an actor, not an administrator. It was, perhaps the sort of job Barker should be doing, but Barker was not there, so, having seen from the start that C.E.M.A. could have great significance for the arts, and especially the theatre, in peace and war, Lewis felt a moral obligation to accept the position.

The Welsh tours had completely justified all that he had believed theatre was for and could do. How he loved the simplicity of these productions, *words* communicated to the audience, not the spectacle. It reminded him of the Charles Fry recitals and the old pastoral tours, but with an artistic grounding that those had lacked and that the last thirty-five-odd years had given to him. Released from the trappings of West End production by patriotic duty, he could do the tragedies in the style he most enjoyed, and to audiences he most loved to serve. For him the touring itself, wearing as it would have been to many aging men, was part of the romance of the enterprise. Coinciding as it did with the damage to his home and the destruction of his past, it allowed him a temporary return to his youthful adventuring. Now, maybe looking back wistfully over his shoulder at men like Douglas, just beginning their career, he took up the responsibilities for which his maturity and experience had fitted him. He gave his resignation from the Old Vic to Guthrie, who wrote understandingly wishing him well: "Looking ahead, I hope the C.E.M.A. job turns out to be as interesting and forward-looking as it promises to be, and gives you more fun than you anticipate." He began it in December 1942, and wrote of his new role in the C.E.M.A. bulletin for that month:

I am an actor first, and a Welsh actor at that: any success I have had as a director is due to my knowledge of acting; I fear lest my appointment be also due less to my abilities as an organiser than to a successful and convincing performance of the part of an organiser that has taken in even the Council.

C.E.M.A. had been re-organised. In March, the Pilgrim Trust had withdrawn, having done its groundwork, and the Council became entirely state-financed, receiving its funding as a Grant-in-Aid from the Exchequer. Lord Macmillan and Dr. Jones resigned their positions and the new chairman was Lord Keynes, eminently suited for the post by his broad vision of economics and the arts. Maynard Keynes, a man of almost overwhelming brilliance, great charm, wit and determination, thoroughly enjoyed the wheeling and dealing and the manipulation required of committee work and Council policy. ("A personality compounded of silk and steel," Lewis's predecessor, Ivor Brown described him.) He and Lewis in combat, which they were often to be, were like rapier against broadsword.

When Lewis took up his position, with Charles Landstone as his devoted Assistant Drama Director, sixteen companies were working under C.E.M.A. and there was an exciting project of theatre restoration. The beautiful Georgian Theatre Royal at Bristol had suffered severe water damage after bombing and C.E.M.A. set about restoring it. It was as much of a gala occasion as possible in wartime when the theatre re-opened in April 1943 with a production of *She Stoops To Conquer* in which Sybil played Mrs. Hardcastle. Ivor Brown wrote an oration for her to speak, and Queen Mary, a great theatre-lover then living at Badminton, attended the performance, telling Sybil that she considered the Theatre Royal to be "her own theatre".

Within a few months Lewis was able to start acting and producing again, centring himself in London, where he and Sybil found themselves in all sorts of makeshift digs and flats and friends' houses, and a week-end home at Shamley Green in Surrey, where Patricia and Mary, tiring of the remoteness of North Wales, had found a glorious Elizabethan house to rent. It was two miles from the village and they bought a pony and trap to transport themselves and the children. Lewis and Sybil and various friends and relations

211

had many memorable feasts there, Mary and Patricia contriving all kinds of unlikely and appetising meals from their rations, combined with the produce of a flourishing kitchen garden. And it was here that I first become conscious of Lewis, sturdy and comfortable as a good armchair. I remember him, from my lofty position in an orange high-chair, as a fierce, sometimes alarming man when he sat and argued at his family—praising or blaming Churchill, Lord Keynes, the Labour party, the Archbishop of Canterbury ("It is impossible," he said on several occasions, "to be the Archbishop of Canterbury and a Christian," though he admired William Temple greatly as a man). Sunday lunch would stretch on into the afternoon, while the grown-ups still sat and shouted at each other; and when we children were allowed up from our after-lunch rest, there would be a brisk walk over the common, arguments and discussions still winging back and forth. If Lewis had words to learn he would march off into the woods on his own, walking-stick flashing, streaming out his speeches at the top of his voice, oblivious of any sylvan audience. At tea-time you might be lucky enough to sit next to "Grandaddy Lewis" and, with shrieks of delight, face the attacking monster, formed by his rampant hand, as it stalked across the tablecloth towards you.

During this time Lewis played in John Steinbeck's *The Moon Is Down*, presented by Basil C. Langton, whose Travelling Repertory Theatre was an active associated company of C.E.M.A. A patriotic piece, with much of Steinbeck's poignant realism, it depicted a Nazi-occupied country whose spirit still survived, despite bloodshed and oppression. There was a clear, but not explicit parallel with Norway, and King Haakon attended a performance. Paul Scofield (long recovered from mumps) played the part of a young miner sentenced to death, and made an auspicious start to his London career. Lewis then undertook two productions for C.E.M.A. companies, which brought him almost to the end of the war and his two important offices.

His directorship at C.E.M.A. covered several difficult matters of policy. He dealt with them all consistently and far-sightedly, often sticking thunderously to his guns in the face of opposition, (usually Lord Keynes's), showing—according to your view—either obstinacy, foolhardiness or wise courage. One problem, also symptomatic of the different attitudes of the two men, was the thorny matter of exemption from Entertainments Tax. Charitable organisations were eligible, and entertainment that was for "partly educational . . . purposes, by a society, institution or committee not conducted or established for profit". C.E.M.A. did not work with any company until it received exemption under this clause. The Old Vic and Sadler's Wells had received it as a charity since 1934. The Customs and Excise Department, which considered applications and from 1942 found itself swamped with requests, gratefully accepted the expert advice of C.E.M.A. This led to some confusion about a link between tax exemption and association with C.E.M.A.: all companies recommended by C.E.M.A. were granted exemption, but not all exempted companies were associated with it. Freedom from Entertainments Tax was almost equivalent to receiving a state subsidy; in return, a company had to undertake to plough back any profits for future work. As more companies received exemption, one or two commercial managers began to explore the possibilities, and Lewis became alarmed as he foresaw the abuses that might follow.

One such manager was Hugh ("Binkie") Beaumont whose West End company, H. M. Tennent Ltd., grew in prestige and influence during the 1930s. In 1942 he proposed to set up a non-profit-making company, Tennent Plays Ltd., to bring John Gielgud's *Macbeth* to London. He wanted not only to avoid Entertainments Tax but also to associate with C.E.M.A. and receive support from it. To Keynes, the proposal was a delight—it could bring enormous prestige to C.E.M.A. and excellent theatre to London. He welcomed the idea of supporting a full-scale West End production rather than confirming C.E.M.A.'s guarantee to low-budget flexible touring companies which might be more worthy than artistic. But to Lewis, the plan was little better than a capitalist plot. Why should a commercial management cash in on a scheme designed to encourage projects that were genuinely non-commercial and which might otherwise not take place at all? Regarding it as an entirely unsuitable, unethical use of Treasury funds and tax exemption, he was not afraid to confront Keynes boldly with his disapproval. But Keynes was unmoved; the more sombre and angry Lewis became, the more glitteringly Keynes's wit sparkled.

Lewis lost this battle. Tennent Plays Ltd. presented Gielgud's season at the Piccadilly with a £5,000 guarantee against loss from C.E.M.A. It was a gamble, for air raids were at their worst and invasion threatened. It might have been disastrous but it was not. Audiences flocked to see *Macbeth* and, later, the legendary production of Congreve's *Love for Love* at the Haymarket. Tennent Productions made so much money that Beaumont had to search for something into which to plough his profits back—he finally offered money to C.E.M.A. to pay for factory concerts. Ironically, this very success of the season seemed to endorse Lewis's stand, that Tennents could

213

get on very well without the help of Treasury guarantees. And, more lastingly, over the following years, Lewis's fear was fulfilled: tax exemption used by an ambitious man would mean the concentration of many West End productions under one powerful commercial firm; and this would enable a few people to wield an unhealthily large influence in the theatre. Danger rose from the fact that such a management would always be able to outdo others in getting actors, plays and theatres, and could juggle between its commercial and non-commercial branches to the disadvantage of ventures that were purely non-commerical. Both Keynes and Lewis were aware that the problem Tennents presented must be decided in principle if C.E.M.A. were to serve its highest purpose. They both saw a future for it far beyond the duration of the war; throughout 1943 and 1944 discussions were held which would contribute to the constitution of the Arts Council.

There were certainly abuses of tax exemption and association with C.E.M.A. Tennents Plays Ltd. did not, as the Old Vic did, subtract the tax equivalent before calculating box-office percentages for royalties, theatre rents etc., and so could offer better terms to authors and landlords. (Because actors at the Haymarket were paid a flat rate of £10, this difficult matter did not affect star salaries which, in normal commercial theatre, were often based on percentage as well.) Another difficulty rose over the definition of the hopelessly vague phrase "partly educational" in the exemption clause, especially when it came to the bawdy Restoration comedy *Love for Love*, which created censorious protest. Fortunately, the Customs and Excise Board, working in close and friendly cooperation with C.E.M.A., did not allow censorship to be an issue. (Instead, in the Finance Act of 1946, the phrase "over the year" was added to "partly educational" to obviate consideration of the educational content of individual plays.) During 1943 Keynes himself decided to break the link with Tennents; later its non-profit-making subsidiary was wound up. Much later, in 1957, Entertainments Tax was itself abolished, so, in the long run, Lewis could feel that his policy had held sway even though he had lost a first battle.

Lewis had to fight another battle during the period of association with Tennents, a battle in which he stood up against a play whose message, paradoxically, he heartily endorsed. J. B. Priestley, whose writing and thinking he so greatly admired, wrote *They Came to a City*, which Lewis classed as socialist propaganda; and when Tennent Plays Ltd. proposed to put it on in association with C.E.M.A., Lewis protested, despite his own socialist convictions. This piece of near-sophistry brought up, as he knew it would, the whole question

214

of C.E.M.A.'s power over the artistic policy of an associated company, and the role of the Drama Director in C.E.M.A. The Council
had never had any power of veto over its associated companies,
though Mary Glasgow, as secretary, had the right to attend board
meetings, and had sat in on those of Tennent Play Productions Ltd.
There was no wish to change this; C.E.M.A., choosing bodies it
was prepared to support, then left them free to pursue their aims.
In this disagreement, Tennents, a capitalist firm, went right ahead
with their socialist production, and with the support of a public
body, despite Lewis's disapproval as Drama Director of that body.
Lewis had to accept it. The principle of freedom of action for
associated companies was underlined. But the difference of opinion
had shown that his voice had less power than he could wish within
the Council itself. The Drama Panel included Keynes as chairman
ex officio, Ivor Brown as vice-chairman, J. B. Priestley, Ashley
Dukes, Herbert Farjeon, Athene Seyler and Emlyn Williams. Lewis
and Charles Landstone simply attended its meetings and acted on its
decisions. Now he argued that the Drama Director should be
consulted and brought into discussion more actively, and this point
he won. (Later, when the Executive Committee of the Arts Council
was created in 1945 it was deliberately intended not to have artistic
views, only to administer funds; specialist panels for Drama, Music,
Literature and so on, were formed to advise, and only to advise, and
the role of the Drama Director was defined as administrative, not
one of artistic liaison between theatre companies and the Council.)

Throughout his directorship Lewis's dearest concern was the link
between C.E.M.A. and the Old Vic. In 1944, when Guthrie wished
to bring the company back into London, negotiations began with
the Council to establish a permanent London theatre devoted to the
classics. Discussions were by no means tranquil. Lewis now found
himself cast as a peacemaker, though this did not stop him shouting
his own opinions against any opposition and thumping the table as
usual. Lord Keynes found the attitudes of some Old Vic trustees
difficult to take assuming as they did, that theirs was the only
possible theatre company to be considered. True the Old Vic and
Sadler's Wells had several advantages: already established, loyal
middle-class audiences, a stock company of actors yet to make their
name, and its connections with well-known artists willing to serve
it a season at a time. Lewis could keep communications open
between Keynes and the joint administrators of the Vic, who were
Guthrie and Lewis's old friend and manager, Bronson Albery.
Gradually, an agreement was forged: C.E.M.A. advanced £5,000
for an Old Vic season at the New Theatre, one of Albery's own

theatres. Laurence Olivier and Ralph Richardson were released from the Royal Navy Volunteer Reserve, and with John Burrell, became directors. Sybil joined the company, which also included Margaret Leighton and Joyce Redman. A rich season was launched, with fine productions of *Peer Gynt*, *Arms and the Man*, *Richard III* and *Uncle Vanya*, and C.E.M.A.'s guarantee was untouched. Lewis rightly considered himself godfather to the whole union and would have liked to have taken part himself. But he was already busy with the Travelling Repertory Theatre.

Looking back over Lewis's arguments with Keynes, we can see a certain consistency in the fundamentally different attitudes they held. From the start, Lewis had his own clear vision: that strong, centrally-based network of state theatre which Barker had dreamt of, first-class theatre spread through the nation on a co-ordinated policy. All his efforts went to strengthening the bonds between various bodies that could form such a network. Doggedly he made plans and slowly shifted ground to bring a National Theatre nearer existence. In 1944 the National Theatre Committee, on which he still sat, began official negotiations with the Vic. Next year he represented the Committee at a meeting when a joint committee was formed to link the National Theatre and C.E.M.A. for the first time, through the Old Vic. A slender enough connection, but a beginning. Meetings were also held about the constitution of the Arts Council, the body that was to continue and develop the work that C.E.M.A. had begun; at all of these Lewis urged for a tighter control of drama activities, as he had in every specific problem during his directorship. He initiated the idea, for example, that Entertainments Tax exemption should be granted only to managements that accepted the discipline of association with the Arts Council, and that the Council should pool and administer a share of all profits, perhaps up to the amount of the exemption. But he knew, even while making his suggestion, that such a scheme would have given the Council more real power than Keynes wished it to have.

To Keynes the idea of discipline and control by the Arts Council was entirely alien. He had his own vision and enthusiasm for the arts and artists, believing passionately that the nature of art was not to be directed or linked to a coherent attitude and policy. "The artist," he said in a broadcast about the new Arts Council in 1945, "walks where the breath of the spirit blows him." He admired the independence of his own first candidate for a subsidy, Donald Wolfit, who had fiercely refused to use even the programme acknowledgment "in association with C.E.M.A.". "Let him be," Keynes advised Mary Glasgow. "He'll always be a lone Wolfit." Encouraging a catholic, uncentralised and laissez-faire policy for the Arts Council, he saw it as a neutral intermediary between the Treasury and the recipient of funds, providing freedom for the artist, not, as Lewis saw it, a framework. No wonder that their views on particular issues so often clashed when their overall aims were so different. Both thought the other a mere amateur. Lewis felt that Keynes was a stage-struck patron and administrator, not a professional theatre man; Keynes was impatient of Lewis's sharp distrust of commercialism. Ivor Brown described Keynes as being more interested in standard-bearing than in culture-raising; it was true that the brilliance of the Gielgud-Tennent season excited him more than the humbler tours of halls and factories. Moreover, these "shoestring" ventures smacked of a worthiness that was almost "churchy", and that he could not abide.

So Lewis found himself out on a limb. Barker, at a distance, retreated from the move to link the Old Vic with the National Theatre committee; Keynes crushed any suggestion of explicit artistic policy from the Drama Department of the Council. In early days even Tom Jones, disliking the idea of discipline from above, had opposed Lewis's effort to keep dramatic projects under some kind of central control.

Perhaps the differences with Keynes were less about the widest issues of art and morality and the nature of patronage, than about a view of theatre itself. Keynes, as chairman of C.E.M.A., dealt with theatre as one branch of the arts; Lewis, actor and director, knew it to be a unique social force working through an artistic co-operative. Since any performances is a living communication between company and audience, individualism is less important than in some other arts. Lewis's ideal theatre had people working together through love and discipline. As in a family, loyalty, close bonds and common goals were essential for harmony and healthy growth; discipline was a condition of its corporate happiness. Though relations between Keynes and Lewis often neared breaking point, Lewis's courage and integrity had to elicit admiration and respect. Formal meetings often brought angry arguments and explosive rhetoric. But in the more relaxed atmosphere of Keynes's home, with his wife, the dancer Lydia Lopokova, to decorate it with her liveliness and beauty, many much more informal and far-ranging talks offered the kind of disinterested discussion Lewis loved. In the long run both men were unselfishly devoted to the task of founding a body which would support, not shackle, the arts. If Keynes defended them against authoritarian tyranny, Lewis contributed by defending them against exploitation and bureaucracy.

In March 1945, as the war at last approached its end, Lewis tendered his resignation as Drama Director, praised and thanked by all at C.E.M.A. and by R. A. Butler, now Minister of Education. He was delighted to be asked to serve on the Council itself; almost more so to discover that Keynes had suggested the invitation. At about the same time, he resigned as president of Equity, ending an extraordinarily rich period of his life when he had been able to serve and influence his whole profession. Was it altogether by chance that he was the second to hold both these offices, just as he had been the second director at the Gaiety? The role of successor does seem to have suited him. Though he did so much pioneering work, he rarely explored totally new territory. Not founding any movement or society, yet a key figure in several, how often he would emerge after the initiation of a project during what might be a difficult period of reaction, consolidation and growth. The test of a good second leader would have to be in the development of the organisation itself. His personal achievements are less relevant than those of a founder or explorer. People recognised, respected, sometimes even ridiculed Lewis for his devotion to the theatre rather than to his own career in it. They forgave his rages because of his selflessness. I think he was often quite consciously carrying on the work of Barker, the lost leader, and even perhaps, on a less conscious level, living on as standard-bearer to his brother Will.

After such hard and dedicated work, this chapter of his life ended with a doubly happy conclusion. The Allied victory came, and on VE day itself, by a master-stroke of the celestial playwright, John arrived home after nearly five years in prison camp. On the march since January and finally liberated at Lübeck at the end of April, he arrived back at an hour of jubilant confusion, unable to announce his arrival. He made his way to "Thirty Trees" the house at Ashtead, near Epsom, where Patricia and Mary were now living—and so John's war ended, as Lewis's lullaby did, with a weary solitary man, measuring as steadily as he could, the long walk home from the station in the dark. The triumphant reunion was one that only the Cassons knew how to celebrate, as telephones rang for Sybil in Manchester with the Old Vic, and for Lewis in Bristol with the Travelling Repertory Theatre, and from them back to John in Surrey: nothing that made any sense except "Welcome,"— "Welcome back!"—"Welcome home!" Yet, in reality, the same scene was being played all over England. Now it's over, now at last we can start again and make some sense of things. "Now thank we all our God!" and pray that the suffering has been of some use to us and to the world.

Within a couple of weeks Lewis's own glory came when he heard in secrecy that he would be knighted in the Birthday Honours. How proud he felt! Never one to scorn signs of rank or status, if the bearer lived up to his position, he saw his earlier war medals and his titles as true symbols of honour, recognition that, like Othello, he had "done the State some service". Now he accepted his knighthood in a medieval spirit of fealty, and of all the hundreds of congratulatory letters he received, he valued perhaps most of all the brief note which Barker sent, the only surviving letter from him:

Ritz Hotel, June 27

My dear Lewis

Long years ago—you'll have forgotten—you came to spend a Sunday with me in the country; and instead of enjoying yourself, you spent the day fixing me up an electric bell. And I was grateful, even if (probably), I scolded at you for wasting your time. You've found wider and better ways of showing your unselfishness and public spirit since then; and I find myself back—on my way to Paris—just when the Powers That Be have found at last a more or less suitable way of acknowledging this. And I'm so glad and I hope you are. God bless you.

Warm remembrance to you both—and the rest.
I hope all is well with them.
as ever
H G–B

12

Knight of the Theatre
1945–1948

The news of Lewis's knighthood reached Sybil in a mysterious message she received in Belgium, which read: "Remember our black Scottie? That's what's coming to me." The Scottie's name had been Knight, and this was Lewis's ingenious way of telling her his secret while she was on tour with the Old Vic in the war-wasted towns of Northern Europe. Within a few weeks Lewis was off on a similar tour, and letters flew between them as they pursued each other through Belgium and Germany, coinciding for one glorious week in Paris. Both tours were organised by E.N.S.A., run by their old friend and colleague, Basil Dean, who from his base at the Theatre Royal, Drury Lane, controlled a vast network of wartime entertainment for the troops. They had worked together at the Gaiety; they had all contributed to the effort to keep theatre alive in the first war; they had all plunged into a series of ambitious artistic productions in the commercial West End during the Twenties and Thirties. Now, in different ways, they were the people whose faith and experience had been called upon, for their own and another generation, in the Second World War.

Lewis, on his own tour, thought particularly of the meeting of the generations. He was playing Warwick in his new production of *Saint Joan* in which Ann played Joan, over twenty years after Sybil, and several years younger. A challenge to any young actress, it was doubly so for Ann; she rose to it magnificently. Closely resembling Sybil in vocal and facial expression, and in drive and fervour—so closely that John, seeing the production in England, felt he was seeing Sybil's *doppel-gänger*—critics inevitably accused her of imitating her mother. But she did find her own Joan. Having recently become a Roman Catholic, but, as she said to Shaw, "a Protesting one", she was in a position to explore Joan's situation for herself and make the fighting saint real for herself, not a reconstruction of performances remembered from childhood. Lewis was the usual stern and critical taskmaster, but in no danger of imposing his wife's interpretation on his daughter. Basil Langton played De Baudricourt

220

and the Inquisitor. It was a splendid choice of play for troops trying
to put Europe together again after the Allied victory.

In Lübeck, it was Lewis who was the *doppel-gänger*, for he drove
over the exact road John had taken only two months before, in the
final march to liberation. Yet in parts of Belgium it was his own
ghost that Lewis met, finding little towns and villages associated
with the battlegrounds of the First World War and already looking
as remote from war as the field of Waterloo. One day in Bruges he
took a train to Ypres, and cycled six miles and back to visit the grave
of his cousin Alec.

In Hamburg he set out to explore the town and its environs,
eager—as in all his travels—to see what kind of people and places he
was among, taking a tram right to the end of the line, through a
working-class district and the beginnings of country and market
gardens. He was appalled at the amount of war damage he saw:
"We are supposed to pride ourselves on the accuracy of our
bombing," he wrote to Sybil, "so we can only conclude that the
smashing up of miles and miles of fine workmen's flats and small
houses was deliberate, for whole districts of wealthy homes are
almost untouched. Of course there *are* works and garages among
the houses in the poor district and they're gone too, and I suppose
the fires were so bad that they did most of the destruction, but I find
it very difficult to believe that the destruction of the houses as such
was not intended." He added, " . . . the tramload of dear old tired
women shopping was so exactly like Bermondsey".

He and Sybil wrote to each other every day. Though the vagaries
of the Forces' postal service, and frequent disorganisation within
E.N.S.A., meant long gaps and delays, most of the letters eventually
reached Swan Court since by then it was habitable again—and they
have survived. They are now a revealing record of Lewis's thoughts
and feelings particularly for his views on the political events of those
decisive months. As usual he read the papers every day and his
written comments to Sybil were the equivalent of their breakfast
table talks on the state of the world. He saw not only much of what
was going on in the British liberating army at first hand, but also
met and exchanged views with a good cross-section of people, from
the British officers who wined and dined the company at various
places, to some Belgian journalists who interviewed him, as well as
all the people he met casually on trains or trams, in the streets and
shops and in the theatres. He was always listening, watching,
questioning, reading, arguing, and when possible, implanting a
humane and rational doctrine, sometimes at the risk of being dis-
courteous.

On one occasion a group from the company, invited to an elegant party, included Ann, who was a staunch pacifist, and several other socialists and pacifists, as well as Lewis, and they all felt a double duty to behave like good guests and at the same time to tackle the British officers boldly on several controversial issues. The conversation alternated all the evening between sparks and sparkle. Lewis set out to topple the arguments of Colonel Armytage, the Commanding Officer, their host, who held firmly to the belief that the German people would have to be punished for the monstrous acts perpetrated by the Nazis. Belsen stood a few miles away, horrifying, still half-living proof of these monstrosities.

Strangely, Sybil had visited the camp at Belsen a few weeks earlier and he had not yet received her account of it. By the time he arrived in Hamburg no visits were permitted, even if he had wanted it. There, amid an unbearable stench which she was told was of "living children's bodies", Sybil had been shown the tiny sordid huts that had housed all the prisoners and were now being burnt; the twisted bony creatures, who, the doctor told her, he hoped would recover; and, worse, the fleshless contorted bodies of those he could not save, all reeking with the odour of putrefaction. All who witnessed these horrors, undreamed of before the camps were liberated, were deeply affected and needed to speak passionately about them. But Lewis was worried by the insistence he heard from many officers that the whole German people should be held responsible for the camps, and by the continual "rubbing-in of Belsen" as he put it "as a proof of their iniquity". He put the point forcibly to Colonel Armytage: "If I am to be held even more responsible for what our government is doing (because our system is more democratic), I must know more of the facts. No one tells me how they (that is I) are treating the political prisoners in India, therefore I am supposed to assume that they receive nothing but humane treatment. It is more convenient to assume that, as the Germans did." He went on to describe what he had heard about the Canadians in charge of the prison island where the SS men were being kept. The Canadians, he had been told gloatingly by some R.A.F. officers, were treating the SS, "as the Nazis treated the Jews". He was angry because he felt that Colonel Armytage and others played down these stories, or assumed they were not true, or indeed were themselves kept in ignorance. The important point was that, whether they were true or not, Lewis and others in his position did not know, so it was senseless to consider that the German people knew what was going on in the concentration camps. He also tackled the Colonel on the question of duty and obedience. "At what point," he enquired, "is it the duty of 1) a soldier or airman 2) a policeman 3) a civilian in wartime to refuse to carry out an order which he knows or thinks is against international law or international conscience?" "I was very fluent!" Lewis commented in his account of this discussion to Sybil, and later wrote a charming, almost grovelling letter to Colonel Armytage, who himself had sent a note asking Lewis not to think of him as a complete "Colonel Blimp". "It's not a bad technique," Lewis concluded, "to go pretty far in what you want to say and then later say how dreadful it was of you to say it! Then the doctrine has some sinking-in effect without hurting their feelings."

By the next day, Lewis's thinking had gone off into the kind of daring propositions he usually launched at Sunday-supper arguments. There were, he suggested to Sybil, similarities between British and Nazi regimes, in that British industry and business, including the theatrical business, got rid of undesirables by eliminating them through sacking, the equivalent of death. (Of banishment, I should have thought.) But a democratic society has to keep undesirables within the community and govern them with or without their consent. No partiality, patriotism or any other sentiment, prevented Lewis from carefully examining and comparing the models and structures of society and the principles of social conduct, in family, business, school, church or state. "In essence," he said, "the Nazi does remove the heretic or potential rebel from the general community at will, and without law (as we do as employers) by death or the concentration camp. The *cruelty* of the concentration camp is quite another matter. But even that originally began on a basis of *educating* recalcitrant people to be better citizens (Nazi version of course) by rigid training."

As well as protesting about wholesale condemnation of the German people, Lewis found himself up against what he called "*Daily Express* propaganda" about Russian atrocity. He met this in the horrifying tales of some soldiers on the train from Paris and was particularly irritated because of their great influence over popular opinion. "When pressed," he observed, "they have never actually met any of the 'Red Army' but of course as actual fighting men they get credit for first-hand knowledge."

During the tour the General Election took place in Britain, and Lewis was delighted at this first overwhelming victory for the Labour party which he had supported so long. "Well, Labour will have to get to work this time!" he wrote. "There can be no shirking on the ground that they had insufficient parliamentary majority." He wondered if Churchill would be a sufficiently staunch patriot to go to the Peace Conference at Potsdam as second to Attlee, and lowered his estimation of the ex-leader when he declined to go. He was interested to see what Cabinet Attlee would appoint: "It must be very like casting a very important production."

In August came Hiroshima, with its colossal indiscriminate effects. Lewis could find no victory in it: "How far we have travelled down the Nazi road." He dismissed all optimistic suggestions that the nuclear threat was so large that it would end the actual practice of war, ". . . which has been said I suppose at every stage since the invention of gunpowder". And he lamented that only one member of the Commission which developed atomic fission spoke of the possibility of peaceful development. He was disturbed at the inconsistency of punishing the Germans for the crime of making aggressive war while Japan was to be allowed to keep her emperor. He was appalled that the second bomb was dropped so prematurely at Nagasaki, and puzzled why the British coalition was broken *before* Hiroshima, instead of afterwards when its predicted effect of ending the war was actually achieved.

So, with a fairly even weight of hope and fear about the post-war world, Lewis returned to London and received his knighthood. A family dinner at the Savoy celebrated it, and John tells how the personal moment suddenly grew bigger as they listened to some Labour M.P.s also celebrating at a neighbouring table. Lewis felt so moved by the coinciding of his own honour, the Labour victory and the coming of peace, that he almost stood up and made an impromptu speech about it (as he was always threatening to do in public places), wanting so much to say that this moment of history was a great opportunity, and that if everyone put their backs into it, and set about things in the right way, the future might really be the golden dream for which everyone hoped they had been fighting. But social reality blurred the edges of the scene. He did not make his heart-stirring Agincourt call to action.

Underneath the euphoria, Lewis had several worries in his mind, mainly to do with the family. John decided to leave the Navy and go into the theatre, starting right at the bottom as assistant stage-manager for £10 a week at the Glasgow Citizens' Theatre, where the producer was Matthew Forsyth, a staunch member of Lewis's old company, who had himself been assistant stage-manager for *Saint Joan*. It was a huge risk for the father of three children, but it paid off well; within a couple of years he succeeded Forsyth as resident producer and was well set on a theatrical career. Still, for a while things were pretty insecure financially, but Lewis worried more than he needed, harking back as usual to the deep-seated fears of his teens.

Christopher was also in a precarious position in Dublin. So were Russell and Rosemary, as well as Eileen and her family. Lewis helped as much as he could, but continued to worry, especially when he realised that his own earning capacity might well begin to diminish. Ann was doing well, but Mary was another cause of concern. Her marriage, shaky for some time, did not weather the war years. She and William Devlin now separated by mutual consent, he to pursue his theatrical career with Hugh Hunt at the Bristol Old Vic, while she came to London with her four-year-old daughter (myself) and began to look around tentatively for a career. This was no easy task. Her chief education had been in the theatre; she had turned away from acting ten years before and was not to be induced to return. Gradually, she managed an exact reversal of the change Sybil had made. Where Sybil had started to be a professional pianist and, when thwarted, turned her hobby, acting, into a career, Mary, too, began to turn a hobby (singing to the virginal) into a career and embarked, under the Arts Council, on a number of lecture-recital tours of mainly Elizabethan music.

There was also the problem of Bron-y-garth. This beautiful old house, designed for a life of genteel elegance, was in danger of becoming a white elephant. After Mary and Patricia left it in 1943, it had been put to good use as a home for evacuees. Now, much work was needed in the grounds and the house, and Lewis found himself weary of organising the work and reluctant to undertake the expense unless he could see its real purpose in the family future. It would be hard to find a house that evoked deeper feelings than this mysterious and powerful place. Lewis had seriously considered getting the house exorcised, because although he and Sybil loved it and found snatched moments of peace and contentment there, he was conscious that its charm, good or bad, amounted to a kind of enchantment.

Looking at it in a more businesslike way, he knew that Patricia's parents, Betty and Reggie Chester-Master, were much in need of a home; that his sister Elsie hoped to use it as a convalescent home for mental patients; and that it remained an ideal holiday place for his children, nieces and nephews and all their offspring—even if he and Sybil might soon be too old for the frantic midnight dashes by train or car which had exhilarated him a decade before. Overcoming a sudden desire to get rid of the place, he decided to let things be, relying on John and Patricia to share the responsibility with him.

He was pre-occupied now with plans for the Travelling Repertory Theatre. It had started quite humbly as a C.E.M.A. touring

225

company, run by the actor Basil C. Langton, a Canadian who had trained with Michel St. Denis, George Devine and Glen Byam Shaw at the Old Vic School and shared many of their ideals. He drew upon several actors who had worked with Lewis, including Ann, Freda Gaye and Douglas Campbell. At first Lewis took an interest simply as one of the C.E.M.A. companies during his directorship; but when the prospect of directing Ann in *Saint Joan* came up, he jumped at the chance and worked energetically at the task of reinterpreting the play with a new generation of actors. He was able to pass on to Langton all his long-held ideals about repertory theatre which went well with the ideal of ensemble theatre that Langton had studied at the Old Vic School. On the E.N.S.A. tour they began to plan towards the old dream of a London repertory season. It seemed that a new socialist Britain might really be prepared to welcome some fine ensemble theatre along the lines of the Vedrenne-Barker seasons. C.E.M.A., now fully constituted as the Arts Council of Great Britain, supported the company, a guarantee that might just give financial security enough to bridge the gap while a regular audience built up. At first no London theatre was available. The company went on a provincial tour, rehearsing and adding productions to their repertoire. Then, early in 1946, the King's Theatre, Hammersmith, became free and they opened in March. For the first time, Lewis was actually directing and acting in a London season of classical and modern plays, and the season was admirable. He played the Chorus in *Romeo and Juliet* with Basil Langton and Renée Asherson as the lovers, and Roebuck Ramsden in his fifth production of *Man and Superman*, which had come to symbolise his ideals of the work a theatre company should be doing. Ann played Ann Whitefield, a part to which, with her beauty, intelligence, vivacity, and wit, she must have been wonderfully suited. There were two new plays, one, *The Wise Have Not Spoken*, by Paul Vincent Carroll, described as "an Irish *Heartbreak House*"; the other, *In Time To Come*, a play about Woodrow Wilson, by Howard Koch and John Huston. Long ago, Sybil and Russell had met Wilson in America and taken a great shine to him. Lewis, admiring his idealism, was pleased to portray him in the theatre. He took great trouble over voice and appearance, making himself a beautiful nose that really did give him a resemblance to the thin wiry Wilson. Sybil, who had left the Old Vic Company, despite Olivier's pressing invitation to join an American tour, was able to play Mrs. Wilson, thoroughly enjoying her supporting role of bringing comfort and warm milk to "the great man". Of course, as soon as the very idea of a repertory season was mentioned, Lewis had urged the inclusion of a Greek tragedy, and the *Electra* of Euripides was chosen, with Ann in the leading role, Basil Langton as Orestes and Sybil as Clytemnestra which Zillah Carter played on tour. It was an excitement to work on such stuff again, and in Murray's translation: Lewis, who had played Castor in 1906 at the Court, found it satisfying to direct Ann, who absorbed many of Sybil's qualities, but was more controlled and suited to quite different parts. Notices were mainly good and encouraging, the audiences small but enthusiastic. Yet somehow, to Lewis's regret, it remained a by-water not to be channelled and fed so as to grow into the great mainstream of English theatre. Financially the season failed, and the Arts Council decided to dissociate the company.

Just after the T.R.T. season ended, Barker died. Ever since 1940 Lewis had kept a secret hope that the man he would always believe to be the leader of the English theatre might be persuaded to undertake his true role again. As C.E.M.A. developed, he knew Barker should be there, guiding its drama policy; as the Old Vic established its link with the National Theatre Council, he wondered if Barker would step in to lead the way; because he realised how Barker disliked anything makeshift, he turned sometimes to the possibility that, in the end, Tennent Plays Ltd. under Beaumont's glittering management with John Gielgud as star, might lure Barker back to create a London repertory theatre. Or perhaps T.R.T. even would take off under his direction? These frustrated dreams rose from Lewis's conviction that among all who favoured the establishment of a national repertory theatre, whether Lord Esher, Lord Keynes, Tyrone Guthrie, Geoffrey Whitworth, Basil Langton or himself, there was one man, Barker, in whose hands that theatre could become the living glory it ought to be. Now Barker was dead. As some too lukewarm tributes showed, he might be remembered only as a Shakespearian scholar and an interesting figure of Edwardian theatre. Lewis was enraged to hear Hesketh Pearson's radio portrait of Barker, which painted him as something of a namby-pamby aesthete. He took to paper to write a heartfelt tribute of his own; but *The Times*, to whom he sent it, did not print it.

Indeed, times seemed out of joint in all ways theatrical. More and more Lewis found disappointment and frustration. Most of all he was depressed by the lack of interest in speech and rhetoric, a manner of speaking that was flowing, vibrant and limpid, conveying the range and depth of the English language through a variety of pitch, tone and rhythm as rich as singing. Since the end of the First World War, rhetoric had dwindled as the dominant feature of theatrical art, and with hindsight one can see why. During that explosive era of European culture before 1914, other theatrical reforms became more influential. The advances in theatrical technology, coming on top of the avant garde ideas of Gordon Craig and the Russian designers, provoked a passionate interest in décor and all the theatre's visual aspects. Agreed, rivalry between rhetoric and scenic splendour had been waged for three hundred years, since Ben Jonson broke with Inigo Jones. But there grew up also an alternative to both of these, the development of naturalistic acting, begun in England with the "cup-and-saucer" plays of Tom Robertson, spreading through Europe via screen-acting and the sometimes misunderstood writings of Stanislavsky, and breeding the American "Method" of the 1950s. The idea that acting could be a sincerely-felt re-creation of the actor's spontaneous actions and reactions was beguiling, especially when psychology was becoming a fashionable topic. As microphones and cameras became important, directors looked for subtlety in facial and vocal expression, and gradually many actors shied nervously away from anything large-scale which might be considered "ham". After the horrors Hitler had perpetrated, suspicion of emotive declamation probably increased antipathy towards the study of rhetoric. At any rate, after the Second World War, Lewis found even fewer professional actors who knew and understood what he meant by stage speech; for the rest of his life he complained, sometimes quite peevishly, about the decay of the art of acting. A brief correspondence with the actor Peter Ustinov indicated the misunderstandings that could arise.

Ustinov claimed that, at some Drama League conference, Lewis said that every line of dialogue has only one possible intonation. Lewis denied that he had said exactly that: "Every written sentence has millions of possible variations of phrasing and intonation, depending on the character of the speaker, the context of the sentence, the amount of deliberation before speaking it, and God knows what else." Then he explained his theory more clearly: "But what I do contend is that each of these variations connotes a definite balance of thought and emotion, and that any change from that form represents a parallel change in thought and emotion. Conversely, if dramatist, author and actor agree absolutely on the thought and emotion that the line is to express at that moment, there can only be one form to express it." Ustinov answered the letter, maintaining that even when dramatist, director and actor agreed on the thought and emotion, there were still many ways of expressing it: "In my short experience I have often noted, that through the genius of a certain actor, the dramatist can be awakened to the subtlest shades of meaning behind his line—and yet can be satisfied in a future production by a completely different rendering which is as right." He ended with a comment on different actors' interpretations of the same part: "Laurence Olivier, John Gielgud, Donald Wolfit and Alec Guinness all have completely different conceptions of Hamlet, and yet all their conceptions are justifiable, even if one does not agree with any of them."

A part of the disagreement derived from modern actors' dislike of imposed intonations. For some reason a feeling had grown that while a director might take responsibility for the actors' moves, he had no right to dictate his speech patterns. Yet to Lewis, verbal orchestration was the most important part of a director's craft. Poel and Shaw had both dictated the "tunes" to their actors, Barker had helped the actor to find his own tune. Though Lewis tried to do this, as his career progressed he found fewer actors capable of exploring a range of vocal expression, and so he became dogmatic, just at a time when an autocratic method of directing was less acceptable.

Ustinov's comments suggest that he did not quite understand the theory behind Lewis's thought. Lewis believed simply that every variation of intonation reflected a variation in thought, emotion or "God knows what else". When Ustinov accepted the different renderings of his own lines, was he not actually accepting the fact that the lines, like the part of Hamlet, were open to different meanings? All might be valid, if they were true to the spirit of the play, but Lewis would insist that only one way of performing a part would convey exactly *any one meaning*. Most actors and directors, and many writers, accept various interpretations of the meaning of a text, but reject the idea of intonation as a means of precise expression. Yet the two ideas are compatible. An actor or director should surely seek precise means of expression to communicate exactly what he thinks the author intended, even if, indeed particularly when, ambiguity, non-communication or obscurity *is* the meaning.

What disappointed Lewis in so much that he now heard in performances, rehearsals and acting classes, was an over-emphasis on self-expression and a great suspicion about rhetoric. He wrote a memorandum on the Method during a trip to New York in 1957, praising it for its training in relaxation, concentration, personal imagination, auto-suggestion and imaginative interplay between one actor and another, and saying that these had always been essentials of good acting. But he argued that English-speaking actors lacked other important qualities which teachers should emphasise, including ample, controlled breath, a vocal range of at least two octaves, a generous giving of one's whole personality to the audience and rhetoric, the conscious design and control of words translated into sound, melody and silence. "Stage speech," he ended, "should show how expressive the sound of the designed speaking of chosen words can be, rather than merely show how dull, flat and meaningless is the sound of ordinary speech." In more down-to-earth terms he summed up the actor's task to someone who was complaining about an inattentive audience: "Actors are there to make people listen, and if you cannot do it one way you must do it another."

During the last years of Lewis's theatre-going life there were signs that an interest in theatrical rhetoric was growing—Dylan Thomas's *Under Milk Wood* which Lewis loved and studied; the poetic style of some of Pinter; Brecht's use of theatre as a dialectical tool; and the development of the Royal Shakespeare Company. Sadly, by this time Lewis's hearing was impaired, so he was not fully capable of judging whether the rejection of what he most valued and had offered most to the theatre, was as total as he feared. Because this branch of theatre was neglected for much of his career, I think his own thoughts about it had little chance to evolve. He could not always adapt his own approach to the demands of a culture that saw artistic values as relative and often subjective. In this one respect I believe that an amazingly forward-looking man tended to hark back to a theatrical era which, although experimental, based its values on a more fixed social and cultural order than any in the post-war Western world.

To return to 1946, Lewis found himself again working with one of his children. At Glasgow he appeared in two plays at the Citizens' Theatre, where John was now firmly established and soon to become director. Lewis did not always behave too well, taking direction only reluctantly from Matthew Forsyth, but (as John related), as soon as Matthew took the bull by the horns and rallied him, he apologised profusely and became meeker in his attitude. During this season there came the unexpected news of Ann's engagement to Douglas Campbell and a journey down to London for a February wedding as cold as his own had been, and rather more austerely dressed, owing to the strictness of clothes rationing. But the champagne flowed. I myself made my first public appearance as bridesmaid, and the couple rushed off for a honeymoon even shorter than Lewis and Sybil's, before, similarly, going into a repertory theatre together. (Not in Manchester, but in the more obscure town

230

of Kidderminster—which goes to show how the provincial theatre movement had spread in the intervening forty years.)

In April 1947 Lewis made his first post-war appearance with the Old Vic Company, as the Duke of York to Alec Guinness's Richard II, directed by Ralph Richardson at the New Theatre. Administrative links were very complex. The programme read: "By arrangement with Bronson Albery/The Joint Council of the National Theatre and the Old Vic, in association with the Arts Council, presents The Old Vic Theatre Company in . . ." This structure owed much to Lewis's endeavours with Keynes, Guthrie, Geoffrey Whitworth, Lord Esher and others; and, fragile and unwieldy as it must have seemed, it represented what was gradually developing into a National Theatre Company.

The cold of that February, and of the whole bleak winter in England had another result. In the Isle of Wight, J. B. Priestley found himself snowed up in a draughty house with nothing to do but brood about the state of the nation and write a play. And there *The Linden Tree* was planted and took root, the story of a family trying to cope with the strains and glooms of post-war rehabilitation and the establishment of a strong "Welfare State". Priestley sent it to Michael MacOwan to whom he had promised a play for the relaunching of his London Mask Theatre. And to play the leading character, Professor Linden, he thought immediately of Lewis, a perfect part for him—a history professor in a dreary provincial town celebrating his sixty-fifth birthday in 1947. A man of integrity and dedication, fierceness and kindness, a lover of family, work and beauty. His department want him to resign, his students do not value his work, his wife is tired of her dull, difficult life, and the rest of his family is unsympathetic and involved in its own problems. He refuses to give in and remains to do what he considers to be his work. Only his youngest daughter stands by him. Lewis, having to play nearer to his real self than ever before, was able to express some of his own ideals through it—perhaps those he had wanted to express that night at the Savoy. The Linden family represents the span from youth to old age in its attitude to the past, present and future of English life. It is the professor who understands that the dreariness of post-war England is, paradoxically, (and because of the social revolution), something to be proud of:

> Call us drab and dismal if you like and tell us we don't know how to cook our food or wear our clothes—but for Heaven's sake, recognise that we're trying to do something that is as extraordinary and wonderful as it's difficult—to have a revolution

231

for once without the Terror, without looting mobs and secret police, sudden arrests, mass suicides and executions, without setting in motion that vast pendulum of violence which can decimate three generations before it comes to a standstill. We're fighting in the last ditch of our civilisation. If we win through everyone wins through.

Running through the play as a *leitmotiv* which expresses its English character is Elgar's Cello Concerto. Professor Linden knows that it says more than the nostalgia for a bygone era that inspired it, because now the musician is his daughter:

Young Dinah Linden, all youth, all eagerness, saying hello and not farewell to anything, who knows and cares nothing about Bavaria in the 'Nineties, or the secure and golden Edwardian afternoons, here in Burmanley, this very afternoon, the moment we stop shouting at each other, unseals for us the precious distillation, uncovers the tenderness and regret which are ours now, as well as his, and our lives and Elgar's, Burmanley today and the Malvern Hills in a lost sunlight, are all magically intertwined.

Ironically, in the last great part he created, Lewis needed only to be himself, like a Method actor, and he found it difficult. For one thing, he would keep trying to portray Professor Linden's age, forgetting that he himself was seventy-two, and the character sixty-five. (Right into his nineties he used in the poem *Carcassonne* to put on an "old" voice to do the man who had lived "nigh seventy years"!) And Michael MacOwan found that often the construction line was too visible. This was partly because of Lewis's long experience as a director, experience which always endangers an actor's immersion in a character. It was also because of his whole anti-immersion, anti-naturalistic approach to acting. Later, when Brecht's work was better known, Tyrone Guthrie accurately described Lewis as a Brechtian actor, his performance commenting on, and drawing attention to, the thoughts and feelings of the character at each significant moment. But Priestley's play was quite explicit within a realistic convention. It worked best when MacOwan succeeded in getting a subtlety from Lewis that was more Chekhovian. The whole production was an immense critical and box-office success, running for a year at the little Duchess Theatre and winning the Ellen Terry Award as the best play of 1947. It was "a microcosm of post-war England", wrote W. A. Darlington. "Daily life in England nowadays," wrote *The Times* critic, "is ugly, inconvenient and dispiriting, but a man's business . . . is to set to work to improve it." And Lewis's performance was seen as integral to its meaning, "A bit of a silly, largely a saint and perfectly enacted by Lewis Casson . . . that is old Linden, the tree whose young branches stretch outwards and away . . . He is left suspended, not quite sacked, not quite despondent, a beautiful figure of resolution."

13

Experience is an Arch
1949–1969

The branches of the Casson tree continued to spread. Ann's first son, Dirk, was born in 1948, seventh of Lewis's ten grandchildren. Many of his theatrical "children" were now at the height of their careers. Because history moves so much more slowly than the visions of some of its dreamers, it was only in his last twenty years that Lewis saw many of the ideas he had fought for most strongly being fulfilled at last. He was not always involved in them personally, or even able to recognise them, as they were intertwined in the day-to-day running of his own career and life which continued to be very active until the last five years.

Bron-y-garth at length was sold and Lewis and Sybil looked for a more practical replacement. Allowed to join in the search, I thoroughly enjoyed the game of exploring all kinds of strange houses and imagining life there. Appropriately, having abandoned the land of Lewis's childhood, they turned to Kent, which was Sybil's, and eventually found Cedar Cottage, a charming, rather ramshackle Elizabethan cottage on Wrotham Hill. There were lots of pleasant neighbourly associations. Aylesford was only a short drive away; Russell and his family had lived in Wrotham village for a while; nearby was Stanstead where the Barkers had lived, and Kingsdown where Sybil had sent her boys during the First World War. Even Dymchurch, the well-loved holiday resort, was within manageable driving distance. So books, pictures and furniture that Patricia salvaged from the Bron-y-garth sale were squashed into the cottage, and it became, for the next ten years, an extension of their London home, as ever a retreat for the family and many friends. Sybil pretended to become a successful gardener and Lewis pottered around in a workshop room. Weekends there contained the usual long argumentative Sunday lunches and long brambly walks. ("There *was* a path here," Sybil would insist as Lewis tried to beat back the nettles and thorns that always seemed to block our way.) And in the evenings, perhaps family music. Sometimes, during those years, I was the only grandchild around and would sit in a

234

corner reading, and at the same time half-listening to the absorbing but incomprehensible conversation of the grown-ups. Their talk was always scattered with the names of actors, artists and politicians whose lives and ideas were spoken of familiarly, whether or not Lewis had actually known them. (Thus it came to me as a great surprise to discover, when I was about fifteen, that the Laurence Olivier I had grown to worship on stage and screen was none other than the "Larry" who featured regularly in these conversations.)

Retrospectively one sees how, very gradually, Lewis's career began to wind down. Only five more Shakespearian parts lay before him. John Gielgud, one of the few actors to make Shakespeare a commercial possibility in the West End, mounted two splendid productions at the Phoenix Theatre in 1951 and 1952. There was *The Winter's Tale* in which Lewis played Antigonus, and greatly enjoyed his final scene, "Exit pursued by bear", which he performed with a good hearty yell, and then *Much Ado About Nothing*, for him closely associated with William Poel. In fact, when he wished to explain Poel's methods, he often chose the first few lines of that play to illustrate them. Now, playing Leonato himself, he was a living illustration yet again. In the same year he appeared at the Old Vic, as Friar Lawrence to Alan Badel's Romeo and Claire Bloom's Juliet. In the previous year Queen Elizabeth had laid the foundation stone of the National Theatre with great ceremony, and Lewis must have joined the company with some optimism. But no building was raised; the National Theatre seemed no nearer existence. Ironically, however, there was an important link. Several of the Old Vic company, including Douglas Campbell, were invited in the following year to go out to Canada with Guthrie and take part in what seemed a crazy scheme of mounting a Shakespeare Festival in a tent in Stratford, Ontario. They became the nucleus of a company in the first purpose-built thrust-stage theatre. Lewis followed its progress with enormous enthusiasm, because it fulfilled so many of his Shakespearian ideals, with its focus on the actor in his space and the swift exciting transition from one scene to another. Not only did Douglas achieve many of his finest performances, but later Ann acted there, and over the years five of Lewis's grandchildren have played at Stratford.

As a new Shakespearian tradition was being founded, Lewis ended his own Shakespearian career in a season with Donald Wolfit, who was, in a sense, the last of an old tradition. Wolfit played Lear, giving a huge and powerful performance which some thought too starry and old-fashioned, and others richly satisfying. Lewis provided a strong Gloucester and also played Tiresias to Wolfit's

Oedipus. What make-up he did for Gloucester's blinding I do not know, but he had a wonderful time making the sightless eyes of the blind prophet out of ping-pong balls! Finally, he played, suitably enough, the Welshman, Owen Glendower, in *Henry IV* Part I. "It would be worth the journey to Hammersmith," said one critic affectionately (the season was at the King's), "to see Sir Lewis Casson's Glendower again after an interval of nearly twenty years."

So Lewis ended half a century of Shakespearian acting, bridging the years from Poel to Guthrie. As one of an audience his span was even longer, from Henry Irving at the Lyceum to the Royal Shakespeare Company at the Aldwych. Strangely, he never appeared with the Stratford company himself.

While Sybil did not act in these productions, they were together in all the new plays in which Lewis now appeared. The usual pattern was to find her a good part, and if there was a suitable supporting part for him, so much the better. Over the next few years he created a variety of old gentlemen of varying humours from gruff to syrupy, none particularly rewarding, but all with a substance, an integrity and a humour. This was true also of several revivals in which they appeared together.

Two original scripts were very special to them both. The first was Clemence Dane's play about Queen Elizabeth I, *The Lion and the Unicorn*. She had written it some years before, with Sybil in mind, but chances to put it on kept melting elusively away. In 1951, when Charles Cochran had expressed interest in staging it during the year of the Festival of Britain, they were full of excitement and anticipation. Sybil had always admired, practically envied, Elizabeth's strong, independent nature. Apart from the all-important devotion to Lewis and the family, it was a nature she shared, and one part of her almost regretted not having followed a more rigorously solitary mission in life. The play centred on Elizabeth's last years and her relationship with Essex. Lewis would be perfect as Sir William Cecil, her "Spirit". But just as they were about to start rehearsals, Cochran died; suddenly, and horribly, electrocuted in his bath. Cochran, who had given Sybil her first West End chance: Cochran, whose battles over actors' rights had led to the founding of Equity. A true friend and enemy was gone; somehow they never had the heart to go on with the Elizabeth play.

They did, later, do a new play by Clemence Dane, *Eighty in the Shade*, which she wrote to celebrate their golden wedding in 1958. Based on Ellen Terry and her daughter Edith Craig, it again gave Lewis very limited scope as an old family friend and beau. An admirer, Cecil Wilson wrote in the *Daily Mail*: "To make it a worthy Casson occasion it should at least be a pair of parts, but Sir Lewis takes such a modest back seat that the evening rests entirely on his enchanting wife." He did not take a back seat in the rows over the script, with Winifred (Clemence Dane) refusing to alter a syllable and Lewis raging over her obstinacy. Tempers reached a pitch on the opening night in Brighton, the wedding anniversary itself. A great friendship was almost broken. But somehow Lewis was pacified, the double event was celebrated with a large, joyous party, and everyone pretended not to have heard discordant voices. Guests included at least one friend from Manchester days, Nicolai Sokoloff, who had directed the music there. The family gave them a beautiful globe, to bring everyone close; by this time John's branch had settled in Australia, and Ann and Douglas were in Stratford, Ontario with their four children.

The search for a new play continued, both of them poignantly eager to find Sybil a play that would suitably crown the end of her career, and be another *Saint Joan*. It seemed possible when they found that the historian Hugh Ross Williamson, a Catholic convert, was as excited as Sybil was over yet another independent and spiritual woman, Saint Teresa of Avila, and would like to write a play about her for Sybil. For many months the new creation was debated, with almost as many altercations as over Winifred's play. But Williamson was always ready to make changes and revisions. Perhaps too ready, for what emerged was a play without much backbone. Lewis felt that he had started on the wrong foot by over-emphasising Teresa's obedience, instead of the great revolutionary spirit that made the whole question of obedience so critical for her. The clash, Lewis felt, was the essence of the play. And he suspected that Williamson's own experience was the cause of the problem. "Now he [Williamson]—always a rebel—has gone over to Rome," he wrote to John, "he finds the obedience chafing and by a reverse process has to emphasise it. It's to some extent the same problem as Saint Joan's—genius versus the status quo, and unfortunately he's written the status quo part—mine as the Father-General—better than the rebel Teresa." For whatever reason, the play lacked vigour and astringency. Sybil's superb performance, portraying both the firm practicality and the mystical inspiration of Teresa, gave some of us in the younger generation an inkling of what her Joan was like. Lewis played the Father-General with warmth and dignity.

The main pleasure of this Teresa experience became their visits to the Carmelite monastery at Ware to meet some of Teresa's order. They were so delighted with the nuns' simple warmth and humanity that they went back after the play, and soon the trip became almost an annual visit. One of the nuns had seen Lewis in *Prunella* years before, and they all called him their "Father-General". Conversations were conducted through a grille, which did not hinder communication at all. Sybil and Lewis would speak poetry to the nuns, and on one occasion Mary, who went with them, took her virginal and sang Elizabethan songs. And they also visited the Benedictine Abbey at Stanbrook, where Dame Laurentia had lived, the nun who had corresponded with Shaw. These visits were a gift of peace to Sybil and Lewis. They loved the eager intelligence of the nuns for whom, it was so clear, closed doors did not a prison make.

For those with a real interest in Sybil's and Lewis's career, the lack of good material was becoming noticeable. "After years of accomplished flirtation with drama without pretensions," wrote Harold Hobson in his review of *Teresa of Avila*, "would it not renew the splendour of the English theatre if Dame Sybil and Sir Lewis appeared again in a play of weight and value?" But it was too late. *Teresa of Avila* was the last original play (1960) in which Lewis appeared. He had been offered a part in a play by Robert Bolt, and it would have been his introduction to the just-emerging group of new British playwrights. But he had chosen instead to take a small part in a Noël Coward comedy with Sybil, relishing the idea that at eighty-five two West End managements were after him.

The truth was that by 1960, Lewis was less able to cope on his own. "Up to eighty," he used to say, "I felt exactly the same as I did when I was younger. All my faculties seemed to be pretty nearly as good as they were, and I seemed to be as alive as anything." He had had a few problems with his hearing but nothing really to worry about. Gradually, however, the depressions that had dogged him all his life, made serious inroads into his energy and resources. More and more he needed Sybil's constantly invigorating presence to sustain him through the moils and toils of daily living. Yet his intelligent interest in every facet of human life continued undulled, and his warm concern in the affairs of friends and family. This very concern often gave him grief because he wanted still to take on the full responsibility of being head of the family, and shoulder the burden of anyone with a problem. His advice was eagerly sought as father, husband, uncle, grandfather, colleague or friend; counsel always wise, compassionate and perceptive. But he felt inadequate and worried because he knew he would not always be able to help over financial problems as he would have liked.

This picture would lead one to imagine that Lewis gradually reduced his activities when he reached his eighties, but this was not so. From 1954 until 1962 he and Sybil embarked on a series of tours and visits all over the world that turned them back into international stars and made them new explorers. John's family had settled in Melbourne, Australia, and the first plans were built round the idea of visiting them and doing some recitals. The British Council was delighted to sponsor them, so in June, 1954, just after celebrating Sybil's fiftieth year on the stage, they set sail to revisit Australia after more than twenty years. There was only one branch of the family to leave in England and that was mine. Christopher and family were settled permanently in Dublin, and Ann had gone to Canada with her children only a month or so before. Two years before, my mother had married my schoolteacher Ian Haines, and now we three waved off Sybil and Lewis on their new adventure and settled down to nearly two years of communication through letters.

Dramatic recitals were less common than they have since become. Lewis and Sybil contributed to the resurgence, and for him it was a revival of much of his early work. He greatly enjoyed devising and preparing their three programmes; they spoke excerpts from plays, which he would introduce and arrange so that a scene was almost self-contained; and in this way they managed to do Euripides, Shakespeare, Shaw and Clemence Dane in the simple style Lewis loved best. Just enough movement to set up the scene; then all the concentration on language and mood. He wore a dinner jacket, Sybil some rich, simple full-length dress, and their scenery was curtains, a couple of chairs and perhaps a table. For many audiences it was an exciting new experience to have their imaginations stirred by this bare convention. For some, though, there was embarrassment at the spectacle of two old people acting a scene of youth and fire, or the sound of Lewis imitating the sound of a Greek bugle with his back to the audience as if in some kind of ostrich effect. Such conventions have been developed much more since then; Lewis's belief in them was a few years ahead of his time just as much as it was old-fashioned. Nevertheless, their presentation of poetry was probably most satisfying, especially poems halfway between drama and lyric. Browning was a favourite of them both and Lewis's renderings of *The Bishop Orders His Tomb at Saint Praxed's Church* and *My Last Duchess* were masterpieces of irony. His skill in portraying a character critically and yet sympathetically, from the inside and the outside, was never more apparent. He also did a beautiful Reverend Eli Jenkins from *Under Milk Wood*, and a heart-breaking poem of Edith Sitwell's in which a man is betrayed by his own sister. The anthology format allowed them to range far and wide, and one of Lewis's most successful pieces was a poem based on an old French ballad, *Carcassonne*, the ballad quite famous, the English adaptation quite unknown. Where Lewis found it I do not know, but it became a classic in his repertoire, like a favourite song, or the party piece of some Edwardian reciter. It tells the story of an old French peasant whose sole ambition is to go to the nearby town of Carcassonne. Lewis raised it into a quite profound experience as he reminded his audience that the passing of time would never change the old man's Carcassonne, "For it is built upon eternal ground"; he reached out to touch the lives of his audience with the knowledge that such a place is "nigh to everyone", and ended "For all the world there is a Carcassonne."

I doubt if another actor alive could speak poetry more beautifully than Lewis. He prepared each piece elaborately, marking the text until it looked like a musical score, to remind himself of the significance and shape of each phrase. An important part of his method was insistence on the onward movement of any speech. Each tiny pause, each subtle inflection, was designed to reveal to the audience the developing pattern of the piece, and to carry them through to the next moment. He was like a skilful merchant gradually unrolling a rich Persian carpet until its intricate splendour lay revealed. Ear and mind were never allowed complete repose until the very end. His method allowed him to explore the complexities and reveal the meaning of even such obscure works as Hopkins's *The Wreck of the Deutschland*. His analysis was as thorough as the most learned of literary scholars could have made it; his mastery over his vocal instrument was as complete as that of a lieder singer, and his theatricality gave to the entire performance the illusion of simple sincerity.

They rehearsed throughout the sea-voyage and opened with a nerve-racking performance in the ballroom at Government House in Perth. A far cry from the Welsh mining valleys, yet something of the same feeling of pioneering, of working at the theatrical frontiers, which excited both of them. Wherever they went they were fêted and lavishly entertained. Many of the performances were gala occasions. The enthusiasm with which they were greeted showed the growing demand for poetry and drama in all the towns of Australia and New Zealand that they visited. And the whole tour was lifted by the grand reunion with John and Patricia and the three grandchildren.

Early in 1955 the British Council extended the tour to India. They longed to see that country in which over many years they had acquired quite passionate interest, admiring Mahatma Gandhi and all that he stood for, and long supporting the freedom of India. Just before leaving England Lewis was excited to receive an Honorary Degree from Glasgow University in company with Krishna Menon, with whom he had already shared many platforms and struck up a fast friendship. Years before this, after appearing in *Sakuntala*, Lewis had been fascinated by the simple conventions of Indian theatre; they had also met the poet Rabindranath Tagore and treasured his translated works. Now they faced the terrifying contrasts of India herself—appalled by the squalor and poverty especially in Bombay and Calcutta, uplifted by the beauty of the country and its religion. In Bombay, New Delhi, Madras and Calcutta they were treated like royalty, usually staying in the mansion of some state official. They performed in colleges and universities as well as giving gala recitals; and, as in Wales, they were delighted with the indigenous theatre which, with the lilt of Indian English, actually reminded them of the Welsh.

Sybil called the Indian trip the "top of our lives", and it did seem a crowning experience. They were completely in harmony with each other, and their staunch support of Indian independence over the years made them very welcome even before they arrived. As usual their warmth and knowledge about everything they saw and heard was wholly captivating. Whether it was health, politics, theatre, religion or the mountains, they knew all about it and were delighted to be shown and told more. In any personal encounter Sybil established the first contact with her unique eagerness and warmth of manner that melted all shyness. As the strangers, hosts or audience relaxed and became expansive about their concerns, Lewis's quiet comments and questions would reveal his understanding of their situation; the whole occasion would become quite a profound interchange of ideas. No wonder the British Council considered them valuable ambassadors. Typical of their experience were visits to various old temples which consolidated their belief in the oneness of religion, a belief already fostered by the books of Sarvepalli Radakrishnai, Professor of Comparative Religion at Oxford and Mysore. Hearing of their presence in New Delhi, he invited them to spend a Sunday morning with him, rounding off their whole understanding of Indian religion in the most satisfactory way. Again, no less a person than Pandit Nehru arranged their trip to see Everest. "More than anything, I want to see the sun rise on Everest," Sybil told him; and he replied, "I will arrange the sunrise and everything for you." Which he did. They were driven to Tiger Hill and provided with hot coffee; and magically, the fog of the day before lifted, and they stood, hand in hand, to watch Kangchenjunga, Everest, Lhotse and Makalu turning to rose precisely on cue.

The tour continued to the Far East where they performed in Hong Kong, Singapore and Kuala Lumpur. Again they sought out all manner of experiences and there were strong social contrasts; they visited the leper colony of Hay Ling Chay Island and gave a recital there for young and old. The leper children then performed a mime and the adults a Chinese play in honour of their guests. Like royalty, they were often feasted, not always with delicacies they could easily appreciate. Lewis's famous indifference to food sometimes came in handy; Sybil insisted that at one meal she was confronted with "old vests, boiled", and was furious to see Lewis tucking in as comfortably as if it were plain beef stew.

Back to Australia then for two plays with Ralph Richardson and his wife Meriel Forbes. And finally, on the last stages of this great adventure, they continued the recitals in South Africa, Rhodesia and Kenya, ended in Israel and Turkey, and returned to London in the spring of 1956 after nearly two years away.

Instead of sinking back into the tranquillity of home life to ponder their memories, Lewis and Sybil felt rejuvenated by their world travels. In a few months they were off again to renew their acquaintance with New York. They had been offered a Graham Greene play on Broadway and it gave them a grand opportunity to cross the Atlantic and see the Campbells, including Benedict, their tenth and last grandchild. Just before this, Lewis acted his last part away from Sybil, in a revival of Shaw's *The Doctor's Dilemma*; also his last appearance in Shaw, whose work and influence had been so integral to his whole career. He had played in the first production fifty years before, and he was happy to complete that circle. After New York another play took them to Australia again, and for the second time their granddaughter Jane Casson was with them, playing granddaughter to her own off-stage grandmother in Enid Bagnold's *The Chalk Garden*.

Both these productions showed that Lewis was still a most volatile member of a company. In New York they were directed by Carmen Capalbo, who ran the Bijou, an off-Broadway theatre which put on three-month runs. Each rehearsal began with a "conference"—a long discussion between director and actors, which Lewis found immensely frustrating; for him there was no such thing as interpretation without execution, and to talk about a scene without actually speaking it was largely a waste of time. Once, indeed, he got so furious with Capalbo that he did not even make peace before leaving the theatre, most unusual for him despite his long history of altercation and dispute.

As for *The Chalk Garden* Lewis kept himself busy directing scenes from *King Lear* with some of the company and teaching Jane to speak poetry. He felt a great need to pass on some of his skills and she was an apt pupil.

He also disgraced himself with one of his most outrageous acting pranks. The story, remembered by many, is told with most relish by the Australian actor, Gordon Chater. Playing the part of an elderly judge in *The Chalk Garden*, he was taking immense pains as usual, to "age up" to portray someone at least ten years younger than himself. In fact he was becoming so decrepit that Sybil was asked to suggest tactfully that his appearance and manner might be a little younger, since at least one member of an audience had been heard to enquire if Sir Lewis was not getting a bit "past it". At the next performance Gordon Chater, playing the butler, opened the door for Lewis to enter. He had been doing this with some trepidation because Lewis, invisible to the audience until he stepped through the door, was always creating surprises for him—standing there with a flower pot on his head, or, on one occasion, not standing there at all. This time, Gordon was confronted with a grotesque sight—eighty-three-year-old Lewis in full juvenile make-up—fair hair, blue eyeshadow, doll cheeks and little cupid-bow lips. He fairly bounced on to the stage and proceeded to flit through the scene, simpering and quivering with youthful charm, to the complete horror of all on stage, who struggled frantically to keep their composure. All were transfixed, but no one was more furious than Sybil, who was heard raging at him in the dressing-room after the show. True to his nature, Lewis soon admitted that he had overstepped the mark and apologised to the management and then to all the actors. Though even then he told Gordon, with a glint, he was sorry only because, "I should have shown you what I was going to look like before I came on."

Soon after this Australian trip Lewis first developed the eye trouble that burdened his last ten years. On a walk with John's family he fell heavily and suffered some concussion. Though he was advised to rest for a couple of days he and Sybil were the sort of people who hated to fuss about their health or take to their beds when there was the faintest possibility of keeping going. So he kept going. A few months later, a black blob appeared in front of his eye. Gradually it increased till he could see only sideways. China-mending and other handyman work had to stop; he found it difficult to recognise people easily; and the worst thing was that reading became impossible. That he found almost unbearable; not to have a book at his side and the newspaper with his morning coffee, narrowed his world quite drastically.

Still foreign adventures beckoned. When they returned to England, Sybil started to make a film and Lewis sank into the background, rather bored. Suddenly he was asked to go out to Rome to play Tiberius in *Ben Hur*. He always enjoyed the precise technique of filming, accepting the small parts that sometimes came his way, beginning with Basil Dean's *Escape* in 1930. *Ben Hur* seemed a mad exploit with the charm of a schoolboy "lark". He packed up his bags and set off "looking about ten years old", said Sybil, "and very naughty". She felt quite forlorn letting him go and hoped Jack Hawkins, also in the film, would look after him. The whole experience was a fantasy. He had to make his own way to a huge labyrinthine hotel where an Australian actor explained that he was living there more or less permanently; Rome was such a splendid centre for epic films that he was never out of a job. Lewis was both fascinated and repelled. He set off for the studio the next day feeling like Alice in Wonderland, and sat for two hours while he was given a most elaborate make-up base which dried into thousands of wrinkles. Fresh from his own antics with greasepaint he was delighted by the technique and by his wig which took another half hour to be put on. Then he was togged out in grand Roman gear, driven to the lot, and shown to the director, William Wyler, who at once condemned the make-up as "too extreme". So back they went to remove the make-up, and then it was time for lunch. Lewis spent the afternoon trying to get a script. He had been told the script was by Christopher Fry, but soon found it had gone through many different hands and no one was sure what the final version of his three speeches was to be. Back at the hotel in the evening, Lewis found his humour beginning to wear thin, and he was glad when the actor George Relph, whom he was replacing, walked in and told him the whole story, including the fact that he, George, had been released but could not get an aeroplane ticket home until they were sure of getting Lewis. Now the absurdity began to take on a more Kafkaesque quality. He spent another morning trying to get a script, suggested he should write his own, and was told "No", he would have to wait now until Monday morning (it was Saturday). Finally losing his patience, he delivered an ultimatum—he would write his own lines, learn them on Sunday, do the scene on Monday, or he would go home, whichever they preferred. They preferred his going home. So he had a car back to the hotel, packed, went on to the airport and arrived home fifty-two hours after he had set off, and regaled everyone with his wild exploits in the land of *Ben Hur*. "The whole place is like a maelstrom," he wrote to John, "vast buildings, an area of about a square mile. Thousands of American and Italian employees. You drive everywhere from one building to another. Hopeless confusion, broken English, no one responsible for anything. Mad! Mad!"

In lumping Lewis's foreign adventures together I have lost the chronology of his story and must now fill in a few more gaps. The *Ben Hur* episode came just before *Eighty in the Shade* and the golden wedding. Next year, while doing the Noël Coward play (*Waiting in the Wings*) Lewis decided to sell Cedar Cottage. Since his eyesight deteriorated he had not been able to drive, and this made the trip a wearing train journey. No housekeeping arrangement had been satisfactory for very long because the house was often cold and damp and it was quite remote, with few neighbours. With so many of the family now living abroad, the house was often empty— probably most richly occupied by me. I spent many half-term holidays there with a schoolfriend, and we filled the place with the long complicated adventures of Dick Turpin, Saint Joan, and various brave people of Queen Elizabeth's time, climbed in the loft, listened to the musical-box and explored all kinds of fascinating family treasure in an old sea-chest, such as a huge autograph album which contained a tiny slip of paper marked "Napoleon Bonaparte's hair"; inside was a single lock of sandy hair. After the cottage was sold I never saw that album again and I never discovered its provenance.

So, for the last few years, the Chelsea flat was Lewis's only home, on the whole a great relief to him. All his children were now on the way to owning their own homes, with his help, or with that of his sister Elsie, who left her house to Mary and Ann; he could feel more secure now about their welfare.

After *Teresa of Avila*, not the most cheering of events, yet another recital tour of Australia was suggested. Because he was depressed and becoming frail, and Sybil's arthritis was a source of pure agony, it seemed a mad idea, and Lewis almost lost his nerve when he saw the plans laid out. But a sea-voyage promised relaxation, the thought of Australian sun and warmth was alluring, and in the event they coped magnificently with a crowded three-month schedule and came back rather rejuvenated than aged. For both of them in their last years, it would always be a puzzle to decide whether the challenge of adventure or performance would lift their spirits and stamina to deal with it, or prove too great a task and crush them. No one regretted this last Australian trip and they returned to fulfil a pleasant engagement at Chichester in the summer of 1962.

Playing in the first Chichester Festival linked past and future in a number of exciting ways. To be in Laurence Olivier's company was a joy and a beautiful reversal of roles from the time he had been a pageboy in *Henry VIII*. To act on the first English thrust-stage was tremendously exciting after all they had heard and seen of Stratford, Ontario, and though the stage was far too large and presented many problems, it did open up new possibilities. Only recently Lewis had spoken about the importance of the new stage for the theatre of the future: "The theatre . . . will have to concentrate on things that the proscenium theatre and the film and television cannot do at all. They will never give you an actual solid actor that you can believe in to the extent you can if you can see a three-dimensional actor within a few yards off, talking to you."

Olivier had chosen one playwright, Chekhov, who many thought could not possibly work except on a proscenium stage. But his production of *Uncle Vanya* was a triumph. Michael Redgrave, Joan Greenwood, Fay Compton, Joan Plowright, Sybil and Lewis and himself all created that elusive atmosphere of dullness, absurdity, exasperation, passion and poignancy. Amazingly and sadly, this was the only time Lewis played Chekhov, making of Ilya Telyegin, "Waffles", a wonderfully comic, tranquil, down-trodden old man, "an oasis of peace in the discordant atmosphere", *The Times* critic wrote. Sybil and Lewis spent the season in a peaceful cottage at Fishbourne, looked after by their granddaughter Jane.

The venture had another dimension for Olivier was using the season as a stepping-stone to the National Theatre, at last to be opened at the Old Vic: Lewis could take much credit, through his earlier work, for this final realisation of the great Barker dream. Though he and Sybil returned to Chichester in the following year, they could not accept Olivier's invitation to join the first National Theatre season in September 1963, though their hearts were certainly there.

Between the Chichester seasons they were able to do their recital programme in England. Called *Some Men and Women*, it ran for two weeks at the Haymarket after touring. Some critics found the anthology a little old-fashioned, but that did not matter because, by this time, Sybil and Lewis were such an institution that audiences and critics grasped the opportunity to "meet" them. "The atmosphere is less that of a recital than of a drawing-room entertainment," wrote *The Times* critic, "with Sir Lewis as the genially grizzled host, giving rock-like support to his bubblingly impulsive partner, who is continually breaking the formality of the proceedings to pass a friendly word with the guests." And another long-standing admirer, Philip Hope-Wallace summed up their "image" beautifully:

This couple is 'wonderful' in the sense that the Fire Brigade and the District Nursing Service are wonderful and as the Metropolitan Police used to be. They have indeed 'done the State some service'. When not giving two-person Shakespeare in Dunedin or New South Wales, they will be found shaking hands with lepers or reading *Oliver Twist* to Nigerian nurses on their off-days.

During the period of these recitals they had a holiday that forged more links with the past. My stepfather, Ian, had a great love of the Lake District which Mary shared, and they arranged to take Sybil and Lewis to visit their favourite places and to see all the old Casson haunts. They went to Seathwaite and explored the churchyard there, which is stuffed full of Cassons. Most important was the grave of "Wonderful Walker" and the stone where he sheared the sheep. Lewis proudly signed the visitors' book "great-great-great-grandson of Wonderful Walker", and then they all went to look at Walla Barrow Crag and thought about "all old friends round . . ."

At last Lewis's failing eyesight made his work too difficult to continue without great effort. Remembering lines was also a problem. He played a butler in *Queen B*, an eccentric comedy by Judy Guthrie, in which Sybil toured, and he coped by memorising the position of every single piece of furniture and prop, like a stone-blind person. He learnt the lines by putting them on to a tape recorder and playing them over to himself.

As his work lessened, Lewis had more time to reflect on ideas he had developed since his youth. One of the glories of his mind was its great chain of continuity with all that lay in the past. About this period he was invited to give a lecture on William Poel, and, true disciple that he was, resolved to find a way to do it even though he could not see to read. He solved the problem by rehearsing the speech with his friend Freda Gaye, who took note of each point he made. The idea was that he would talk and she would guide him through according to the notes. In the event he spoke brilliantly and fluently for an hour, brushing aside any attempt of hers to prompt his ideas. He spoke of Poel's belief in "art for life's sake", of his definition of theatre as "a laboratory for research into humanity". It was a wonderful opportunity to sum up a philosophy, maybe Lewis's own crystallisation of his ideas rather than a regurgitation of Poel's.

On October 26th, 1965, he was ninety. My cousin Penny and I, then sharing a flat, determined to celebrate this with him by taking him out for a treat which Sybil would not be allowed to join. He was very dependent on her, and sometimes, we feared, he felt that he was becoming less of a person in his own right. The fear was entirely ungrounded because, whenever you talked to him, a moment came when, no matter how much fatigue and depression he was feeling, something you said would arouse some enthusiasm or other, a gleam would come into his eye and strength and confidence into his voice as he launched into a reminiscence, or a pet theory, a ridiculous association or a new insight, that refreshed your mind and heart more than you could ever convince him it had. We racked our brains to think of a suitable treat and finally decided to take him to an opera. Sybil saw the three of us off in a taxi, and we rolled up at Covent Garden to see *Das Rheingold*. The choice could not have been happier. The programme informed us that this was the ninetieth performance of the opera at Covent Garden. And Lewis then announced that *Das Rheingold* was the first opera he had ever seen in London, back in 1894! We all enjoyed ourselves immensely, but the main feature of the evening was the flood of reminiscence the occasion unleashed. As we stood under the great chandeliers in the foyer, Lewis began to tell about his youth in London—not family anecdotes, but memories of what the city was like. Then, reliving his early scientific enthusiasms, he told us of his first experience of the wonders of electric light, radio and telephone, running water— we became aware, suddenly, what an incredible period of change his ninety years had spanned, and all three of us were awed. For a moment the continuity of the generations seemed so poignant a sensation as to be almost physical. (When he went to the film *2001*, able to see its vision of the future only out of the corner of his eye, he wept at the same humbling sensation. "I was alive when they invented the motor car," he whispered.)

Still his career continued. In 1966 Sybil and Athene Seyler starred in a revival of *Arsenic and Old Lace* and Lewis played the last victim of the two amiable sisters. It was a delicious reunion of old friends, more like a tea-party than a theatrical performance. Athene and Sybil were in rich comic form; we all held our breaths whenever Lewis had to negotiate the narrow staircase on the set, most of all when he had to come down it with two suitcases. But he always managed it, and ended by sitting at the table with a beatific smile on his face as he pronounced the last line of the play, "I thought I'd had my last of elderberry wine . . ." as he drank back the fatal beverage.

In splendid theatrical contrast to this intimate comedy was the ritual magnificence of the Encaenia in the summer of that year, when he and Sybil became Honorary Doctors of Oxford University, the only married couple to receive the honour at the same time. It was a coldish day, with the scarlet gowns flapping in the wind, and

248

they stepped out sturdily in the procession to the Senate House. The orations were in Latin, the whole event a medieval ceremony moving in its mixture of simplicity, dignity and pomp. Dame Mary Cartwright, honoured at the same time, was Mistress of Girton College, Cambridge, from which I had come down just three years before, so I was enjoying the linking of my two worlds. (Lewis had already received a doctorate from Glasgow University in 1954 and from the University of Wales at Aberystwyth in 1959 and he was made a Fellow of the Imperial College of Science and Technology in the same year.)

One more trip abroad. Ann and Douglas were living in Minneapolis, where Douglas was acting and directing at the Guthrie Theatre, built in 1963. Guthrie had established close ties with the University of Minnesota, and Sybil was invited to teach a summer acting workshop of one week for the Theatre Department there. It was another chance to combine work with seeing a branch of their scattered family, so off they went for a six-weeks' stay. They gave one recital to a packed auditorium, and, besides having all kinds of outings with the family, went to some of the rehearsals for Guthrie's most exciting project. This was *The House of Atreus*, a translation of the *Oresteia* by John Lewin, performed in the high shoes associated with Greek tragedy, and with magnificent masks, the whole production designed by Tanya Moiseiwitsch. The designs were most impressive with the gods on stilts towering above the mortals and the actors' speech and gestures heightened to match. Over the years Guthrie had trained his audience to a point where a rigorous formality of play and production was warmly accepted. *The House of Atreus* would be the company's masterpiece and reach wide audiences. Even the rehearsals gave Lewis a marvellous chance to see how modern repertory theatre was fulfilling his early dreams. Of course he argued over many points with Guthrie. He was, as he had said so many years before, "never satisfied". Douglas was playing Clytemnestra in a grand manner modelled on Sybil.

Tales of this trip reached me from both sides of the Atlantic, because, shortly after their return, I too set out for Minneapolis to study at the University, and so missed Lewis's final stage appearance in a revival in 1968 of *Night Must Fall* which never reached London. He was in the first scene of the play, wearing the full regalia of Lord Chief Justice, and with a single long speech. Unable to memorise it for live performance, he recorded it, ingenious to the last.

I was back at the end of the year, in December 1968, for the diamond wedding. There were two parties to celebrate this event; one, of theatrical friends whose number was of course immense, and who spanned several generations; the other, for their joint families, attended by over a hundred Cassons and Thorndikes. Of the first party it was said that if a bomb fell on the flat where it was held, there would be no London theatre to speak of. The second party was made memorable by the sight of Lewis moving from group to group, making the guests "mingle", not to fulfil his role of polite host, but so that all possible links should be made, and the generations and distant connections meet each other. He loved to see these circles joined. Meeting my then husband, whose name was William, he immediately called him "Will" as if in recollection of his own brother.

A smaller family group met late on the night of December 31st to usher in 1969. I held Lewis's hand as we all joined in the singing of "Auld Lang Syne". It was the last time I saw him. One late spring morning in Minneapolis we heard the news that he had been taken into the Nuffield Nursing Home. The official diagnosis was a non-functioning of the kidneys, but it was really just the whole frail body winding down until at last it stopped. Later on the same day, May 16th, we heard of his death, with Sybil beside him. A Thanksgiving service was held in Westminster Abbey on June 3rd. True to his destiny, he was the *second* actor to receive this honour; the first being Sir Henry Irving. In October 1971, on the ninety-sixth anniversary of his birth, a memorial plaque was unveiled in the Actors' Church, St. Paul's, Covent Garden: a slab of blue slate, a gift from the old Casson quarry in Blaenau Ffestiniog. It bears a quotation from Euripides:

> What else is Wisdom—
> To stand from fear set free
> To breathe and wait!

Beside it now is another blue slate for Sybil, who lived until she was just three weeks older than he had been.

During those last seven years, she and I often talked of him, especially as I had decided to research his life and career. She enjoyed listening to me read my account of people, places and plays that were so vivid to her. Though facts, names and dates were now vague, she could remember the quality of each event. We tried to explain Lewis's character to ourselves, seeing how many apparently incompatible qualities were bound together in him. He was a rebel and a traditionalist; a romantic and a realist; a theorist and a prag- matist. He never rejected any part of his heritage or his experience, and like an actor who becomes tinged by the parts he has played,

250

retained always some qualities of the roles he had undertaken in life: the analytical mind of the chemist; the practical craftsmanship and sensitive ear of the organ–builder, the zeal of the priest; the eloquence of the teacher; the discipline of the soldier; and he was always the actor, slipping into whichever role was appropriate. All these qualities were drawn together into a whole man who struggled towards a goal he knew was impossible. "Theoretically," he said once, "he [the actor] follows a parabolic curve, ever approaching perfection, but never reaching it." He was surely echoing his own soul when he spoke the words of Tennyson's *Ulysses*:

> I am a part of all that I have met;
> Yet all experience is an arch wherethro'
> Gleams that untravell'd world, whose margin fades
> For ever and for ever when I move.

Chronology of Lewis Casson's life
and theatrical career
October 26th, 1875–May 16th, 1969

Besides major events in his life, all the theatrical performances I have been able to trace are listed here, except for some minor productions and charity performances. Films, radio, television and individual recitals are also omitted. For repertory seasons I have listed the first, but not the subsequent performances of a production. Authors, except Shakespeare, are noted with the first reference to each play. Theatres are in London unless otherwise stated.

1875	Born in Birkenhead to Thomas and Laura Ann Casson, a brother to Frances, born 1872, and William, born 1873.
1877	Birth of his sister, Esther.
1879	Birth of his brother, Randal.
1881	Birth of his sister, Elizabeth.
1883	Birth of his sister, Ann.
1884	Entered Ruthin School.
1891	Entered Michell and Thynne's Organ Factory, Shepherd's Bush.
1892	Entered City and Guild Institute, South Kensington, to study Chemistry.
1894	Assistant at St. Augustine's Church, Kilburn. Joined Randolph Amateur Dramatic Society and Irving Dramatic Club.
1896	Entered St. Mark's College, Chelsea, on a Queen's Scholarship.
1898	Assistant resident tutor at St. Mark's.

1899

February   Neighbour in *The Alchemist* (Jonson), Apothecaries' Hall, directed by William Poel for Elizabethan Stage Society.

1900   Entered Thomas Casson's Positive Organ Factory, Camden Town.

June   Messenger in *Athalie* (Racine), St. George's Hall, directed by Charles Fry.
Joined Charles Fry's semi-professional company and the British Empire Shakespeare Society. Performed in and around London. (Few of these are recorded.)

November   Buckingham in *Henry VIII*, Dumain in *Love's Labour's Lost*, Sebastian in *Twelfth Night*, St. George's Hall, directed by Charles Fry.

1901

June   Duke Frederick in *As You Like It*, Botanical Gardens, directed by Elsie Fogerty.

November   Romeo in *Romeo and Juliet*; Hotspur in *Henry IV* Part I; St. George's Hall, directed by Charles Fry.

1902

November   Posthumus in *Cymbeline*. Royalty, directed by Charles Fry.

1903

November   Polixenes in *The Winter's Tale*; Cassius in *Julius Caesar*; Laertes in *Hamlet*; Don Pedro in *Much Ado About Nothing*; Royalty, directed by Charles Fry.

1904

February   Don Pedro in *Much Ado About Nothing*, touring London town halls, for London Shakespeare League, directed by William Poel.

April   Sir Eglamour and First Outlaw in *Two Gentlemen of Verona*, Court Theatre, for J. H. Leigh, directed by Harley Granville Barker.

June   Servilius in *Timon of Athens*, Court Theatre, for J. H. Leigh.
Mr. Joyce and Aloysius in *Where There Is Nothing* (Yeats), Court, for Stage Society.
Left Casson's Organ Factory to become a professional actor.

Summer   Played in *The Duke of Killiecrankie* (Marshall), touring with Leigh Lovell.
Pastoral tour.

September   Pico del Amare in *The Prayer of the Sword* (Fagan), Adelphi, for Otho Stuart and Oscar Asche.
Joined Vedrenne/Barker company at the Court, to walk on, understudy and play parts.

December   Statue of Love in *Prunella* (Housman and Barker), Court.

1905

March — Lignol in *The Three Daughters of M. Dupont* (Brieux), King's Hall, Covent Garden, for Stage Society.

April — Rosencrantz, later Laertes, in *Hamlet*, Adelphi. Dante

May — in *Beatrice* (Filippi), Court, for Rosina Filippi. Octavius Robinson in *Man and Superman* (Shaw), Court.

Summer — Pastoral tour.

October — Another Gentleman in *The Wild Duck* (Ibsen), Court.

1906

January — Adolphus Cusins in *Major Barbara* (Shaw), succeeding Barker; Castor in *Electra* (Euripides/Murray), Court.

March — Sidi El Assif in *Captain Brassbound's Conversion*, Court.

June — Jokanaan in *Salome* (Wilde), King's Hall, Covent Garden, for Literary Theatre Society.

August — Played in *The Good Natur'd Man* (Goldsmith), tour directed by William Poel for Elizabethan Stage Society.
Messenger in *Atalanta in Calydon* (Swinburne), Crystal Palace, directed by Elsie Fogerty.

September — Magistrate's Clerk in *The Silver Box* (Galsworthy), Court.

November — Mr. Danby in *The Doctor's Dilemma* (Shaw), Court.

1907 — Elected to Council of Actors' Association and joined Reform Group.

March — Directed and played Ghost of Darius in *The Persians* (Aeschylus/Ryan), Terry's, for Literary Theatre Society. His first production.

April — Allen Trent in *Votes for Women* (Robins), Court.

June — Troilus in *Troilus and Cressida*, Great Queen Street, directed by Charles Fry.

Summer — Pastoral tour.

October — Chaplain Brudenell in *The Devil's Disciple* (Shaw); Messenger in *Medea* (Euripides/Murray), Savoy, for Vedrenne and Barker.

December — Joined Miss Horniman's Company on tour.

1908 — Toured as Harry Trench in *Widowers' Houses* (Shaw); Eldest Son in *David Ballard* (McEvoy), directed by Iden Payne.

April — Provost in *Measure for Measure* directed by William Poel, The Honourable Percy Wilton in *The Few and the Many* (Richardson); Dr. Lomax in *Clothes and the Woman* (Paston); Henry Jackson in *The Return of the Prodigal* (Hankin); Gaiety, Manchester.

Summer — Provincial tour for Miss Horniman. Pastoral tour.

September — Opening of the Gaiety, reconstructed.
John Abel in *Marriages Are Made In Heaven* (Dean), Gaiety, Manchester.

255

| October | Directed and played Henchman in *Hippolytus*; also played in *Gentlemen of the Road* (McEvoy); *The Charity That Began At Home* (Hankin); *The Amateur Socialist* (Tarpey); *The Fantasticks* (Rostand); Gaiety, Manchester. |
| December | Married Sybil Thorndike at Aylesford, Kent. |

1909

February	Played in *The Silver Box*; Dr. Hope in *Cupid and the Styx* (Martin); Gaiety, Manchester.
March	Robert Frith in *The Three Barrows* (McEvoy), Gaiety, Manchester.
April	Bue Asbirning in *The Feud* (Garnett); Cyril Hinmers in *Trespassers Will Be Prosecuted* (Arabian); Gaiety, Manchester.
May	William Pargetter in *The Tragedy Of Nan* (Masefield), Gaiety, Manchester.
June	Season with Miss Horniman at the Coronet. Left Miss Horniman's Company.
August	James Roden In *The Fires of Fate* (Conan Doyle), Haymarket. Minor productions.
October	Birth of first son, John.

1910

February	Directed *The Marriage of Columbine* (Chapin), Court, for Play Actors.
February–June	Doctor in *Justice* (Galsworthy); Osier in *The Sentimentalists* (Meredith); Mr. Brigstock in *The Madras House* (Barker); the Statue of Love in *Prunella*, directed by Barker; and Fenwick in *Chains* (Barker) and played in *Trelawny of the "Wells"* (Pinero), directed by Dion Boucicault, Duke of York's, for Charles Frohman's Repertory season.
August	Fletcher in *Smith* (Maugham) U.S. tour for Frohman.
September	Death of his father, Thomas Casson.

1911

July	Returned to Gaiety, Manchester.
August	Directed *Sir Anthony* (Chambers), playing Robert Morrison, and *Lonesome Like* (Brighouse), Gaiety, Manchester.
September	Directed *The Vikings at Helgeland*, playing Sigurd the Strong, Gaiety, Manchester.
October	Succeeded Iden Payne as Artistic Director of Miss Horniman's Company at the Gaiety. Directed *What the Public Wants* (Bennett), playing Holt St. John; *The Little Stone House* (Calderon); *Chains*, playing Tennant; *The Cat and the Cherub* (Fernald), playing Wing Shee; Gaiety, Manchester.

November   Directed *Our Little Fancies*, (Macnamara); played Anthony in *Strife* (Galsworthy); Gaiety, Manchester.

December   Directed *Twelfth Night*, playing Antonio, Gaiety, Manchester.

1912

January   Birth of second son, Christopher.

February–   Led Canadian tour of Miss Horniman's company with
March   *Candida* (Shaw); *The Tragedy of Nan*; *Mollentrave on Women* (Sutro); *The Silver Box*; *She Stoops to Conquer* (Goldsmith); *The Return of the Prodigal*; *Cupid and the Styx*; *Mary's Wedding* (Cannan); *Makeshifts* (Robins); *The Little Stone House*; *Reaping the Whirlwind* (Monkhouse); *Man and Superman*.

April   Returned to Manchester, directed *The Perplexed Husband* (Sutro); *The Thieves' Comedy* (Hauptmann); Gaiety, Manchester.

May–June   Season with Miss Horniman at the Coronet.

June   Directed *Hindle Wakes* (Houghton), Aldwych, for the Stage Society and subsequently for Miss Horniman, Playhouse.

August   Directed *The Subjection of Kezia* (Ellis), playing Matthew Trevaskis; *Beauty and the Barge* (Jacobs and Parker); *The Question* (Wickham); *Pilkerton's Peerage* (Hope), playing Earl of Addisworth; Gaiety, Manchester.
              Death of his mother, Laura Ann Casson.

September   Directed *The Polygon* (Brighouse); *The Charity That Began At Home* (Hankin) playing Basil Hylton; *Elaine* (Chapin), playing John Curtis; *Race Suicide* (Fyfe); *The Pigeon* (Galsworthy), playing Professor Calway; *The Shepherd* (Forrest); Gaiety, Manchester.

October   Directed *The Devil's Disciple*; *Prunella*, playing the Statue of Love; Gaiety, Manchester.

November   Directed *Revolt* (Calderon), playing Vernon Hodder, Gaiety, Manchester.

December   Directed *Wonderful Grandmamma* (Chapin), Gaiety, Manchester.

1913

February   Directed *Miss Tassey* (Baker); *The New Sin* (Hastings); Gaiety, Manchester.

March   Directed *Old Heidelberg* (Förster), playing Staatminister von Haugel; *The Whispering Well* (Rose); Gaiety, Manchester.

April   *The Marriage of Columbine*; *Jane Clegg* (Ervine); *The Dream Child* (Down); Gaiety, Manchester.

May   Season with Miss Horniman at Court.

September   Directed *A Family Affair* (Magian and Max); *The Apostle* (Loyson); *The Price of Thomas Scott* (Baker); *More Respectable* (Casey); *Hiatus* (Phillpotts); *Nothing Like Leather* (Monkhouse), playing Mr. Push; Gaiety, Manchester.

October	Directed *The Shadow* (Phillpotts); *Julius Caesar*, playing Brutus; Gaiety, Manchester.
November	Directed *The Way the Money Goes* (Bell); *The Pie in the Oven* (Bell); Gaiety, Manchester. Resigned from Miss Horniman's Company.

1914

January–April	Joined the Scottish Repertory Theatre at the Royalty, Glasgow, as artistic director and directed: *The Honeymoon* (Bennett); *Sire de Maletroit's Door* (adapted from Stevenson); *The Little Damozel* (Hoffe); *The Point of View* (Phillpotts); *Walker, London* (Barrie); *Yellow Fever* (Ray); *The Devil's Disciple*; *East is East* (Hubbard); *Columbine* (Arkell); *Mollentrave on Women*; *An Episode* (Schnitzler, adapted Barker); *The Threshold* (Malleson); *A Man of Ideas* (Malleson); *The Liars* (Jones); *The Man of Destiny* (Shaw); *Campbell of Kilmohr* (Ferguson); *Marigold* (Garvice and Abbott); *Mr. Hopkinson* (Carton); *Loving as We Do* (Robins); *Womenkind* (Gibson); *Man and Superman*, playing John Tanner.
May	Birth of first daughter, Mary.
	Minor productions in London
August	Outbreak of First World War. Enlisted in Army Service Corps.

1915

	Sergeant in Motor Transport in France. First concert party. Commissioned in Royal Engineers.
April	Death of his sister, Frances.
September	Battle of Loos. Death of his brother, Will.
November	Birth of his second daughter, Ann.

1916

	Battle of the Somme.

1917

August	Wounded. Awarded Military Cross. Worked for Basil Dean in Army Camp Theatres.

1918

Winter	Returned to France.
Summer	Appointed Secretary of the Chemical Warfare Commission at Ministry of Munitions.
	Armistice.

1919

January	Constant in *The Provok'd Wife* (Vanbrugh), King's Hall, Covent Garden, for Stage Society.
March	Le Bret in *Cyrano de Bergerac* (Rostand), Garrick.
June	Inauguration of the British Drama League.
August	First Conference of the British Drama League.
	Appointed to sub-committee on Repertory Theatres.

October	Directed *The Trojan Women* (Euripides/Murray) for matinées at the Old Vic, playing Poseidon and Talthybius.
November	Directed *Sakuntala* (Kalidasa, translated Binyon), Winter Garden, for East–West Society.
	The Trojan Women, Alhambra, for the League of Nations.
December	*The Trojan Women* at the Holborn Empire.

1920

February–April	Directed *The Trojan Women*; *Candida*, playing Morell; *Medea*, playing Messenger; *The Showroom* (Bell); *Tom Trouble* (Burley); Holborn Empire, in management with Bruce Winston.
May	Robert Darzac in *The Mystery of the Yellow Room* (Bennett), St. James's.
June	Played in *The Mystery of the Rose*, St. Paul's, Covent Garden, for Elsie Fogerty.
September	Began directing Grand Guignol seasons at the Little, for Jose G. Levy:
	First Programme: directed *How To Be Happy* (Verber); *GHQ Love* (Rehm), playing Her Husband; *The Hand of Death* (de Lorde), playing Henri Deniare; *Oh, Hell!!!* (Thorndike and Arkell). Additions: directed *The Medium* (Mille and de Vylars), playing Bervil, *What Did Her Husband Say?* (Maltby).
December	Second Programme: directed *What Did Her Husband Say?*; *Eight O'Clock* (Berkeley), playing The Chaplain; *A Man In Mary's Room* (Unger); *Private Room No. 6* (de Lorde), playing Count Lutzi. *The Tragedy of Mr. Punch* (Thorndike), playing The Blind Man. Additions: directed *The Shortest Story of All* (Morrison); *The Person Unknown* (Maltby).

1921

March	Third Programme: directed *Gaspers* (Collins); *The Love Child* (Fenn and Pryce); *Seven Blind Men* (Descaves), playing Stevens; *Dead Man's Pool* (Bridges), playing Col. Redcliffe; *The Kill* (Level); *The Chemist* (Maurey), playing The Solicitor.
June	Fourth Programme: directed *Latitude 15°S* (MacClure), playing Sam Farquar; *The Vigil* (de Lorde); *Rounding the Triangle* (Crawshay-Williams), playing He; *The Old Women* (de Lorde), playing the Doctor; *Shepherd's Pie* (Frapie and Fabri). Joined Council of the British Drama League.
October	Fifth Programme: directed *Haricot Beans* (Chaine and Beauplan); *The Unseen* (Renaud); *The Old Story* (Hirsch); *Fear* (de Lorde); *E. and O. E.* (Williams). Addition: directed *Crime* (Level).

1922

January	Sixth Programme: directed *Amends* (Crawshay-Williams); *Changing Guard* (Not-Bower), playing the Doctor; *De Mortuis* (Logan); *The Regiment* (Francheville), playing Captain Graff; *Cupboard Love* (Crawshay-Williams).
April	Seventh Programme: directed *Amelia's Suitors* (Maltby); *Progress* (Ervine), playing Professor Henry Corrie; *The Nutcracker Suite* (Crawshay-Williams); *Colombine* (Arkell), playing Prologue; *At the Telephone* (de Lorde), playing Rivoire.
May	Eighth Programme: directed *A Happy New Year* (du Clos); *The Sisters' Tragedy* (Hughes), playing John; *To Be Continued* (Bastia); *The Better Half* (Coward); *The Hand of Death*.
July	Season at the New under Lady Wyndham's management: directed *Rounding the Triangle* playing He; *Jane Clegg*, playing Mr. Morrison.
September	Directed *Scandal* (Bataille), playing Admiral Gravières; and Préfet, New.
November	Directed *The Cenci* (Shelley), playing The Judge; *Medea*, playing the Messenger, New.

1923

	Began partnership with Bronson Albery.
January	Directed *Advertising April* (Farjeon and Horsnell), Criterion.
	Scandal; *Advertising April*; *Jane Clegg*; *Medea*; provincial tour. Addition: directed *Cymbeline*, playing Arviragus and Philario.
September	*Cymbeline*, New.
October	Directed *The Lie* (Jones), New.

1924

January	Elected to Executive Committee of British Drama League.
February	First broadcast for B.B.C. *The Tragedy of Mr. Punch* and *Columbine*.
March	Co-directed *Saint Joan* (Shaw), with Shaw, playing Chaplain De Stogumber, New.
May	Directed *Man and the Masses* (Toller), New, playing The Guide, for Stage Society. *The Lie*, provincial tour.

1925

January	*Saint Joan*, Regent.
March	Tom Edgeworthy in *The Verge* (Glaspell), Regent.
May	Directed *The Round Table* (Robinson), playing Passenger, Wyndhams.
December	Directed *Henry VIII*, playing Prologue and Griffith, Empire.

1926
March   *The Cenci*, Empire.
May   *Saint Joan*, Lyceum, cut short by General Strike.
June   Directed *Granite* (Dane), playing Nameless Man, Ambassadors.
             Henry VIII; *Saint Joan*; provincial tour.
December   Directed *Macbeth*, playing Banquo, Princes.

1927
February   Directed *The Greater Love* (Fagan), playing Polusky and Col. Schutz, Princes.
March   Directed *Angela* (Bell), playing Valentine Guiseley, for British Hospital for Mothers and Babies.
April   *Medea*, Princes.
June   *Medea* and *Saint Joan*, Théâtre des Champs-Elysées, for International Theatre Festival.
September   Old Vic season at the Lyric, Hammersmith: Petruchio in *The Taming of the Shrew*.
October   Shylock in *The Merchant of Venice*.
November   Benedick in *Much Ado About Nothing*.

1928
January   Henry in *Henry V*. End of Season.
February   Directed *Judith of Israel* (Baruch), playing Arrophernes, Strand.
March   Dinner in honour of the Cassons given by the British Drama League and the Société Universelle du Théâtre.
April   Directed *The Lie*; *The Silver Cord*, (Howard); *Jane Clegg*; *Much Ado About Nothing*; *Henry V*; *Medea*; *Saint Joan*; *Macbeth*, playing Macbeth; touring South Africa.
1929
March   Season at Wyndhams for Leon M. Lion: directed *Major Barbara*, playing Adolphus Cusins.
April   Directed *Mariners* (Dane), playing Benjamin Cobb.
May   Directed *Jane Clegg*, playing Henry Clegg; *Medea*. End of season.
June   Charles Denbury in *Exiled* (Galsworthy), Wyndhams. Directed *Madame Plays Nap* (Girvin and Cosens), playing Napoleon, for Daniel Mayer Management on tour.
December   *Madame Plays Nap*, New. Foundation of British Actors' Equity Association.
1930
January   Reverend Herbert Messiter in *The Devil* (Levy), Arts Theatre Club.
March   Socrates in *Socrates* (Bax), Prince of Wales, for the Stage Society.
May   Directed *Moloch*, playing Professor Zeigher, Strand.

August   Directed *The Squall* (Bart); *Ghosts* (Ibsen) playing Pastor
                Manders; *Granite*; *The Matchmaker's Arms* (Dukes);
                provincial tour. Played in *Escape* (Galsworthy), the first
                all-British talkie film to be made in the English countryside.
                Joined Executive Committee of Shakespeare Memorial
                National Theatre Committee.

1931
March   Directed *The Medium*, playing Bervil, Palladium.
April   *Saint Joan*, His Majesty's.
May   Directed *Marriage By Purchase* (Passeur), playing Armand
                Fontaine, Embassy Theatre Club.
August   Michael Townsend in *Late Night Final* (Weitzenkorn),
                Phoenix.
September   Directed *The Painted Veil* (Maugham), playing Walter
                Fane, Playhouse.
November   Lennox in *Bluestone Quarry* (Munro), Duchess, for the
                Stage Society.

1932
February   Directed *Saint Joan*; *Macbeth*; *Captain Brassbound's Conversion*;
                Milestones (Bennett and Knoblock); *Madame Plays Nap*;
                Advertising April; *Granite*; *The Painted Veil*; touring Egypt,
                Palestine and Australia.

1933
April   Returned to England.
                Inherited Bron-y-garth, Portmadoc, from Lucy Casson.
May   Baron Stein in *Diplomacy* (Sardou), Princes.
October   Stanislas Rosing in *Ballerina* (Ackland), Gaiety.
November   Directed *On The Rocks* (Shaw), playing Sir Jafná
                Pandranath, Winter Garden.

1934
February   English Chaplain in *Nurse Cavell* (Roberts and
                Forester), "Q" then Vaudeville.
June   Dr. Braddock in *Men In White* (Kingsley), Lyric.
September   Directed *Moonlight Is Silver* (Dane), Queens.
October   The Mayor in *Overture 1920* (Bolitho), Phoenix, for
                Embassy Theatre Club.
                Supt. Harrison in *Line Engaged* (De Leon and Celestin),
                Duke of York's.
November   Reverend Percy Huntbach in *Flowers of the Forest* (Van
                Druten), Whitehall.

1935
January   Delegate from British Drama League to Moscow Arts
                Festival.
February   Glendower in *Henry IV* Part I, His Majesty's.
                Directed *Days Without End* (O'Neill), Grafton, for the
                Stage Society.

July	Peter Quince in *A Midsummer Night's Dream*, Regent's Park.
December	Lord Palmerston in *Victoria Regina* (Housman), Broadhurst, New York.

1936
August	Directed *Hands Across the Sea* and *Fumed Oak* (Coward); *Village Wooing* (Shaw); *Hippolytus*; *My Son's My Son* (Lawrence); provincial tour.

1937
February	George Loveless in *Six Men of Dorset* (Malleson and Brooks), provincial tour.
June	Judge Vlora in *Judgment Day* (Rice), Phoenix.
September	Directed *I Have Been Here Before* (Priestley), playing Dr. Gortler, Royalty.
December	*The Trojan Women*, Adelphi, for the League of Nations.

1938
April	Directed *Coriolanus*, Old Vic.
May	Baron Krug in *Power and Glory* (Capek), Savoy.
September	Directed *Henry V*, Drury Lane.
November	Directed *Man and Superman*, playing Roebuck Ramsden, Old Vic.
December	Sir Anthony Absolute in *The Rivals*, Old Vic.

1939
January–April	Joint director, with Esmé Church, of Old Vic Mediterranean tour: *The Rivals*; *Hamlet*, playing Polonius; *Trelawny of the "Wells"* playing Sir Williams Gower; *I Have Been Here Before*, playing Dr. Gortler; *Libel* (Wooll), playing Judge Tuttington. Also in the repertoire: *Henry V* and *Viceroy Sarah* (Ginsbury).
June	Col. Pickering in *Pygmalion* (Shaw), Haymarket.
September	Outbreak of Second World War. Joined ARP Service.

1940
	Appointed Advisor on Professional Theatre for C.E.M.A. Became President of British Actors' Equity Association, Vice-chairman of London Theatre Council and Provincial Theatre Council.
April	Co-directed *King Lear* with Granville Barker, playing Kent, Old Vic.
May	Gonzalo in *The Tempest*, Old Vic.
September	Directed *Macbeth*, playing Macbeth, South Wales tour for Old Vic.

1941
January	*Macbeth* tour in Northern England.
March	*Macbeth* tour to North Wales.

June	Co-directed *King John* with Tyrone Guthrie, playing Cardinal Pandulph and later The Bastard, tour in England and Scotland, and New.
September	Directed *Medea*; *Candida*; South Wales tour for Old Vic.

1942

January	*Medea* tour in North Wales.
May	Directed *Jacob's Ladder* (Housman), provincial tour for Old Vic.
September	Played in *Cathedral Steps* (Dane), an anthology in praise of Britain, St. Paul's Cathedral and the ruins of Coventry Cathedral.
November	Appointed Drama Director of C.E.M.A.

1943

February	Directed *Days Without End*, tour for Mary Newcomb Players.
June	Major Orden in *The Moon Is Down* (Steinbeck), Whitehall, for Travelling Repertory Theatre (T.R.T.).

1944

January	Directed *Sheppey* (Maugham), tour for Stanford Holme Company.
September	Directed *Jane Clegg*, tour for T.R.T.

1945

January	Directed *Saint Joan*, playing Warwick, tour for T.R.T.
June	Received the K.B.E.
July	*Saint Joan* tour in Belgium, France and Germany for E.N.S.A. Resigned as Drama Director of C.E.M.A. and as President of Equity.

1946

March	T.R.T. season at King's, Hammersmith: directed *Saint Joan*, playing Cauchon; Chorus in *Romeo and Juliet*; Sylvester Tiffney in *The Wise Have Not Spoken* (Carroll).
April	Directed *Man and Superman*, playing Roebuck Ramsden.
May	Woodrow Wilson in *In Time To Come* (Koch and Huston).
June	Directed *Electra*, his last production. End of season.

1947

January	Dr. Marshall in *A Sleeping Clergyman* (Bridie); Priest in *The Righteous Are Bold* (Carney); Glasgow Citizens'.
April	Duke of York in *Richard II*, New, for the Old Vic.
August	Professor Linden in *The Linden Tree* (Priestley), Duchess.

1948　　End of London run. *The Linden Tree*, Glasgow Citizens'.

1949
February   Simon Brocken in *The Foolish Gentlewoman* (Sharp), Duchess.
September   Eustace Mills in *Treasure Hunt* (Farrell and Perry), Apollo.

1950
August   Lord Randolph in *Douglas* (Home) at the Edinburgh Festival.

1951
June   Antigonus in *The Winter's Tale*, Phoenix.

1952
January   Leonato in *Much Ado About Nothing*, Phoenix.
September   Friar Lawrence in *Romeo and Juliet*, Old Vic.

1953
February–   Season at King's, Hammersmith with Donald Wolfit: Tiresias in *Oedipus Rex* (Sophocles) and Gloucester in *King Lear*.
September   Glendower in *Henry IV* Part I. End of season.
November–   David Anson in *A Day By The Sea* (Hunter), Haymarket.

1954
–June   Honorary Doctorate at Glasgow University.
                Dramatic recitals with Sybil, touring Australia and New Zealand.

1955   Extension of tour to India, Hong Kong and Malaya. Northbrook in *The Sleeping Prince* (Rattigan); Mr. Fowler in *Separate Tables* (Rattigan); touring Australia and New Zealand.

1956   Dramatic recitals in South Africa, Rhodesia, Kenya, Israel and Turkey.
June   Dr. Warburton in *The Family Reunion* (Eliot), Phoenix.
October   Sir Patrick Cullen in *The Doctor's Dilemma*, Saville.

1957
January   Dr. Frederick Baston in *The Potting Shed* (Greene), Bijou, New York.
July–   Judge in *The Chalk Garden* (Bagnold), touring Australia and New Zealand.

1958
–June
December   Golden Wedding, celebrated in Brighton.

1959
January   Sir Horace Darke in *Eighty in the Shade* (Dane), Globe,
               preceded by provincial tour.
July   Honorary Doctorate at the University of Wales at
               Aberystwyth.
               Fellowship at Imperial College of Science and Technology.

1960
September   Osgood Meeker in *Waiting in the Wings* (Coward), Duke of
               York's.

1961
October   Father-General in *Teresa of Avila* (Williamson), Vaudeville,
               preceded by provincial tour.

1962
February   Dramatic recitals with Sybil in Australia.
–April
July   Telyegin in *Uncle Vanya* (Chekhov), Chichester Festival.

1963
May   *Some Men and Women*, dramatic recital with Sybil,
               Haymarket, preceded by provincial tour.
July   Telyegin in *Uncle Vanya*, Chichester Festival.
September   Harding in *Queen B* (Guthrie), provincial tour.

1965
October   Ninetieth birthday, celebrated in London.

1966
February   Mr. Witherspoon in *Arsenic and Old Lace* (Kesselring),
               Vaudeville.
June   Honorary Doctorate at Oxford University, with Sybil.

1967
June   To Minneapolis, U.S.A., last foreign trip.

1968
April   Lord Chief Justice in *Night Must Fall* (Williams), provincial
               tour.
December   Diamond Wedding, celebrated in London.

1969
May   Death at Nuffield Nursing Home, London.
June   Service of Thanksgiving in Westminster Abbey.

1971
October   Plaque placed in Actors' Church, St. Paul's, Covent
               Garden.

Bibliography

From a large number of sources, I have selected the published books on which I drew most, excluding plays. A detailed bibliography is appended to my doctoral dissertation, "The Dreamer and the Maker: A Study of Lewis Casson's Work in the Theatre", presented to the University of Minnesota, June 1972.

Casson, John: *Lewis and Sybil: A Memoir*, Collins, London, 1972.

Cole, Marion: *Fogie: the Life of Elsie Fogerty, C.B.E.*, Peter Davies, London, 1967.

Dean, Basil: *Seven Ages: An Autobiography 1888–1927*. Hutchinson, London, 1970.

—— *Mind's Eye: An Autobiography 1927–1972*. Hutchinson, London, 1973.

Forsyth, James: *Tyrone Guthrie*, Hamish Hamilton, London, 1976.

Hawkins, Jack: *Anything for a Quiet Life*, Elm Tree Books, London, 1973.

Howe, P.P.; *The Repertory Theatre: A Record and A Criticism*, Secker, London, 1910.

MacCarthy, Desmond: *The Court Theatre, 1904–1907*, ed Stanley Weintraub, University of Miami, 1967.

Macleod, Joseph: *The Actor's Right to Act*, Lawrence & Wishart, London, 1981.

McPherson, Mervyn (ed): *The Grand Guignol Annual Review*, Little Theatre, London, 1921.

Maltby, H. F.: *Ring Up The Curtain*, foreword by Lewis Casson, Hutchinson, London, 1950.

Payne, Ben Iden: *A Life In A Wooden O*, Yale University Press, London & Newhaven, 1977.

Pogson, Rex: *Miss Horniman and the Gaiety Theatre, Manchester*, Rockliff, London, 1952.

Purdom, C. B.: *Harley Granville Barker, Man of the Theatre, Dramatist and Scholar*, foreword by Lewis Casson, Rockliff, London, 1955.

—— (ed): *Bernard Shaw's Letters to Granville Barker*, Theatre Arts Books, New York, 1957.

Ricketts, Charles, R. A.; *Self-Portrait*, compiled from letters and journals by T. Sturge Moore, ed Cecil Lewis, Peter Davies, London, 1939.

Speaight, Robert: *William Poel and the Elizabethan Revival*, Heinemann, London, 1954.

Sprigge, Elizabeth: *Sybil Thorndike Casson*, Gollancz, London, 1971.

Thorndike, Russell: *Sybil Thorndike*, Thornton Butterworth, London, 1929.

Thorndike, Russell, and Thorndike, Sybil: *Lilian Baylis*, Chapman & Hall, London, 1938.

Trewin, J. C.: *The Theatre Since 1900*, Andrew Dakers, London, 1951.

—— *Sybil Thorndike*, Theatre Monograph Series No. 4, Rockliff, 1955.

—— *The Gay Twenties*, Macdonald, London, 1958.

—— *The Turbulent Thirties*, Macdonald, London, 1960.

Trewin, Wendy: *All On Stage: Charles Wyndham and the Alberys*, Harrap, London, 1980.

Webster, Margaret: *The Same Only Different*, Gollancz, London, 1969.

Whitworth, Geoffrey: *The Making of a National Theatre*, Faber and Faber, London, 1951.

Williams, Harcourt: *Old Vic Saga*, Winchester Publications, London, 1949.

Index

Plays are listed by title. Theatres are in London unless otherwise stated.